How Eskimos Keep Their Babies Warm

Also by Mei-Ling Hopgood
Lucky Girl: A Memoir

How Eskimos
Keep Their Babies Warm

And Other Adventures in Parenting
(from Argentina to Tanzania and everywhere in between)

MEI-LING HOPGOOD

ALGONQUIN BOOKS OF CHAPEL HILL   2012

Published by
Algonquin Books of Chapel Hill
Post Office Box 2225
Chapel Hill, North Carolina 27515-2225

a division of
Workman Publishing
225 Varick Street
New York, New York 10014

Library of Congress Cataloging-in-Publication Data
Hopgood, Mei-Ling.
    How Eskimos keep their babies warm : and other adventures
    in parenting (from Argentina to Tanzania and everywhere in
    between) / Mei-Ling Hopgood.
        p. cm.
    Includes bibliographical references.
    ISBN 978-1-56512-958-0
    1. Parenting—Cross-cultural studies.   2. Parent and
    child—Cross-cultural studies.   I. Title.
    HQ755.8.H657 2012
    649'.1—dc23   2011036571

10 9 8 7 6 5 4

For Monte, Sofia, and Violet

Contents

How Eskimos Keep Their Babies Warm

Introduction

❧

Travel is more than the seeing of sights; it is a change
that goes on, deep and permanent, in the ideas of living.
—Miriam Beard, *Realism in Romantic Japan*

I'm sitting on a patio in Buenos Aires, nibbling on cinnamon cake, talking with a group of friends about the way local parents raise their kids. We are a Chinese American, a Bolivian American, an African American, a Portuguese woman, and two Argentines—three moms, one expectant mom, and two maybe-somedays. Our husbands and significant others dip in and out of the conversation. The subject turns to raising a child in a culture that is different from our own, and the conversation goes something like this.

"It's crazy," I say. "There are so many things that moms and dads do so differently here, things I'd probably flip out about if I were in the States."

Another American mom chimes in. "I know! I don't know what to do when all these parents on the playground offer my kid a cookie. I say no sometimes. But I've had to relax about that and so many other things."

"Doesn't all that sugar make the children hyper?" someone asks.

"That's not true," says an Argentine, who is stewing a bit at the end of the table. "My son falls asleep earlier than anyone, with or without a few cookies."

"What *about* bedtimes? I mean, come on, Argentine kids are up at all hours," another woman says.

"Yeah, I can't believe they're running around restaurants at midnight!"

"But it all works out," I interject, knowing that I've been guilty of letting my child stay up past 11:00 p.m. more than once.

Raising a child abroad has been eye-opening. There are so many surprising, instructive moments of comparison and contrast, from the way Argentines pamper pregnant women (I was offered seats on trains and buses and urged to cut to the front of almost any line) to the attitudes about food (fresh purees are fed to kids instead of prepackaged baby food).

The experience made me think back to all the observations I'd made in passing, pre-parenthood. I saw kids enthusiastically eating strange foods at a bar in a swamp town in Brazil and in the tent home of a family in rural Thailand. I watched in awe while moms and dads carried babies on their backs, hips, and chests as they climbed mountains, loaded trucks, and even drove motorcycles. My biological siblings in Taiwan suggested, to my amusement, that I might fold a thousand cranes for good luck when I was pregnant and insisted that I should drink only hot beverages after birth to ensure that my body healed properly. My Korean sisters-in-law slept with their kids well into toddlerhood with no guilt, and fixed streamed rice wrapped in seaweed nori wrappers for snacks and hot soup for breakfast. My birth sister, who was raised in Switzerland, told me how some kids grew up learning three or four languages in school.

These things once seemed like cultural eccentricities that might have made me marvel, laugh, or gasp in horror. But now that I'm a mom, I realize that in many cases there are interesting, darn good reasons for why people do what they do. It occurred to me that if I asked the right questions, I could learn a ton about parenthood from people in different cultures. So I set out in planes, trains, automobiles, cruising the Internet, looking for smart fathers and mothers who were willing to share their stories. I dug into the vast research of scholars schooled in other cultures, then hunted down some of those experts, as well as pediatricians, psychologists, and child developmental specialists, to ask them to help me understand what I was learning. I was familiar with the advantages and neuroses of parents in and from middle-class America: how much we care about our families and the myriad inventions that have helped make our kids healthy and happy. I'm grateful for my BellaBand, BabyLegs, my Maclaren stroller, for WebMD and the many available innovative, modern baby products. But I wanted to step out of my comfort zone into communities that were not so familiar, to see what I might be missing.

Reading these chapters might make you think that I'm a mother who calculates her every move and decision. Once my first child was born, instinct tended to be my guide. The parenting books, magazines, and blogs were entertaining and occasionally helpful, but sometimes the advice made me feel inadequate, as if the wrong move meant certain disaster for my family. (Really, I didn't need to do any more worrying.) I was so absorbed with the developments and challenges of the day that I'd forget what we'd been through six months before. The trials of breast-feeding and the first tooth faded into the recesses of my strained mommy brain as we moved on to preschool, viruses, and temper tantrums.

Observing real parents dealing with the similar challenges in distinct environments—often much more difficult or harsh than the reality I knew—forced me to think about what I was doing. Meredith Small, Cornell anthropologist and author of *Our Babies, Ourselves: How Biology and Culture Shape the Way We Parent,* a book on how culture and biology impact parenting, wrote:

> The parental practices we follow in the West are merely cultural constructions that have little to do with what is "natural" for babies. Our cultural rules are, in fact, designed to mold a certain kind of citizen. A !Kung San woman of Botswana, for example, carries her baby at all times. She lets the baby breast-feed in a way that we in the West have unkindly, and tellingly, called "on demand." A San child would never be left to sleep alone. In contrast, American babies, for example, are often set in plastic seats or in strollers for long periods of time; they feed on a prescribed schedule;

and the accepted rule is for each baby to have a bed, if not a private room, to itself. In general, the two styles reflect the place of person within society. Feeding, sleeping patterns, and how a baby spends the day quickly become a lesson in expectations. San children live in a tightly knit small community, where social integration is important. In America, social independence is favored, and so babies are regulated and encouraged toward independence. The cultural milieu, then, is a powerful and barely studied force that molds how we parent.

When I saw how early the Chinese potty trained, how the French talked to their children about food, how members of a Lebanese American extended family methodically taught their kids to feel deeply responsible for and connected to one another, I was compelled to think about what I wanted for my own child in a wider context. I began to examine, in many cases for the first time, not only how I was raising my child but also my entire value system. In the book *Parental Behavior in Diverse Societies,* Harvard anthropologist Robert LeVine and his coauthors put it this way: "By exploring the contexts of parental behavior in other cultures, we uncover universals and variables in the parental predicament and are able to place our current problems in a broader perspective."

My conclusions weren't always pretty, but I kept exploring, and the more I discovered, the more I wanted to know. What I heard and saw sometimes seemed strange, but at the same time much of it felt familiar. Being a good parent was such a universal concern, even if we had unique visions of what should and should not be done. I became a mom on a mission, searching the globe and, as a consequence, myself, for the secrets that could help me become the best parent I could be. This book is my quest.

⁓ 1 ⁓

How Buenos Aires Children
Go to Bed Late

The hour hand has long since crossed twelve midnight, and my toddler is *tirando fuego*—on fire—shaking her hips to a salsa song with a handsome Argentine almost twice her age.

Sofia's polka-dotted dress balloons into a mushroom cap as she spins in circles. Her ponytails are frazzled and crooked, and her heavy eyes remind me where her little body is supposed to be. Yet my baby is jubilant, ad-libbing, throwing in a wiggle here and a head shake there. Her dance partner, who is not quite two and a half years old, is stomping and shrieking encouragement. Sofia throws him a kiss.

We are breaking the rules again. The sleep routine we've cobbled together is toast, and I'm laughing and wilting inside. My child is so happy, winning her own *Dancing with the Stars* competition. I hate to be the foot that quashes her Christmas Eve joy, but I know all too well that her father and I will pay for this in the morning. I've tried to put her down a couple times, but she is not having it, not one bit, not with the music, the fireworks lighting up the Buenos Aires sky, and her doting audience. One part of me is feeling guilty for this whooping transgression that would set sleep experts' fingers a-wagging, but the other Argentine parents at the party, true *porteños* (Buenos Aires natives), don't even flinch at the fact that our children are up at this hour. This is a special night, Nochebuena, when all Argentines celebrate Christmas and families are expected to be together. Besides, late nights for children are no big deal. Go to almost any *parrilla* (a traditional Argentine meat grill) or pizzeria in Buenos Aires, especially on a weekend or summer night, and you'll spot kiddies of all ages out on the town.

This should feel normal to me now that we've lived in Argentina for four years. My husband and I tend to eat and sleep earlier than most Argentine families, but we frequently break the routine and let Sofia stay up and out, though not usually to this extreme. Yet I haven't completely shaken my hang-up, the sense I might be committing a grave parenting offense. In Buenos Aires sleep schedules don't get in the way of a good party. This idea once seemed crazy to me, a mom whose American friends go to great lengths to get their kids to bed, in their own bed, in their own room, before eight o'clock every night, but millions of Argentines have been raised this way. By following their lead, was I dooming my child to developmental, academic, and social failure, or were there lessons to be learned from more relaxed *porteño* moms and dads? As I watched my daughter shimmy across the living room, I needed some answers, fast.

WHEN MY HUSBAND and I moved to Argentina in 2004, we were married without kids and accustomed to staying up. In the States we spent plenty of weekend nights at bars until closing time, which usually meant 1:00 or 2:00 a.m. But Argentina kicked our butts. Friends would invite us for 9:00, 10:00, or 11:00 p.m. dinners, which entailed a *picada* (appetizer), a meal, a dessert, and then endless conversation. We would find ourselves falling asleep in our coffee at 3:00 a.m. Try as we might to soldier on, we'd often be the first to excuse ourselves and end up sleeping until noon the next day, blinded by the midday sun when we emerged from our bedroom. I was in awe: *How do these people do it? They work in the morning and even have kids. Do they ever sleep?*

These questions took on new urgency after we had our first child in Argentina, so I started asking around to local friends, moms and dads, pediatricians, and even cultural experts. Late nights, it turns out, are in this city's cultural genes. Many people who live in Buenos Aires are descendants of Spanish and/or Italian families who moved to Argentina in the 1800s and early 1900s. Those immigrants brought with them the habits of the southern Mediterranean, where people ate after the sweltering sun set and didn't worry much about letting the kids stay up.

In their new land, also plentiful in daylight hours, people kept close their *nonna*'s pasta recipes, the traditional weekly family gathering, and the delayed dinner and bedtime hours. One historian that I spoke with, Dora Barrancos, head of the Interdisciplinary Institute of Gender Studies at the University of Buenos Aires, shared her theory that many immigrants were still single when they arrived, so they were able to paint the town at all hours, and these habits became a way of life.

For a while, the daily siesta helped regulate the sleep deficit. Then city residents rid themselves of that pesky little detail because business owners decided they wanted to use every hour they could to earn more money. Thus Buenos Aires evolved into a city of people who truly never seem to sleep, where restaurants owners don't unlock their doors until 8:00 p.m. and lines don't begin forming outside clubs until 2:00 a.m. It is a badge of honor, this lateness. The city's official website brags, "In Buenos Aires you eat at nighttime, after 10 and on into the morning hours. While in cities like Paris, New York and London restaurants are packed at 8:30, in Buenos Aires, that doesn't happen before 11 p.m."

We were out for a stroll one summer night at about ten o'clock and observed our neighborhood, Palermo, brimming with families. Most of the *parrillas* were only then filling with customers. The smell of steak wafted to the sidewalk where young Argentines, dressed in their clubbing clothes, sipped champagne and waited for a table. Nearby, plenty of mothers and fathers chitchatted, leaning against their strollers, in which their babies were wide awake and babbling. Other parents were holding toddlers who were laughing and pointing at other children who were just ambling in. Waiters set up high chairs, and more than a couple kids danced between tables. In any number of hot spots—even upscale places—I saw children, from a few weeks old, being cradled by grandparents, snoozing in their carriers, playing with pieces of bread on wooden tables.

These scenes were jolting when we first moved here. Once upon a time, when motherhood was further off, I wasn't so tolerant. I cast a stink eye now and then at parents whose misbehaving spawn disrupted my quiet meal. Then I had a child.

In Buenos Aires, the social lives of adults and children blend rather fluidly. Despite the fact that most middle- to upper-class parents have the kind of access to babysitters that many Americans can only dream of (child care is much cheaper), they don't hesitate to ditch the nanny and bring the kids along, especially if it's a family event. Most Argentines—even single and childless folks—don't seem to think of little ones as a drag in many group settings. On the contrary, they believe children add a certain lightness, humor, and even hope.

I ran this idea by Soledad Olaciregui, a Spanish teacher and the co-owner of a business that helps foreigners understand Argentine culture called Maneras Argentinas (loosely translated: Argentine Ways). She and her business partner had helped me out with a travel guide on the city of Buenos Aires that I put together for *National Geographic Traveler*. Olaciregui didn't have children when we first met, but by the time I was inquiring into bedtimes, she was the mother of a ten-month-old girl. She agreed with me that other cultures separate adult and kid time and space a lot more than hers does.

"It really surprised me that in England there are restaurants that display signs that say, 'Prohibited to enter with children,'" Olaciregui said. "There are places that let in dogs but not kids! I think in Argentina this would be unthinkable."

Sure, there are limits. During school nights, a lot of kids stick to a routine, though it tends to skew later than many Americans could ever accept. Kids don't go to late-night bars or dance clubs, and they usually don't attend speeches or formal events. But it's not uncommon to see a child tagging along with his parents at a rowdy soccer game or a big nighttime show. My friends tell me they saw five-year-old children weeping with joy alongside their parents at the first Rolling Stones concert ever in Buenos Aires in 1995. Some parents even bring their babies to the movies, cradling them with one hand while they reach for popcorn with the other.

Most at-home events—birthday parties, barbecues, and so on—welcome kids; it's rare to get a no-children-allowed request. (We've received invitations like that only from families in which at least one parent is not Argentine.) Weddings, which usually last from 8:00 p.m. to 7:00 a.m., almost always feature children.

"At our wedding, my niece Catalina, who was five, ate, danced, and had a blast the whole night," my friend Macarena Byrnes told me. "She only fell asleep—on two chairs pushed together—for about a half hour, and when she woke up she was very angry with everyone because we had let her sleep and she missed out on some of the fun."

Her son, Bauti, was born a week before Sofia, and we became close as our children grew up together. I'd always been madly envious of the sleep habits of her son: he went to bed by himself without fail by eight o'clock, slept through the night, and woke around eight the next morning. He took naps that could last from two to four hours. Bauti was a powerhouse, incredibly coordinated and strong, a nonstop ball of energy; he played hard and slept hard.

Although Bauti was a master at his routine, Byrnes didn't worry about breaking it on nights when he wasn't going to school in the morning.

"Everyone, from the day we are born, is used to going to bed late if necessary," she said. She's married to an American, so she knows how early life can be in the States. When she first visited her in-laws in Maryland, she was astounded that some Americans actually eat at 5:00 p.m., an hour at which most Argentines have just begun to sip their afternoon cup of tea.

That is not to say all Argentine parents keep their kids out late; some subscribe to an earlier routine. Still, most families I've met think spending quality time with relatives and friends is more important than getting their kid to bed at the same time, in the same place every night.

Juana Lugano, who likes to call herself my Argentine mother, often invites my family to join her own children and grandchildren for their almost weekly dinner at her apartment on the weekend. (It's where we have spent two of the last three Christmas Eves.) The dinners never get started before nine o'clock. More than once she's bumped the start time up to eight thirty to accommodate our American preference to eat and sleep earlier.

(Her children hardly ever show up before nine.) Even she admits that the kids can become "terrors" if it gets too late.

"But it would be such a shame if the children did not share these moments with their family," she said.

MATEO ACOSTA IS five years old and has dewy, brown Paul McCartney eyes, with lashes that extend for miles. From his mom he inherited his straight hair, from his dad, his love of yerba maté, and from his country, he got his daily routine.

Like many Argentine children, Mateo goes to bed late and wakes up late. When he was very young, his mother, Mariana Garcia (a reporter), and his father, Martin Acosta (a photographer), started their jobs at the largest newspaper in Argentina at around noon and stayed until at least eight or nine, while a nanny cared for their son.

As a toddler, Mateo would often wait until his parents got home to go to sleep, and then they ate, played, and read together. His parents never forced him straight into bed. Instead, they chose to linger, wanting this to be an intimate time when Mateo "could enjoy Mama and Papa," Garcia said. She often stayed with him—cribs in Argentina are often large enough to fit a small adult—until he fell asleep, usually around 10:00 p.m. or later.

"The truth is that we never had an overly rigorous method to teach him to sleep," Garcia said. She never had hang-ups about his nighttime waking or whether or not Mateo should be falling asleep in her arms. If he wanted to be in their bed, they let him. Their view was that it mattered less where everybody was sleeping, as long as everyone was getting a good night's sleep. That way, the whole family was happier.

Going out was simply part of the happiness equation. On evenings that were obviously meant for adults—Argentine parents do welcome those childless breaks, too—they would take turns babysitting or arrange for their son to stay with a nanny or his grandparents. But often he tagged along with his mom and dad. We got to know Mateo pretty well, at birthday parties, *parrillas*, and Korean and Chinese restaurants. He's come to our apartment for curry dinners, Halloween, and Chinese New Year parties. His parents would take turns entertaining him, or friends carried him around, tickled him and told him stories. He ate what the adults ate, from *morcilla* (blood sausage) to sushi. We all went to a party on my birthday when Mateo was about two, and he played with the breadsticks, olives, and dips on the coffee table most of the night. No one minded. My husband and I watched him evolve from a pudgy baby who fell asleep in his baby carrier while his parents sipped wine and talked politics, to the boy who watched *Shrek 2* on my iMac and could describe in detail each character's peculiar traits.

"We tried to find an equilibrium between our own routines and Mateo's life," Garcia said when I told her how I was impressed with the fluidity in which she and Acosta seemed to integrate their son in their social lives.

"It is not easy," Acosta once warned me. They, like all parents, made sacrifices. They didn't go out when their son was tired or sick or when they themselves didn't have the energy to chase him around. They didn't see their single friends as much, and they couldn't go out on a whim. Mateo had some meltdowns; I've seen him throw tantrums in restaurant booths and throw chopsticks at his mom. But in Buenos Aires, even if a child has a fit in a public place, almost no one glares. In fact, fellow customers, waiters, or restaurant owners might come over and help. The payoff to this public suffering is that your child spends more time with you and your family, and you can continue to see your friends more than once in a while (which helps you stay sane).

"In general, it seems to me that parents go everywhere with their babies," said Garcia. "Later, there's a period of time (during toddler-hood) when the kids briefly turn into savages and you have to lay off for a while. But then they return to being domesticated, and you can start going out again."

Mateo had just turned five when I interviewed his mother, and she told me she adored going on "dates" with him. He sat properly, ate, and chatted about his day at school.

"I love it. It's just *barbaro,*" she said, using a common Argentine term for "fabulous." Garcia and Acosta stuck to a 10:00 p.m. bedtime on weeknights once he started elementary school; tardiness is not taken as lightly as it is in preschool. Students and parents are held accountable when they show up even five minutes after start time. Still, during the weekend and summer vacation, Mateo's mom relaxes and allows him to stay up. "Yesterday, for example, we went to my mother's house and we left at midnight," Garcia said. "He went home and slept like a baby."

This is not to say that Mateo is a perfect sleeper. Garcia

quipped, "Any parent who says their kid sleeps all night, every night, is lying." She simply expected her child to adapt to her schedule, just as she adapted to his.

That simple idea appealed to me, though it was easier said than done. Not getting enough or not even close to enough sleep, is one of the most vexing problems of parenthood. It takes a lot of experimenting to find the right balance for each child in each family. I was embracing the Argentine way to some extent but I still wondered if it was better for my social calendar than it was for my daughter's health.

WESTERN SLEEP EXPERTS and parents have made their matter-of-fact preference more than clear: routines are key, and the earlier the better, for children and for parents. Little room is made for exceptions. A cultural norm has turned into a rule. Parents who admit to letting their child stay up often do it with a lot of explanations, apologies, and guilt.

Yet if you dig a little, you will find that many child development experts will admit there is nothing intrinsically wrong with setting later bedtimes, if children make up for it somewhere: sleeping in, taking naps, and so on.

"As long as they're getting enough sleep, it doesn't make too much difference," Richard Ferber, sleep guru and director of the Center for Pediatric Sleep Disorders at the Children's Hospital in Boston, told the *New York Times*. The problem, some experts say, is when parents break those routines, which Argentines do on a regular basis.

I called the National Sleep Foundation in Washington, D.C., to quiz their experts on what I was experiencing in Argentina. I half expected to get a stern verbal thrashing, because I was clearly not always heeding their advice about enforcing a consistent bedtime and ensuring quiet time every evening that was "free of loud music and bright lighting." The organization—dedicated to improving the quality of life for Americans who suffer from sleep problems—hooked me up with one of its board members, College of the Holy Cross professor Amy Wolfson, author of *The Woman's Book of Sleep*. Wolfson listened thoughtfully as I described the Buenos Aires night scene over the phone.

"I'd hate to judge a culture," Wolfson said immediately. She wondered if Argentines and their bodies could be more used to this lifestyle. Scientists have found that our circadian rhythms—the biological clock that regulates how our body functions—are adaptable; years of late-night reveling may have produced people who can thrive later with fewer ill effects.

Still, Wolfson said that by and large erratic sleeping habits—"falling asleep in a restaurant, sleeping in a stroller, and then sleeping in the car, waking up and falling asleep, waking up and falling asleep"—are not a good idea for anyone. Inconsistent patterns can lead to bad habits and possibly sleep deprivation and disorders, and scientists have shown that children (and adults) need a certain amount of uninterrupted sleep for body and mental development.

"It's definitely better to have more consistent schedules," Wolfson said. "Does that mean that it's terrible to let your kids stay up once in a while or you should be stressed about it? No. There's a happy medium. But I think regularly depriving a child of sleep is not a good thing."

Some Argentine doctors aren't big fans of their own culture's habits either, though they are more willing to make exceptions for the social reality of the families they treat. During one of Sofia's checkups, I asked her pediatrician, Oscar Albanese, for his opinion on the impact of late nights on kids.

"Every place has their customs and habits," he told me. "This happens to be a bad one." Too many parents let their littlest ones stay up well past midnight too often, he said. The danger comes when kids end up exhausted and never make up for the loss.

Any parent knows what a nightmare it can be to deal with a tired, cranky child. Research has shown that the long-term impact of chronic sleep deprivation can be serious. Lack of sleep has been identified as a factor in behavior problems, tantrums, hyperactivity, and poor performance in school. Some scientists theorize that sleep problems in the formative years can lead to permanent brain changes that can impact cognitive functions. But does sleep have to occur in a certain way, in exact amounts, at the same time and place to be healthy?

Despite their late nights, families in Buenos Aires seem to make up at least some sleep in the morning. I'm constantly blown away when friends tell me that their toddlers usually snooze until nine or ten o'clock in the morning and complain when little ones wake up at an outrageous seven thirty. Society doesn't get moving until around eight, long after many Americans would have already hit the gym, showered, and made their way to work. I feel like I'm the only crazy wandering the streets if I head out for a postdawn jog. Gyms don't open before seven, and most breakfast spots start pouring coffee at eight at the earliest. Morning preschools don't open their doors until nine o'clock, about an hour or so later than your average American school, and many families still prefer to send their kids to preschool during the afternoon. If we take Sofia to the playground before ten on a Saturday morning, we are usually the only ones there.

My pediatrician told me he advises parents to get their kids to bed by 9:00 or 10:00 p.m., and encourage them to sleep until at least 7:00 or 8:00 a.m. (This was a relief to me, given that that was approximately the schedule Sofia kept.) He admitted, however, that meeting that ideal in the reality of Buenos Aires can be a tall order.

"So often the way we sleep depends on the light, the climate, the way people have grown up," he said. "Those things are hard to change."

Sleep in the real world. This idea intrigued me and got to the heart of my questions. Western scientists have told us that adults need seven or eight hours of sleep during the course of a twenty-four-hour period, and toddlers should get more, eleven to fifteen hours between nighttime sleep and naps. So what happens when we start molding that biological need to our own cultural and social behaviors and desires? Industrialized nations such as the United States and England embraced the eight-hour early-to-bed, early-to-rise routine (preferably in nice plush beds) in order to accommodate a more productive workday and life. In places such as Argentina, Spain, and Egypt, families prefer to stay up later, enjoying dinner during the cooler hours, perhaps sneaking a nap during the hot daytime hours. In African tribes such as the !Kung and the Efe, people tend to fall in and out of sleep all night, socializing, caring for babies, tending fires, and shooing away predators. Do we really know which models are better and which are worse?

That's one of the questions that journalist Jeff Warren asked in his exploration of human consciousness, *Head Trip: Adventures on the Wheel of Consciousness*. After talking to various experts and even experimenting with different sleeping methods, he told me that he came to this conclusion: "There are no ideal sleep patterns. When you dig around you find there are many different flavors of sleep."

But, he continued, "the 'ideal' distinction is important. I actually think there are 'better' sleep patterns in terms of patterns that are more suitable for different cultures. And if you're not getting a certain amount of sleep you will definitely feel it. The key is realizing you can get these hours in many different ways."

Scientists have obsessed over sleep, sliced and diced it in all kinds of laboratory settings to figure out how much we need and when, and why we can't seem to get enough. But as Wolfson and anthropologist Carol Worthman will tell you, not many scientists have looked at sleep from a non-Western cultural vantage point in homes and camps versus laboratories.

Piqued by this gaping omission, Worthman, a professor at

Emory University, did just that, digging through more than fifty years of research to compare the sleeping habits of several cultures, ranging from the Hiwi tribe in southern Venezuela to the Gabra nomadic people who live in a rocky desert on the border of Kenya and Ethiopia, and citizens of modern-day Egypt and America.

Worthman discovered that many, if not most, people blend fluidly their social and their sleep universes. In many cultures, adults and children rarely, if ever, sleep alone. They are in huts, tents, mats, crowded apartments, cuddled up with their parents, sisters, brothers, and the family dog (cat, chicken, etc.). People fall in and out of sleep during campfire talks, nighttime religious rituals, and family parties.

"In our culture, quality sleep is going into a dark room that is totally quiet, lying down, falling asleep, doing that for eight hours, and then getting up again," Worthman told the *New York Times Magazine*. "But that is not how much of the world has slept in the past or even sleeps today."

The Efe or the !Kung African tribes "stay up as long as something interesting—a conversation, music, dance—is happening and they participate; then they go to sleep when they feel like it," Worthman and Melissa Melby wrote in "Toward a Comparative Ecology of Human Sleep," featured in a book on adolescent sleep. "Additionally, no one, including children, is told to go to bed, and individuals of any age may nod off amid ongoing social intercourse and fade in and out of sleep during nighttime social activities." The Balinese, who practice nighttime religious rituals, always bring their children along, where they might fall asleep at will. (I thought of all the kids in Buenos Aires who are used to falling asleep in random places; generations of children have snoozed on chairs pushed together in busy restaurants or on sofa cushions at parties.) This way contrasts greatly with the advice that many Western sleep experts give: that you should contain your children's sleep and that they always should be put to bed in the same quiet space.

"American parents put their infants to sleep under conditions of minimal sensory load, but later expect their children to titrate arousal and focus attention appropriately in a world with high sensory loads and heavy competing demands for attention," she observed.

Worthman and other scientists have wondered if industrialized society's attempts to force sleep into an eight-hour block has contributed to sleep disorders in adults and children alike. Some scientists believe that segmented sleep—a pattern that consists of two or more periods of sleep and "peaceful" wakefulness—is the natural way for humans. (Babies often sleep this way.) Some studies have shown that segmented sleep can leave people more alert.

"Sleep can be considered a biologically driven behavior of the child that is strongly shaped and interpreted by cultural values and beliefs of the parents," wrote Dr. Oskar Jenni and Bonnie O'Connor in an article on culture and sleep for *Pediatrics* in 2005.

"It is important to note that many 'problems' with sleep during childhood, such as difficulties falling asleep alone or waking at night and seeking parental attention, are based on culturally constructed definitions and expectations and are not necessarily rooted in sleep biology," they wrote. They point to research that shows people in Japan (in contrast to the United States) don't worry about insomnia and rarely consult doctors about it as a problem. Italian parents reported it "customary and preferable to have infants sleep in their rooms with them irrespective of the availability of separate rooms, and considered the American norm of putting children to bed in separate rooms to be 'unkind,'" they wrote.

"Clearly, there is a need to understand better the effects of cultural norms on children's sleep behavior and their interplay with biology. Such an understanding is fundamental to comprehending what constitutes a sleep problem, when and for whom, how best to approach it, and perhaps even to work to modify some cultural standards and practices as a means of improving quality of life for children and families."

While there are minimal biological sleep requirements for children, Jenni and O'Connor asked: "Are the cultural standards provided by our own society optimal for the development of our children? The large diversity of children's sleep behaviors among societies and cultures may in fact indicate that an 'optimal cultural standard' does not exist."

In other words, we just don't know enough to say which way is better. Could learning to sleep amid noise and chaos have developmental advantages?

For my own child's sake, at least, I liked to think that might be true.

OUR DAUGHTER WAS born in Buenos Aires on September 7, 2007, and keeping with local tradition, Sofia was out on the town at night less than two weeks later. We eased into it. One evening when my husband and I needed a little break, we bundled Sofia up, put her in a stroller, and walked a couple blocks to the Mexican restaurant we frequented. We went early, shortly after eight o'clock, and the staff had just begun putting the silverware and candles on the tables. The cheery waitress congratulated us and quickly cleared out a cozy little space near the front window but out of the cool breeze. We were the only customers in the place for at least an hour. Our baby slept pleasantly while we ate chicken fajitas.

Most of the time, we kept Sofia to a fairly regular schedule, with one- or two-hour naps twice a day and bedtime sometime between nine and ten. Later, at around eighteen months, she stopped taking a second nap, but her bedtime remained the same. She slept pretty well during the first six months of her life in the Pack 'n Play beside our bed, waking for her night feedings only, and transitioned to her own room without much scandal, at least at first. I wasn't worried about not making the crib routine every night; we were fortunate in that Sofia could and would fall asleep in most settings.

Still, my daughter was a waker (payback, my own mother says, for my disdain for sleep during childhood). Frustrated, we tried the prescribed methods, the strict reading-bath routine, the Ferber method, and the Weissbluth way. The advice that friends insisted would do the trick didn't. Sofia woke even if she slept with us. I asked our pediatrician if I was doing something wrong: Was it the bedtime or the going out? He smiled and said, "You just didn't get one that sleeps a lot this time."

In fact, Sofia sometimes seemed to sleep better when we were out; she liked all the fuss, the kisses and the attention. Sometimes restaurant hosts gathered her up and took her on a brief tour of the kitchen, introducing her to the chef. At one of our favorite elegant places—a candlelit white-linen spot, where the waiter pours your wine and bows slightly when taking your order—the owners offered us a giant booth with large, comfy cushions so she could snooze while we ate and hung out with friends. Sometimes we hired a babysitter, but often we didn't have to.

"Bring *la gordita,*" our friends would insist if they had a party, and we usually did. When we were out, like the other mamas around me, I often paid more attention to Sofia's tired signs than the actual hour. When she'd had enough, I fed her and then found a place for her to rest: in my or a contented auntie's arms, on a cushion, on a mat on the floor, or in a bed. We'd sometimes battle a few raucous bouts of crying-child-fighting-sleep, but before long, she'd drifted off. The night Barack Obama was elected president, she slept with four other kids in my friend's extra bedroom and woke up briefly in time for his acceptance speech.

As time went on, our approach evolved. Once Sofia entered

preschool, we went out less (though we still made plenty of exceptions) and tried to be stricter about hitting bedtimes and naps. Even if she was in bed at by nine thirty or ten, that was at least an hour earlier than most of her classmates (who tended to sleep an hour later as well). Almost daily we were one of the first students in the entire school to show up, even if we were a few minutes late. Other students in her class meandered in at nine thirty or ten. Because elementary and secondary schools are more strict about attendance, parents become more conscious of routines as their children get older, my friends tell me, but administrators do struggle with problems with tardiness. (Showing up late seems to be a genetic trait among many Argentines).

Eager for more expert opinion and reassurance, I rang Jim McKenna, who runs the Mother-Baby Behavioral Sleep Laboratory at the University of Notre Dame. He is a well-known specialist in parenting and infant development and an outspoken promoter of co-sleeping, having conducted landmark studies tracking mother and baby sleeping patterns. He listened quietly as I described our sleep habits and challenges and stopped me when he heard a tinge of anxiety in my voice.

"We have to stop thinking that there is just one way to sleep," he told me. "We can sit around and say this is how we want babies to sleep, or this is how they should sleep, but babies are not designed that way."

Babies get the sleep they need, he said; they just may not do it exactly when or where we think they should.

"I always laugh when I go by newsstands and see articles that advertise the six steps to solving an infant's sleeping problems. Those steps are always unrealistic and unbiological. If we just chilled out and let babies be babies, they would ultimately sleep better and parents would sleep better."

The Argentine way is refreshing, he said.

"Your child being valued enough by you and integrated in your life is more valuable than enforcing a rigid sleep routine. In Western culture we look for simplistic recommendations with dire consequences. But I think the way in which many Europeans and South Americans have a much more proximate physical relationship to children is much more suitable to healthy development."

He reminded me, "It's not really the sleep arrangements that dictate the development of a child; sleeping is just one component of an overall system of relationships children have that make them who they are. In other words, it's never the sleeping arrangements that decide how a child will turn out, it's the overall nature of the child's relationship with the parents.

"Including your child in your nighttime activities—it helps to prepare the child for the social life in which she is expected to function," he said. "It's not like you want your child staying out until two a.m. five days a week. But the value of your social world has value to your child . . . The fact that she is integrated in your activities, it shows the nature of your relationship with her."

It was a relief to hear this, and several of my friends agreed.

"I was happy that I could spend so much time with Henry during his first year while still seeing friends and going out," said Cintra Scott, a New Yorker whose son is a year older than Sofia.

"I think that was good for me and him. As a baby, he could sleep through the roar of restaurants and he didn't seem to bother anybody."

It was a bit harder to take her son out when Henry turned two, got active, and had preschool in the morning. But she and her husband still did it. Once, Henry's dad left a party, brought his son back at midnight when the babysitter had to go home, and put him in a bed in the host's home.

Scott told me, "I do think we'd be more isolated if we lived in the States now. I don't think we'd go out as much with Henry if restaurants and parties were not as welcoming, and babysitters cost us more. We'd probably end up staying home more."

The truth was I liked being more relaxed about Sofia's bedtime and enjoyed having my daughter around whenever she was welcome. Time was flying, and each day and night was precious. If my husband and I paid a little bit on the sleep side, we decided, so be it.

COULD OUR FAMILY live like this in the United States? When we would visit, I would trim back our behavior, bending to the potential judgment of others. I knew better than take my toddler to a fancy restaurant, although I had no qualms about choosing a family-friendly place, even if the hour hand was creeping toward eight. And that didn't mean that I'd have to go to some family place that served only chicken fingers and burgers. Ethnic restaurants often seemed more tolerant of babies and kids at slightly later hours.

I found friends—with and without kids—to be more accommodating than I expected, too. My husband and I made sure to ask if Sofia could come along, and when it was time for her to sleep, I cuddled her down wherever we were. Often our hosts were surprised that we didn't make a big deal of bedtime.

The difference in our approach was loud and clear at a Super Bowl party we attended in Chicago when Sofia was sixteen months old. We knew kids were invited, so we happily bundled her up and brought her along. The festivities began around five o'clock in the afternoon, and Sofia dove in. She happily munched on chili, carrots, pasta, cheese sticks, tortilla chips, and whatever anyone offered her, all the while chasing around a three-year-old girl, Melissa, who was dressed as a princess, and kissing a one-year-old named Danny. She hooted when spectators shouted at the game, and she danced when Bruce Springsteen played the half-time show.

As the clock rounded seven, Melissa's mom said she would have to go home, because her child's bedtime was seven thirty, and she was adamant about sticking to her daughter's routine. Regularity—bathing, storytelling, being in her bed at the exact same time every night—was how Melissa's parents ensured that everyone in their home got a good night's sleep. They didn't make exceptions and discouraged people from calling or coming over after seven at night. Melissa's parents drove separately to the Super Bowl party so that when bedtime neared, mom could leave to tuck her in while dad stayed to watch the end of the game.

Danny and his parents stuck around a little longer (and Sofia kept kissing him) at least until the third quarter of the game. They didn't have to be anywhere the next morning, but it was late (about eight thirty) by American family standards.

Sofia pushed on. The lone child, she flirted with the men and "borrowed" the cell phones of the women there, proclaiming, *"Hola!"* into the receiver. We could have left if we wanted—we had to get on the road the next day very early, but we decided against it. We all made it into bed by eleven, and our daughter slept late the next day during our drive to Michigan.

I completely appreciated and respected Melissa's parents' approach. More than once, mostly around the hour of 3:00 a.m. when my child was calling for me from her crib, I wondered if I'd sabotaged any chance of a normal sleep schedule with any number of the decisions I'd made. I'm willing to bet Melissa's family gets more sleep than we do, though there are plenty of parents with a moderate approach to routine who have kids who sleep like angels. My brother in Detroit let his toddler stay up until whenever she wanted, and she slept the night through (in her parents' bed). Even my stricter mommy friends let their kids run wild once in a while at birthday parties or other occasions, though usually not later than nine or ten o'clock tops.

But our way feels right for us. In the end, the outings have become part of Sofia's routine. She can fall asleep anywhere and is highly socially adaptable. Sometimes she gets thrown off when we take her out too late, but then we pull back to get her on track. Most of the time we try to have her at home and in bed at a regular time, but we don't hesitate to make exceptions.

Christmas Eve in Argentina during her fifteenth month of life did test the limits of Sofia's late-night stamina, and ours. It would be the latest we'd ever let her party. Sofia powered on past midnight, and then 1:00 a.m., dancing. When we noticed that she had started resting her head on a chenille chair, we knew the madness had to end. We thanked our hostess and left a half hour later. Our girl promptly fell asleep in my lap on the bus ride home.

All around us, the city hummed with holiday excitement. Families, toddlers, teenagers, seniors—everyone, it seemed—were sitting in plastic chairs in front of their homes, leaning on the balcony rails of their terraces, walking their neighborhoods, still a long way from Sleepytown. Buenos Aires felt as lively as ever. We swiftly spirited Sofia into our apartment, up the stairs and into her bed, before she could figure out that the party was raging on without her. When our own hazy adult heads hit the pillows, we couldn't believe we had made it to 3:00 a.m., a feat we had not accomplished since our daughter had been born. I tried not to think about the almost inevitable fact that Sofia would be awake in a matter of hours. We fell asleep to the sizzle and crack of stray fireworks, the murmur of our neighbors lingering on their patios, and the shimmering echo of laughing children.

Sleeping Arrangements

In many societies, children sleep with their parents at least through infancy and sometimes much longer. Some do so because they don't have much space, but also because they believe co-sleeping to be an essential way to feed, comfort, protect, and bond with their babies and children. Here is a sampling of sleep arrangements in some traditional communities compiled by Carol Worthman and Melissa Melby:

- In the leaf huts of Efe foragers of Africa, no one sleeps alone. Two adults, a baby, other children, a set of grandparents, and even a visitor routinely crash in the same small space.
- Gebusi women in Papua New Guinea sleep together in a narrow area, about seven and a half feet wide, packed like sardines along with infants and children of varying ages. Men and older boys lie on sleeping platforms in a nearby space.
- For the Gabra nomads in northern Kenya and southern Ethiopia, sleeping arrangements include separate beds for husband (and small boys) and wife (with infant and small children) in the sleeping portion of the tent.
- The Balinese in Indonesia are social, even in sleep: "Being alone for even five minutes is undesirable, even when asleep, so widows and widowers who sleep alone are viewed as unfortunate and even socio-spiritually vulnerable," Worthman and Melby wrote.
- The Swat Pathan in Afghanistan and Pakistan allow a bed for each person, but no one gets his own room.

❧ 2 ❧

How the French Teach Their Children to Love Healthy Food

We hope to see the best of ourselves in our kids, in their faces or bodies, in their demeanors, values, and tastes. I know moms who hope their sons will inherit their baby blues, and dads who prefer that their daughters end up with their dark brown skin. Hoping to instill brand loyalty early, fanatic baseball and soccer fans purchase tiny jerseys with the logos of their favorite teams well before their children are born. When not taken to extremes, these are natural desires. We want our children to resemble us, embrace our values, and fit into our lifestyle. One of the traits that I most passionately hoped that Sofia would get from me was my taste for vegetables.

Most of my life, I've been a big fan of veggies—from the leafy greens to roots, from crucifers to cucurbits. Even when I was young, I gobbled up spaghetti squash with butter, sautéed eggplant, Chinese broccoli in oyster sauce, and cabbage with carrots. I ordered mushrooms on my pizza and dill pickle, lettuce, and tomato on my burgers. Truth be told, I love most foods, almost to the point of obsession.

My husband, Monte, is a midwestern meat-and-starch kind of guy. When I met him, he wouldn't have anything to do with vegetables, aside from corn. Monte had mastered moving a salad around on a plate so it looked like he'd eaten more than two leaves and could artfully separate out any stray onions or chunks of tomatoes on a plate. His palate has evolved over the thirteen years in which we've been together, and he has even tried to eat some vegetables; he once told me (only half joking) that in honor of my birthday, he would eat more spinach that year (he didn't). As a rule, I can pretty much bet that if it's green, Monte isn't going to like it.

I've nagged my poor husband about this aversion far too often over the years, which seems to be hereditary since his father and his three brothers share his distaste for vegetables. I worried about his health and felt limited in my culinary repertoire, which wasn't that extensive to begin with. Most of all, I was concerned about the impact it might have on Sofia. It's hard enough to get little ones to eat their veggies when they are bombarded with fun, colorful processed alternatives and kiddie menus that consist of pizza, burgers, and fried chicken nuggets. I feared that once our daughter noticed that Daddy doesn't like broccoli, any hopes for healthy eating would be shot. We agreed to work at it, because Monte knew it was important that Sofia ate well.

I was checking around to see how we could cultivate our child's budding palate, when I found an article in *Today's Dietitian* on kids and eating in rural France. A group of American chefs, health professionals, and educators told tales of visiting schools in the Loire Valley in central France for the International Exchange Forum on Children, Obesity, Food Choice, and the Environment organized by a group called Field to Plate. Attendees spoke in wide-eyed awe of meeting the trained chefs in charge of school lunchrooms who used fresh produce to make multicourse meals that included such scrumptious (and nutritious) offerings as a salad of butter lettuce with smoked duck and asparagus with vinaigrette. Meals were served on ceramic plates and eaten with silverware—no paper or plastic here. Kids drank water—not milk or sweet juices—from glasses. Food in France, the organizer of that trip noted, was considered a pleasure afforded to adults and children alike. Little ones tried all kinds of foods that Americans might consider too strong tasting, such as mussels or Roquefort cheese. They were expected to eat what their parents ate, so kids meals weren't necessary.

My mouth watered at this simple idea. So, for tips on how to convince kids to eat well, I decided to ask the French.

LUNCHTIME AT LA MIMARELA in the tiny southern French village of Saint-Laurent-de-la-Cabrerisse is simply a vision—and I can't believe toddlers are eating this cuisine. The first course features fresh, parboiled green beans dressed with olive oil, vinegar, and salt and pepper, served on colorful plates. The two- and three-year-olds eagerly grab them up with their little fingers. Esteban, a curly-headed blond, proclaims, *"Je vais manger tout!"* I'm going to eat it all! His lunch mates laugh and make the beans dance on the table and in their mouths while an adult at the table gently reminds them to use their silver *four-chettes* (forks). Chubby Kara wants to pass on the beans, but little Julien reminds her of the cardinal rule of eating at La Mimarela preschool: everyone must try everything at least twice.

"C'est bon!" Julien insists. It's good! The others start repeating the praise, an exuberant chorus of toddler peer pressure. Kara finally gives in, reluctantly; she tries one, squints up her face, and moves on. The children gobble up the next course of roasted chicken with wedges of potatoes and ask for more. Then comes the cheese course—a cut of fresh brie—served by the chef himself on a wheeled trolley. The children eat their cheese with a baguette. The sweet dessert finale, as always, is fruit, and on this Monday, it's a whole beautifully ripened banana.

Each meal at La Mimarela is a specially orchestrated event, planned by an in-house dietitian and professional chef. The vegetables and fruit often come from the school's own garden, the local open market, or nearby farms. During one week in February, Monday's lunch menu opened with steamed leeks in a vinaigrette, followed by whole roasted chicken and potatoes, cheese, and cooked pears. On Tuesday, the children ate vegetable soup, baked fish puree, corn and artichoke heart salad, plain yogurt, and apple compote. Roast beet salad with pasta bolognaise was served on Wednesday, and the Thursday menu consisted of baked tomato provençal, papillotes of salmon, and white beans. Friday offered vegetable quiche with mushrooms, puree of carrots, ground beef, yogurt, and seasonal fruit. The *goûter,* or afternoon snack, is usually fruit and whole milk yogurt, and the kids drink water or sometimes fresh fruit juices with their meals.

Food is a central part of the school's holistic philosophy, developed by the director Delphine Le Douarec. She wants the thirty children who attend her school to have good, homemade meals and taste a variety of flavors. And the experience goes beyond mealtime; children work and play in the garden and make art with spices. On birthdays, the chef welcomes the birthday boy or girl into the school kitchen to help make a birthday cake to share with classmates. The hope is that these little things will encourage children to embrace an essential value in French life, especially in this region: *la joie de manger.* The joy of eating.

Saint-Laurent, a hamlet with a population of 685, is nestled in the Languedoc region, about twelve miles west of the Gulf of Lion and fifty miles north of Spain's Catalonia border. The tiny village is named after a twelfth-century goat herder. Today, goat herders along with cantaloupe and potato farmers labor against a backdrop of vineyards, pine forests, olive trees, and *garrigue,* Mediterranean scrubland filled with wild thyme and rosemary. Residents grow veggies and fruits in tidy backyard gardens, shop at open-air markets, and buy their baguettes daily at one of the small *boulangeries* (bakeries). In March, locals scour the nearby woods for patches of wild asparagus and in October, cèpes (porcini mushrooms). Adults and children linger for hours over the preparation and eating of meals—always a few courses or more—discussing life and their food and drink.

"Family and food are the most important things in life," explained Marie-Benedict Vernal, the mother of three daughters, who tends a herd of almost fifty goats. Her friend and neighbor, Riana Lagarde, an American mom who has been living in France for seven years with her French husband, told me, "You always tell your neighbor *'Bon appétit'* right before lunch or dinner. Mealtime is simply a sacred time. My French neighbors shop for food daily to get fresh ingredients, freely share recipes, and constantly ask, 'What are you making for dinner tonight?' rather than ask about your work or money."

One of the most loving things that Vernal can do for her husband and daughters is to provide healthy, well-rounded, tasty meals, she said. Her girls' favorite breakfast is fresh goat's milk cottage cheese, drizzled with honey or homemade strawberry jam, eaten with a fresh baguette instead of a spoon. Lunch is at home; many French primary and secondary school children, at least in the countryside, get a two-hour break for lunch. Vernal's family sometimes eats meat, but more often they cook vegetables from their own garden, paired with rice or pasta. They make soups during the winter and mixed salads during the summer with fresh fruit for dessert. A large head of cauliflower from their garden, topped with béchamel, a buttery sauce, is a common dish. For snacks, the girls prefer a baguette and cheese, not only their mother's homemade goat's cheese, but soft cheese made from cow's milk, a dense *tomme* from the Basque region, and gooey cheeses from northern Brittany.

One scrumptious Friday evening, Vernal invited Lagarde's

family to join them for dinner. Lagarde arrived early, shortly after five. Vernal's three daughters were sitting in a hayloft, nibbling on a round of semi-aged goat cheese watching their mother
midwife the birth of goat twins. Vernal murmured reassurances
to Samsam, the brown mother goat, while coaxing the babies out
gently with an olive-oiled gloved hand. After the birth was over,
Vernal announced that it was time to make dinner and instructed
each girl on her role in the preparation of the meal. Lagarde went
with Vernal's youngest daughter Esther, age six, to choose a head
of frisée lettuce from their backyard garden.

"Grown with goat poo!" Esther proclaimed triumphantly
while tromping around in the garden. Meanwhile, Elaine, the
eldest at ten years old, collected wild stinging nettles for a soup,
and eight-year-old Emmanuelle grated mountains of potatoes to
make pancakes. The mood was bustling, busy, and happy as salad
leaves were cleaned of dirt and snails, and potato pancakes were
fried in a cast-iron pan. Lagarde's husband and three-year-old
daughter arrived with a tarte tatin (a kind of upside-down apple
pie) in hand.

Everyone sat around a large, round wooden table and the
courses began: potato fritters with a dollop of crème fraiche, followed by a pesto–green nettle soup and accompanied by toasted
bread rubbed with garlic. A dish of baked river trout—caught on
a fishing trip the previous summer—followed. Salad, fresh goat
cheese, dried fruits, and walnuts finished the meal. The adults
talked politics, food, and goat herding, and the girls giggled about
boys and school and kicked each other under the table. Everyone

ate almost everything served. Lagarde watched her toddler eat the light green lettuce leaves and lick the dressing off her fingers.

"We try to grow our own food," Vernal said, "but it's not always possible. Sometimes I can trade or barter with other vendors at the farmer's market for honey, eggs, and apples." She shops at the large grocery store in a nearby town for flour and other basic staples once a month. She tells the girls not to waste food, but they don't have to clean their plate. Still, much of the time, they do anyway.

Lagarde later told me, "There is something about gathering and catching your own food that makes children appreciate what's on their plates. It gives them ownership and incentive to eat it. I found the same thing with my three-year-old. If she digs up a potato or a beet or picks up a snap pea, it's hers and she wants to eat it."

Riana, who is a food and travel writer, said that many families in the region eat and think this way; even if they don't eat as well, they "honor their food."

"We are known as *ploucs,* hicks or rednecks to the career-minded, high-rise-living Parisans, but our meals are not so different from theirs: all the family around the table, eating one course at a time, always, always with a baguette."

EVEN IF TRADITIONAL French food has never been my favorite—I find it almost *too* rich—I have to appreciate its profound philosophical influence on eating and cooking everywhere. As the queen of the kitchen Julia Child put it in her book

Mastering the Art of French Cooking, "In France, cooking is a serious art form and a national sport." It is more than just a style; it is an attitude that has informed a way of life.

We Americans appreciate and even love our food, but for many of us, a good meal tends to be a more individualistic pleasure. For many French families, taking pleasure in food is a way of family life.

"In America, you eat while you walk, and you eat while you work," Parisan Camille Labro told me. "For people in France, lunchtime is sanctified. Sometimes in Paris the shops stay open, but in the south of France, I think all shops close between one and four."

I was introduced to Labro, a mother of two, food writer, and cook, through the vast network of food bloggers. Having lived and worked in New York, she seemed like the perfect person to help me compare the way people feed their families in the two countries.

"People take their time to eat, and it's a moment when you sit down, you drop all other activities, and you focus on the food," she explained. "It's almost a habit of the French to talk about the food while they are eating their food, and not even the food they're eating. And it's beyond health—though it's healthier to sit down and eat—it's also a mind health. Learning to take the time. Not to rush through life and to appreciate moments for what they are. People sit at the cafe and have their coffee—or at least stand at the counter. You have to stop and have a relationship with food."

A *good* relationship with food. She made an intriguing point: Americans love food, yet at the same time they fear it. "The relationship is not trusting," Labro said. "'I'll have an egg-white omelet and a salad with no sauce and one toast with rye bread.' What kind of relationship is that?"

The food industry caters to our worries, advertising true and false claims of being organic, without additives, free of trans fats. We are concerned about what and how much our children eat. On the other hand, the French traditionally have eaten several-course meals, and foods made rich with butter and cream. They drink wine daily, even women who are pregnant. Children eat full-fat yogurt and cheese with baguettes and feel full afterward, families told me. The key, as was celebrated in Mireille Guiliano's best-selling book *French Women Don't Get Fat: The Secret of Eating for Pleasure,* is that indulgence is supposed to be done slowly and in small portions.

It's true that the French, like people in so many other countries worldwide, are grappling with a growing weight problem, blamed on more fast food and increasingly sedentary lifestyles. In 2009, one survey conducted by TNS Sofres Healthcare and the Swiss pharmaceuticals firm Roche found that 15 percent of the population in France was obese and that 26 percent of women and almost 39 percent of men were overweight. The French National Institute for Health Monitoring reported that from 2001 to 2007, the number of obese children remained steady at about 18 percent. Those statistics set the nation into a panic; the government launched national campaigns promoting healthy eating, removed vending machines from schools, and even required weigh-in programs at schools in some areas. Nonetheless, while alarming, the French are nowhere as fat as we are in the United States, where two-thirds of Americans were overweight in 2008 and as many as 20 percent of children aged six to eleven were obese, according to the Centers for Disease Control and Prevention.

Americans didn't always eat this badly. We used to eat somewhat like families in rural France, even less than a generation ago, said Ann Cooper, a professional chef and food policy expert who calls herself "the Renegade Lunch Lady." Cooper has appeared in all kinds of media from the *New Yorker* to NPR's Living on Earth, trying to transform school lunch menus and habits.

Where did our diets go wrong? I asked her.

Cooper said it is only in the last thirty years that Americans have made a dramatic shift in how we feed our children. One reason is that mothers went to work and stopped cooking as much, but Cooper also pointed out that "we feed our kids badly by and large because of the marketing of processed foods," such as microwave dinners, prepackaged snacks, and the junk offered at fast-food chains. "Kids' food" became marketable, separate from adult food—and usually much less healthy. Our society became harried and hurried, so cooking and eating became a hassle that had to be made easy. As a result, we started eating hamburgers and drinking Coke and coffee in the car on the way to work and soccer practice. Next, television, cell phones, laptops, and iPads were allowed to infringe on family and mealtime. Meanwhile, strapped school districts spent as little time and money as they could get away with on school lunches and installed vending machines with junk food for the money it would bring in. We are giving kids what they want to eat, we reasoned, and even if it's not good for them, well, better that than nothing. So our children have learned to hate vegetables and love Happy Meals, and we have become fatter and sicker.

Now we are scrambling to reverse the trend. There are some school lunchrooms that serve healthy foods, and plenty of moms and dads who are becoming extra conscious about buying organic products, cutting out sugar, and feeding their children carrot sticks instead of potato chips. Yet even as we try to do better, food still tends to be considered a means to an end (build strong bones, for instance) rather than the end itself, secondary to the other things going on, like making Suzy's soccer practice, attending Johnny's Cub Scout meeting, helping with his incomplete homework, walking the dog, picking up the dry cleaning, and paying the bills.

Kindy Peaslee, a registered dietitian who visited schools in France with Field to Plate, told me, "Our [American] culture is so different and there are so many distractions away from enjoying food at home, taking time to cook and teach our children to cook, and having the means to provide fresh and tasty food that fits the budgets of our schools."

MY MOTHER WAS a stickler about making sure we ate healthy; she outlawed candy, sugary cereals, and junk food. She and my father tried to prepare us home-cooked meals, ranging from casseroles to liver and onions. Still, Mom was never into food and she despised cooking, which was one of the last things she wanted to do after a hard day at the elementary school that she ran. But as she put it, "It wasn't a matter of liking it or not; it was something you just had to do." Dad enjoyed food a lot more than my mother did, and I credit him for introducing us to ethnic foods of all kinds. When he wasn't out for an evening meeting, he'd sometimes whip up a rice-meat pilaf or a stir-fry in his electric wok. When we were little, we almost always ate together at our round dinner table, but later, when the three of us became busy teenagers, we turned into more of a take-out/frozen-meal family. Though we usually preferred ethnic foods (Chinese, Lebanese, Mexican) to fast food, convenience determined our meal choice. We'd eat our microwaved dinners while sprawled in front of the television or quickly at the kitchen counter before running off to a meeting or a basketball game.

I took this eating-on-the-go attitude into adulthood, though I enjoyed cooking and food a whole lot more than my parents did. I bought cookbooks and threw dinner parties, and I loved a good meal out. I'd cook a couple times a week, though I admit often it was something thrown into the oven and occasionally aided by soy sauce or a box mix. With no dining room table, my husband and I would end up eating our meals in front of the television.

I only really began to critique these eating habits after we had our first child. My nanny, who'd been taking care of babies for more than twenty years and who had briefly attended cooking school, started us off right. She made purees from squash, carrots, potatoes, and I followed suit. We cooked the vegetables in our bamboo steamer and mashed them. Sofia liked to chew and suck on corncobs, bananas, and apples while sitting in the kitchen and watching us prepare her meals. My pediatrician gave me a list of foods to introduce, which began with vegetable purees, moved into meats and fruits, and surprisingly, ended with flan. Baby food in jars was not common in Argentina at that time, so I was never tempted to rely on it. The first time we visited the States after Sofia was born, I was blown away by the rows and rows of baby food of every color and origin at a Super Wal-Mart in Illinois. Curious, we tried some. Sofia liked a couple of the fruits, but spit out most of them (and I had pretty much the same reaction). Processed baby foods are a staple in many households; I was a Gerber baby and suspect that if I had Sofia in the States, she would be one, too. There's nothing wrong with that, I think. Following a comparative study of baby foods, even the tough food watchdog organization the Center for Science in the Public Interest concluded that none of them were dangerous, and in fact some can be nutritious as well as convenient. Yet the group also pointed out that the processed stuff usually has fewer nutrients than real food because it is diluted with water and thickening agents—and it costs a lot more.

"Advertising campaigns promote the myth that commercial products are especially good at meeting the nutritional and developmental needs of infants," the study's authors said. "Gerber's public relations and advertising machinery has cultivated an almost sacred image in people's minds of Gerber products. Those perceptions are clearly untrue. Parents, armed with a food processor, blender, or mashing fork, can easily prepare safe, nutritious, and economical food for their infants at home."

Processed baby food seems like part of the regimen that we think we're supposed to follow. It is the same conventional wisdom that warns us about what foods should be introduced to children, and when, from the womb and beyond. The regimen repeats itself in many parenting forums: start rice cereals at six months, then veggies and fruits, and finally pasta and meats. Spices and ethnic foods are not even considered. Understandably, doctors warn against peanuts, honey, and seafood during the first year, fearing life-threatening food allergies, but safe doesn't have to mean bland. Recent research has shown that in families without food allergies, most toddlers can eat many of the same foods that adults do—and they often will if you expect them to. Mexican children gulp down jalepeños, and Japanese tots munch on seaweed and pungent dried fish. In Taiwan, I watched in horror as my four-year-old niece walked up to a plate of steaming whole fish, grabbed out the exposed eyeball with her chopsticks, and popped it in her mouth. A Cheshire cat grin lit her face because she had nabbed the most delicious prize. Even though I'm not going to serve eyeballs for dinner, I learned something from my niece. Each child may have his or her own eating quirks, but we limit them if we start off thinking they'll eat only certain "kids'" foods. Their tastes are shaped by the culture at our dinner tables. And the influence of parental eating habits begins even before a child is born. The Monell Chemical Senses

Center in Philadelphia has found that if mothers ate foods like carrot juice, raw peaches, and green beans during pregnancy or while lactating, their babies were more likely to accept and like those tastes.

I offered Sofia almost anything we ate. My mom, a stickler for good manners, was a little startled at first when my toddler used her grubby hands to take food from my plate. I told my mother that I wanted her to be fearless about trying new foods at a young age. Manners, I argued, could be taught later. Indeed, my effort seemed to be working: at the age of two, while she not surprisingly did like mac and cheese, she also enjoyed hummus, sautéed bean sprouts, and Chinese dumplings.

But I still had to work on our eating habits. More than once, I'd buckled my daughter into her Fisher-Price booster seat and let her suck on noodles in front of the living room television while I ran back and forth to the kitchen. It was a way for me to juggle caring for her and *all the other stuff that I needed to do,* especially when my husband was out of town. But I took to heart what I was hearing from French families: *If you value your food and food time, then your child will. If eating is simply something you have to do, between everything else you have to cram in your day, that is probably how your child will think as well.*

So we turned off our television, computers, and cell phones during mealtime. If our daughter ate before we did, we'd feed her in the kitchen, away from distraction. Most days, we've enjoyed spending time with our food and each other at mealtime. To get our child to eat more, my husband makes up songs about food;

Sofia gets to hear "The Chicken Song" if she eats her chicken, and "The Rice Song" if she eats her rice.

I'm patiently trying to persevere, as prescribed by Chef Alessandra Quaglia and her husband, Jean-Francis, whose mother ran a well-known restaurant in Marseilles. I contacted Alessandra after reading about the cookbook she and her husband had published, *New World Provence,* and asked for her advice. When it came to their preteen sons, Matisse and Remi, the rule in their Vancouver home was always this: "You are allowed *not* to like it but you are not allowed *not* to try it." The owners of well-respected French eateries Provence Mediterranean Grill and Provence Marinaside pointed out to me that palates change and evolve.

"Just because they didn't like it one time doesn't mean I'll never make it again," Alessandra told me. "I have been witness time and time again to them saying they don't like something and then six months or a year later trying it and liking it. Kids are stubborn little creatures and we often heed to their wishes. I cook for myself first! I rarely cook what people consider kid food. Kids should be eating real food, period. How else will their palates develop? It drives me crazy when I see adolescent kids in my restaurant eating pasta with butter. Just yesterday my sons asked me if we could go out for brunch. I jumped at the opportunity and we went out and had the most delicious eggs Benedict with portabella mushrooms and zucchini with a side of salad that had blue cheese and cranberries. They ate it all! It was so satisfying for me to share that with them."

Getting kids involved with food outside of mealtime is also a small, but important thing for the Quaglias and many other families. Camille Labro, for example, told me her son likes to peel quail eggs, and her daughter likes to mix things. Rather than push his children out of the kitchen because they are a distraction or might burn themselves, Frédéric Texier, a chef and father of two who lives in the village of Gréoux-les-Bains in the Provence region, likes his kids to see, smell, and taste what he is cooking and to be curious about the food.

"The children are with me, and they help me," Texier said. "They ask me, 'What is that kind of vegetable? What is that spice?' You have to encourage their curiosity."

Dietitian Kindy Peaslee said these are great ideas for families who want to improve their relationship with food—and can even make a difference with older children who are already choosey about what they eat.

"For example, raise one tomato plant on your patio and have your children take responsibility to water it and pick the harvest and make a salad together," she told me. She suggested visiting the local farmers' market during different seasons and taking the time once a month to let your kids help make the grocery list, shop, and cook the food that you buy together. (Her advice made me recall the times I'd cut out coupons with my father and rode around in the cart while he shopped for groceries.)

"When kids get involved with their eating process and taste freshly grown veggies that they have watered and cared for, it changes mind-sets and creates adventure in their eating," Peaslee said. "It's a process to change kids' tastes for greens. Cooking and preparing part of a meal will help them explore new tastes and make the decision for themselves to discover liking more veggies instead of hearing mom tell them to eat them because it is good for them."

I began trying to involve Sofia more, sitting her in her high chair, letting her fiddle with food or utensils (despite the mess it made), and handing her bits of food to try. My kitchen was small, so even if Sofia was a safe distance from the stove, she was close enough to see everything I was doing. She loved cherry tomatoes, so I'd let her "wash" them before we made our salad. (Mostly this meant she was swishing them around in water, and picking them out, sucking out the juices, then putting the skins back in the bowl.) I took her fruit and vegetable shopping and let her choose a snack. These little things were easy, and fun for both of us.

STILL, THE MOST intimidating part was—and is—the challenge of putting more thought and work into meals each day.

I've always enjoyed cooking, *when I have time,* and I work at home, so I probably have more time than many parents. But sometimes my brain just freezes up. The day ends and I find I haven't thought or prepared in advance. Even the jaunt to the grocery around the block seems overwhelming. I suspect that for parents who do not have a local grocery store, butcher, and pasta shop nearby, it's even harder to wrap their heads around the task, with work and kid activities, the car ride to the store, and the daunting price of fresh produce. There are plenty of times when writing deadlines, my child's playtime, and everything else seem to conspire to deflate any lofty culinary ambitions. On those nights, I can't help but think of cooking as one more in a series of obligations.

How do you do it? I quizzed several families. In reality, most of them are busier than I am. Vernal has her three girls and fifty goats to tend; the Quaglias run restaurants; Labro is a single, working mom; and Texier runs the kitchen in a resort and teaches cooking classes. But all of them told me the same thing: it's not as hard as it sounds.

"It doesn't take longer to cook fresh vegetables than to cook other things," Texier told me. "Fresh vegetables cook in five minutes. Just wash them, and that's it. You have to appreciate the food if you want your children to appreciate the food. Don't push children to eat everything on the plate; just put everything on the table. But really, it's the wrong idea to think it takes longer to cook a fresh product than defrost fish or frozen meat."

Alessandra Quaglia said she and Jean-Francis aren't whipping up gourmet meals daily. They, too, are thinking of how to economize their time in the kitchen.

"Keep it fresh and simple," Jean-Francis advised. They might buy a half chicken, dress it with olive oil, salt and pepper, and cook it on the barbecue grill, then serve it with leftover rice.

"Automatically, if you get fresh and good products, it will be tasty," he said.

That seemed doable.

Sometimes I allow myself a quick fix and turn to boxed macaroni and cheese. (I at least throw in some fresh or frozen vegetables.) Most of the time, whether I'm cooking or Monte is grilling, or if we're ordering in or going out, we do our best to share a real meal together.

Just the other day, despite a pressing workload, I threw together a lunch. It wasn't the most spectacularly healthy of meals, but the ingredients were fresh. I prepared chicken *milanesas* (breaded chicken breasts) and sautéed them in olive oil, and I served them with mashed potatoes and roasted beets. I also baked brownies from scratch—easier than one might think—trying to avoid the trans fats in most mixes. I scurried around our tiny kitchen, while picking at the fresh corn and red pepper soup that our nanny made for Sofia earlier this week. One part of my brain was telling me that the deadlines were looming, and the time was better spent at my desk. The other side reminded me, *This is important.*

At the moment, Sofia is two and a half years old and the list of her favorite foods includes mushrooms, carrots, broccoli, any kind of noodles, vegetable soups with sweet potato and squash, guacamole, Chinese stir-fried pork with vegetables. She gnaws on Italian olives (and spits out the pits like a pro), eats beans, chicken, and like a proper Argentine, has started to enjoy a good steak. Sometimes I let her indulge. She's a big fan of ice cream, chocolate, and peanut butter and jelly, and she gets a sucker every now and then. My husband let her try her first cheeseburger the other day, and she pronounced with every bite, "Good!" As long as she's eating well, I figure she can have a treat. When she doesn't like something, I try to remind myself not to fret; her tastes will change and adapt as the years go by. As she gets older, this whole task is going to get harder. She is resisting food sometimes, saying no more often. I find myself cringing when we are around children who are picky eaters, her beloved cousins or friends who make faces because she likes mushroom pizza or eats broccoli. I have to hope that in the end she will take after me, and eating well will be something she enjoys.

Until then, I'll insist that she can't say she doesn't like something until she "tries, at least twice." My husband, that champ, has even started eating vegetables he'd never have touched before because he knows she's watching us both so closely. The key, I think, is that good food can't merely be something we try to eat or cook but a value incorporated in the way we live.

It's working, I think. During a recent cookout, I found myself nagging Sofia to eat more pasta, potatoes—anything to complement the roasted beets she was gobbling down. My husband reminded me what a happy conundrum we were facing, and for the moment, I softened.

"More beets," she said urgently, and I happily obliged.

The Things Kids Will Eat

A RGENTINA: In this meat-eaters' paradise, toddlers could eat a cow—or most of it anyway. They devour *morcilla,* or blood sausage, and *molleja,* the soft glands of the throat. Babies are sometimes given bread dipped in meat juices to gnaw on.

ITALY: Infants are fed olive oil and various fish, horse, rabbit, and ostrich-flavored prepackaged baby foods, preparing them for the rich meals to come later in life.

TAIWAN: Friends and family from my birthplace recall some childhood favorites: fish eyes, salted watermelon seeds, dried cuttlefish, fried anchovies, wasabi peas, bean pops, lotus seeds, jellyfish, sea cucumber, and eel.

AUSTRALIA: Vegemite, a spread using yeast extract left over from the manufacture of beer, is the household equivalent of peanut butter. It's full of vitamin B and has a sharp and salty flavor, but kiddies who have been raised on it love it. Kraft Foods has long marketed the spread to families, promoting the "Vegemite Kids" and child-friendly jingles.

CAMBODIA: The tabloids had a field day reporting that Angelina Jolie fed her adopted son Maddox crickets when they dined in his homeland. Jolie herself was said to favor cockroaches. But fried crickets, tarantulas, roaches, and other bugs are crunchy goodness for children and adults alike.

GREECE: A Greek friend recalls his grandmother saying that eating the brains of a spit-roasted spring lamb would make him smarter, and eating the eyes would help him see better. Many Greek families love to roast entire lambs, pigs, and goat—head and all—over an open fire. "As kids, our favorite part was when we were allowed to peel the crispy skin off as it rotated," he told me.

BRAZIL: In 2005, Brazil's coffee industry proudly launched a campaign trying to provide a million schoolchildren with breakfast, including a cup of joe. In coffee-growing regions of many countries such as Brazil and Colombia, children drink a small amount from a young age.

KOREA: Even babies get a taste of the spicy pickled cabbage dish kimchi. As soon as a child has teeth, moms and dads start offering him bits of kimchi, rinsed of its hot chili sauce. As time goes on, more spice is left on until the palate adjusts. (Korean and other Asian tots use special training chopsticks to help tiny fingers learn to manipulate unwieldy sticks.)

RUSSIA: Aboriginal children in the Arctic traditionally start at a young age eating the raw meat and blood of deer, seal, and other animals their parents kill. On frigid nights, when food supply and preparation is limited, families eat their kill as is in order to survive; raw meat has more vitamins than cooked meat. Anthropologist Nelson Graburn observed the efforts of Inuit parents, who now go to the grocery store as often as they hunt, as they tried to introduce children to *niqituinak,* an Inuit diet, which includes *maktak* (whale skin and blubber), *qisaruaq* (chewed cud in a caribou's stomach), and foods fermented in oil or served raw. "Inuit uniformly reported that if you do not get children to eat raw meat by the age of three, they never learn to like it," he wrote.

~ 3 ~

How Kenyans Live
without Strollers

Carriage-style? Travel system? Umbrella? Jogging? Front or back
facing? Three- or five-point harness?

My belly was barely protruding and I was wasting countless
hours of the day cruising the Internet, reading safety reports,
checking out parent forums and reviews on strollers. Other parents gleefully responded to my inquisition, filling me in on the
strollers they had used and hated or loved. It was, I found, an
issue that almost universally sparked lively debate among moms
and dads alike. *How durable is the suspension, and does it have a
180-degree seat recline? Can you close it with one hand? Is there a
cup holder or a rain cover?* Given all the options, colors, and extra
features, not to mention the insane amounts of money you can
spend, my husband compared the experience to buying a car. I
planned to use a sling and baby carrier, but a stroller seemed key,
the vital appendage that would help us survive the first few years
of parenthood.

I'd been to plenty of places where parents didn't, couldn't, or had no interest in strollers. During a hiking trip in the Urubamba valley region of Peru, I gasped while pressing myself against the wall of a ravine as I tried to traverse a narrow mountain path. A Quechua woman wearing a full skirt and flimsy sandals swept past our awestruck group with a baby swaddled on her back. In villages in Lesotho, Thailand, and Brazil, mothers I met tied their babies with bright swaths of cloth to their front, sides, or backs. Not once during several visits to my large family in the very modern city of Taipei, Taiwan, do I recall any of my sisters putting their babies in a stroller, even though they owned them. There are real and practical reasons that strollers aren't popular everywhere, ranging from the cost of these contraptions and the quality of available walking space to the belief that a baby needs to be physically attached to a parent during the first year of life. I've always admired the fortitude of parents who wore babies while milking cows, harvesting crops, or climbing mountains. To me, these are impressive examples of how parents adapt to their environment and resources. They seem to prove that we can survive without myriad conveniences just fine. But would I want to?

MANY OF THE roads in Nairobi are to be crossed with a prayer on the tip of your tongue. Streets are pockmarked with holes from flooding and vibrate with the constant drum of traffic. People, cars, buses, motorcycles, and animals weave to and fro with no particular regard for whatever laws might exist.

Aggressive drivers squeeze four lanes out of a two-lane avenue. Sidewalks are precarious, if they exist at all, and pedestrians often find themselves zigzagging among vehicles and walking on the grassy median. When it's raining, roads are impassable because of faulty drainage systems. When it's not raining, the air is filled with dust and smog, and the drill of horns and cursing is deafening. In most of the settlements where the poorest Kenyans live, there are no actual roads, just a labyrinth of dirt paths that separate endless rows of makeshift tin-roofed homes.

Even places that you'd think might be stroller-friendly are no better. Supermarket aisles, for example, are too narrow and crowded. Even if you went with a stroller, it's almost a sure thing that the storeowners would require you leave it with the security guard.

"Kenya is just not a stroller nation," said Maryanne Waweru, a local journalist and a former editor for the largest parenting magazine in Kenya.

"I grew up in a middle-class estate in Nairobi," Waweru said, "and to be honest, I never once saw anyone with a stroller. I lived there for thirty years. Now I live in an upper-middle-class estate, where I have been for the last year, and I've yet to see anyone with a stroller." The only time she has spotted strollers is when she happens to be visiting a shopping mall in an upper-class area, and they are mainly being pushed by foreigners.

How hard was it, then, to get around with a baby? To find out, Waweru decided to join friend and neighbor Patricia Munene on her regular mile-long trip to the local *posho* mill, to buy the flour

that she uses to make porridge for her family. Munene swung her
two-year-old son Mwangi onto her back in one effortless motion,
and wrapped him in a swath of light cotton known as *leso*.

"Have you ever considered buying a stroller for your child?"
Waweru asked her as they walked briskly along the path.

"What is that?" Munene replied.

Waweru tried to explain for about three minutes before
Munene finally understood and huffed, "Oh, that thing for the
wazungu [white people]? Why would I want to waste money on
such a thing?

"Where would I drive it in the first place? Certainly not on
these Kenyan roads that are filled with all sorts of hills and val-
leys [potholes]. There is too much human traffic on the roads.
And besides, motorists do not respect pedestrians or bicycles on
the road, so how do you expect them to respect strollers? They
will knock them down!"

Munene moved quickly, and Waweru felt as if she were half
running to keep up. Meanwhile, Mwangi rested his head on his
mother's back, a smile splashed across his face.

"With that thing I would have to keep looking down to avoid
potholes," Munene continued. "That would waste a lot of my
time. With the child wrapped in a *leso* and on my back, I'm able
to walk fast without having to concentrate on other unneces-
sary distractions." Strollers were expensive; in Nairobi, prams
cost from between forty-five and two hundred U.S. dollars, in a
country where the average salary is less than eight hundred U.S.
dollars a year.

"Will I buy food and clothes for my child, or will I throw away my money on a stroller?" she said.

"But don't you get tired?" Waweru asked, who was now sweating.

"Carrying Mwangi on my back is a piece of cake. My back is used to carrying heavier loads than this."

At the time, Munene worked selling wholesale goods on the outskirts of Nairobi's central business district in a shop owned by her husband, but she grew up in Othaya, north of Nairobi. When Munene was a baby, her own mother would strap her to her back and work in the tea fields. When Munene was a girl and teenager, she also picked tea. She'd regularly lug bags weighing thirty-three pounds on her back. She'd cart around grass to feed cows and collect water in buckets and haul them up the steep hills of the countryside toward home. So carrying her thirty-one-pound son was no big deal.

When they finally reached the *posho* mill, Munene didn't sit down and rest while the flour was prepared but remained standing, swinging her body from side to side, chatting with her son.

Munene and Waweru left the *posho* mill with the flour, the boy now asleep, and stopped briefly at a grocery store where Munene bought some vegetables—tomatoes, potatoes, and cabbage—which she insisted on carrying as well. When they finally returned to Munene's home, Waweru settled into her couch, exhausted, and watched as Munene artfully transferred her child onto another couch while he continued to snooze. Munene moved on to the kitchen, where she began preparing tea, not tired at all. Waweru was amazed.

Munene knew instinctively the benefits of baby carrying that have been widely documented by scientists and that today are pretty well known by many parents, thanks to parenting gurus such as Dr. Robert Sears and the attachment parenting movement. One of the most famous studies, done by Drs. Urs Hunziker and Ronald Barr, found that newborn babies in Montreal whose mothers were asked to carry their babies at least three hours a day (not just when crying) cried and fussed 51 percent less during the evening hours. Other research has found that mothers who carry babies are more in tune with their needs, produce more milk, and are less likely to suffer postnatal depression.

I observed with interest how my Korean sisters-in-law kept their babies swaddled, carried in a sling or in arms during their first several years of life. If they or my brothers weren't holding the babies, someone else was. (Their parents came from Korea to stay in their homes for three to four months after their first baby was born; they cooked meals, weeded the garden, and cared for the child. One sister-in-law had her two sisters, who lived an hour away, move in for a time before the second child was born.) All this holding might seem excessive, but for many Korean families who think parenting is about nurturing and attending to the every need of a child, this kind of physical attachment is essential. And apparently it makes a difference. Meredith Small, in a chapter on cultural perceptions and responses to crying in her book *Our Babies, Ourselves* highlighted studies from the 1970s that said the average American baby spent about sixteen hours, or more than two-thirds of his or her day, "alone"—out of someone's arms, in a stroller, crib, or other contraption. She pointed out that Korean babies, in sharp contrast, spent only two hours alone, or 8.3 percent of their day. While baby carrying and co-sleeping has increased in popularity in the United States since then, it's true that many American parents I know still want their babies to sleep, eat, and think on their own as soon as possible. Yet the downside, according to Small, is that American babies cry more. A study done at Ewha Woman's University in Seoul found that 436 Korean babies ranging in age from one to six months cried on average only thirty-four to fifty-four minutes a day. Another study done by the same researcher compared the crying patterns of Korean babies raised at home and Korean babies raised in institutions such as hospitals and orphanages. The institutionalized babies were picked up half as much and cried twice as much, but they still cried less on average than their Western counterparts.

"With my child on my back, I'm able to bond with him," Munene said. "If I see something along my way that is interesting, I share that with him. It does not matter if he understands what I am saying or not, but the fact that we are able to communicate—the feedback sounds he gives me—that makes me happy because I know he is happy, too."

. . .

ANIMALS HAVE EVOLVED incredible ways to carry
their young. Kangaroo and seahorses developed pouches. Darwin
frogs tote their young around in their mouths and wolf spiders
can carry dozens of their spawn on their backs. For humans, the
invention of baby carriers some fifty thousand years ago was a
"technological revolution," in the eyes of anthropologist Sarah
Hrdy. She has theorized that once humans were able to carry
their babies, as well as their food, they could eat better, work
more, travel, and emigrate from Africa to other continents. Parents created carriers to meet the needs of their lifestyle and the
environment, often adapting the tools they used to carry heavy
loads, from baskets to squash gourds. Some mothers in Papua
New Guinea used a hammock-like bag, sustained by the forehead
(the baby hung along her back). The Chinese used a *mei tai* and
the Japanese an *onbuhimo,* variations of cloth carriers sustained
with straps. Welsh mothers used nursing shawls, and the Maoris
in New Zealand wrapped their newborns in a band of lacebark or
a cloak, according to ethnologist W. J. Phillipps. Native American babies, from the Iroquois to the Shoshone, were wrapped in
moss bags and swaddled to cushioned cradle boards that were
made out of flat pieces of wood or twigs and carried on their
mother's back or hung on a saddle. The idea was that the cradle
board would not only keep the baby safe (until he could walk)
while his parents traveled and worked, but it would also help him
develop a strong, straight back. The board was blessed and often
adorned with gorgeous beadwork and woven fabrics.

The arctic is one of the least child-friendly places on earth. At times, up to ninety inches of snow can cover the icy landscape, and temperatures can drop as low as –100 degrees Celsius. The cold is so strong that breath can freeze in midair, and metal that has been left outdoors will burn your skin. For generations, the native people who inhabited these frigid regions—including the Inuit and Yupik in Alaska and Russia (who commonly refer to themselves as Eskimos) and the Inuit in Canada and Greenland—have had to be vigilant and creative about keeping their babies cozy.

The traditional Inuit baby carrier, called an *amauti* or the *amaut,* is made from the skins of animals that share their lands, such as caribou and birds. The baby is cradled next to its mother's warm body (sometimes her bare back) in a large, often furry hoodlike compartment, where mom can feel any odd movement, cough, or gasp. The loose fabrics may allow the mother to swing her child around for nursing. Bundled together this way, according to the Montreal McCord Museum and Robyn Bryant, of the Avataq Cultural Institute, a mother is acutely in tune with her child's emotional and physiological needs. For example, an infant's wiggle warns her to pull the child to the front and let him urinate on the ground (although in times past, there was a diaper of moss in the bottom of the *amauti* in case of accidents).

Prams or strollers were first invented not as something that could take the load off of women but rather as an aesthetic indulgence for English royalty. In the 1730s, the third Duke of Devonshire asked an esteemed landscape architect named William Kent to build something pretty for his kids to play with. Kent built an ornate, miniature version of the chariots used in those days; the metal shell-shaped basket with wheels could be pulled by a goat and looked a lot like the pumpkin carriage that Cinderella rode to her ball. Kent's gilded pram, which is on display at the Chatsworth House in England, set off a trend among high-end parents that would be echoed centuries later. Other royal families wanted to have a fancy little number for their tots, too, even if it was highly impractical, probably uncomfortable (made of wood or wicker), and fairly dangerous (they were to be pulled by unpredictable animals, such as goats or dogs).

Through the next two centuries, the carriage would evolve from a showpiece for rich families to the more practical piece of machinery it is today. In 1848, American Charles Burton added handles that humans could push, and in 1889 William Richardson created the reversible stroller, which faced either the parent or outward with a shift of the bonnet. In 1965, after listening to his daughter gripe about hauling her bulky pram on a transatlantic flight, aeronautical engineer Owen Maclaren designed a lightweight vehicle with an aluminum frame that started the umbrella stroller revolution. In 1984, Phil Baechler, a newspaper journalist and avid runner who wanted to bring his son along while jogging, established the Baby Jogger Company. Manufacturers have since created strollers to meet almost every imaginable parental need or whim.

Faced with this overabundance of choice, I did a lot of handwringing before purchasing our stroller. After consulting various consumer reports, parent forums on the Internet, and my well-worn copy of *Baby Bargains* by Denise and Alan Fields, I settled on the Maclaren Triumph because of its reputed ease of use in the city. Ironically, after all this fretting, we'd have to run out at the last minute after Sofia was born to purchase another stroller because the Triumph is built for kids six months of age and older. We ended up buying a stroller of a brand I'd never heard of because it was on sale and the seat reclined flat to accommodate our sleeping newborn. It worked like a charm.

I did use a simple sling and later a BabyBjörn quite frequently. By the time we had Sofia, the benefits of baby carrying were well known, and lots of American parents were doing it. I personally enjoyed the feeling of having my daughter close, and it was a lot easier to move about the city during her first year of life (she's a pretty light kid). But our strollers were key: they were a place to hold our child and our stuff, and they gave me a welcome physical break from motherhood. But I never thought about how, when overused, convenience can have a cost.

Some health experts worry that Americans depend on strollers too much. In 2002, the National Association for Sport and Physical Activity (NASPA) task force on infant and preschooler physical activity warned that too many children were being confined in "containers," such as strollers, baby seats, and playpens for too long. The group condemned the marketing of strollers for fifty-pound kids and said that the tendency to keep kids in strollers for years may not only contribute to the growing weight problem among children but also could delay a child's physical and cognitive development. In 2008, Pathways Awareness, a nonprofit devoted to the early detection and therapy of motor and development delays, warned that more American babies were experiencing motor delays because of back-sleeping and a "container lifestyle." Children should be scooting, crawling, and walking, even it means that a tired parent has to chase them around.

How did we end up so dependent on strollers? I rang Jane Clark, head of the University of Maryland's Department of Kinesiology and member of the NASPA task force, who told me she was surprised to find that much of the time, parents don't put their child in a stroller because he is tired. Instead, they strap him in because it's easier to keep him out of trouble and ensure he doesn't get snatched by a stranger. The AMBER Alerts, media reports about missing kids, and movies about lurking pedophiles have sufficiently freaked us out. A BabyCenter.com survey of twenty-four hundred parents in 2008 found "stranger danger" to be the second-greatest fear of parents, even though crimes against children are decreasing. A study released in 2009 by the Crimes Against Children Research Center based at the University of New Hampshire showed that bullying, sexual assault, and other violence against children declined substantially during the last decade. The number of children reporting physical bullying declined from 22 percent in 2003 to 15 percent in 2008, whereas the percentage reporting a sexual assault went from 3.3 percent to 2 percent. Still we worry, and keep our kids restrained and enclosed, and prevent them from roaming around the neighborhood alone or even with friends.

"That overcompensation for the safety of our children has

resulted in unintended consequences: they are getting a lot less physical activity," Clark said. We risk unwittingly perpetuating Newton's law of inertia in our own children: a body at rest stays at rest. A child who is used to sitting in the stroller or car seat most of the time (and having his or her parents help them in and out) is more likely to be sedentary.

Clark thinks more parents should be conscious of the need for a child to be moving from day one. People like to ask her, given her expertise in motor development and coordination, what she'd recommend to help their children's development.

"Vestibular stimulation" is her unequivocal answer.

Vesti-what? She went on to explain. Deep in the inner ear, nestled next to the cochlea (the snail-shell-shaped organ that enables us to hear), there is an intricate maze of canals and ducts called the vestibular system. This crucial network contributes to our ability to balance ourselves, maintain our posture, fix our gaze, and move in a coordinated way. Stimulation of this system—through rocking, spinning, and other movements—has been shown to have a significant positive influence upon arousal level, visual alertness and tracking behavior, motor development, and reflex development. Some research suggests that vestibular stimulation also improves cognitive skills and mother-infant attachment.

Clark said a child who is being carried, rocked, or played with vigorously, or even carried in a sling, moving with his mother or father as they go about their daily business, gets more vestibular stimulation.

"The baby's head is being tipped right and left as the mother moves, for example, as she leans over to put seed into the ground," she told me. "The baby is actually getting a lot of vestibular stimulation. A lot more than you would get if you were in a 'container' [like a stroller or playpen]. A container kind of travels straight on in the world. In fact, most people don't want to tip the container because the child might fall out."

More vestibular stimulation, she said, is believed to improve postural development, which affects a child's ability to sit, crawl, and walk and ultimately impacts the motor skills a person will need in her life. If you want to ski, ice skate, dance, or play tennis, you need hand-eye coordination *and* postural control.

And you also need practice, she said. Clark told me research has shown in particular cultures, children develop certain motor skills sooner than others. For example, she pointed to the work of Charles Super, who in the 1970s conducted a study of babies belonging to a tribe in rural Kenya. Super was trying to sort out well-documented findings at the time that African infants tended to stand and walk substantially earlier than American and European children. The theories that some scholars gave for this difference ranged from genetics to altitude and exposure to sunlight, but Super wanted to go further. For three years, he studied infant development in a Kipsigis farming community in western Kenya, where children on average were learning to sit, stand, and walk at least a month sooner than babies in typical European families. He theorized that a major reason was that 80 percent of mothers deliberately taught their children those skills. Even during the first month of life, many babies were sitting up 60 percent of the time. Walking was practiced from the time a child was about eight months old; when children were one year old, the mothers began to play in a way called *kitwalse* (to "make jump") in which a mother or father makes the child jump in their lap (as we might use a jumper). American babies, Super noted in his 1976 paper, were more likely to spend most of the time lying on the ground (something that would be dangerous in the environment of the Kipsigis) and have more time to practice rolling over or crawling. Super argued quite logically that African babies were practicing motion, so their abilities developed faster.

"Parents in America think if you just water [your children] and feed them they'll just grow and you get your motor skills for free," Clark said. "In many of the African countries mothers have the belief that their children's motor skills need to be taught. And they need to be taught to walk."

FOR ME, OUR strollers were about getting in one piece from point A to point B, but I guiltily admit, the "confining" was a little bonus. Once Sofia became a toddler, I felt like she needed to be strapped in some of the time so I could get things done. That said, I thought it would be an interesting test of fortitude (both Sofia's and mine) if I left our stroller behind during our next international trip. A friend, Vita Thorpe, and her three-year-old son, Jude, had tried it. Thorpe is willowy, young, and turns heads wherever she goes, and wherever she and Jude went during their visit to Buenos Aires, it seemed, they used their stroller. For the first year of Jude's life, she told me that she'd used only a sling, but when Jude got bigger and she moved to Manhattan, she got a sleek black Bugaboo. They maneuvered comfortably and quickly, and Jude ate and slept in his chariot. Whenever we ran into Vita and Jude, he'd be seated, snug and perched on high like a king. However, when she decided to visit the steep paths of Macchu Pichu, she knew she'd have to lose it. The bulky stroller would not cut it on the flights or the Inca Trail. So she learned to wrap Jude on her back by mimicking a woman on YouTube and spent the following two weeks hauling him about.

"Who knew my back was so strong!" she said to me when she returned.

Inspired, I decided to go sans stroller during a return journey from Argentina to Chicago that I'd be making alone with my daughter, who was going on two years old. At first, I intended do things the Kenyan way, visiting a fabric store to try to make a wrap that I would use to tie Sofia onto my back. Unfortunately, I misjudged the length of fabric needed and ended up about a half meter short; I couldn't tie it tight enough. At the same time, Sofia wasn't holding still and when I tried to lift her onto my back, she'd jump down and run away, squealing as I chased her around the house. I grumbled to myself that I should have come up with this idea before she got so nimble.

I ended up falling back on the trusty sling I'd used when she was a newborn. She could sit upright, resting her bottom in the sling, which helped me sustain her weight (then about twenty-two pounds); at least I could go hands-free. I started myself on a toddler-carrying training schedule. I'd tote her the few blocks to and from my house to the bus stop and then from the bus stop to our babysitter's place. I managed that much but found that when the walk stretched out for more than ten minutes, my breath would flag. Sofia started to protest because she was hanging low and the sling cut slightly into her legs. I was forced to use my arms to lift her into a position only slightly more comfortable than if I had no sling at all. At the end of a long walk, the faces of Munene or other moms in the dusty roads of Kenya and in the high mountains of Peru would flash before my eyes. Mostly they were laughing and taunting: *You wimp.*

Our departure day arrived. I hoisted Sofia up and into the sling, while I maneuvered my bags to the American Airlines desk to answer the security questions. The young man at the first checkpoint inspected our documents for far too long. Sofia felt heavier and heavier. Finally, I reminded the guy that I had a two-year-old hanging at my neck, and he let me through.

After that, Sofia and I moved more fluidly as a bundled unit through the tangle of security and immigration lines. I noted, pleased, that people are more likely to help you in Argentina if you had your child on your actual person, especially if you are small and frazzled—me, I mean. (Unfortunately, we've not found this to be the case in United States where fellow travelers would rather families with children travel via hot-air balloons.) People held the door and encouraged me to cut ahead in line. Once at the gate, I put Sofia down and took a deep breath and rested. *So far, so good.* We walked around browsing the stands and stores, when the agent called us to board.

I picked Sofia up to put her back in the sling. A nice Mexican woman gazed at us, observing that the sling looked awful comfy. At that very moment, my docile angel got surly. I'd just handed over our boarding pass when Sofia started to fight me, yelling, trying to get down. I was thrown off balance, trying to restrain Sofia while explaining through gritted teeth to the inspectors that the liquids in my bag were for my obstinate child. Sometime during her tantrum, I lost my ticket.

We eventually boarded—thank goodness for understanding airline agents—settling down in our seats. Sofia promptly drifted off, and I gulped down a glass of wine.

Morning came quickly. Using the sling was easier during our transfer in Miami. Not having to wait for a stroller, we briskly left the plane and passed through immigration and customs. When we reentered security, I had my one-quart plastic bag of three-ounce bottles ready. I pulled off my shoes, whipped out my laptop, put down my baby, and placed our coats on the belt. Sofia, shell-shocked, did only what I told her to do, and hand in hand we ambled in socked feet through the metal detector. It took me a while to get things back in their place, but I gave myself a self-congratulatory mental hug. At least I didn't have to deal with a stroller!

I made Sofia walk for part of the long march to the gate and now we were moving at my daughter's turtlelike pace, making several stops to marvel at the big, pretty murals on the floor. When we arrived, I tried to buy yogurt for Sofia and she took off running twice when I was about to pay. Wallet out, carry-ons askew, I had to chase my laughing child around the airport. *I missed my stroller.* From there, things progressively got worse, not exclusively because of the sling, though it became the object of my ire. Our flight was delayed, and we had to wait for an hour on the plane, deplane and change gates, where we waited another hour. My antsy toddler tried to run down the aisle of the plane and through the airport. There were plenty of moments in which I would have loved to contain her.

When we landed in Chicago three hours late, I wrapped Sofia in the sling (this time she passively accepted her fate) and marched off the plane. Monte was waiting in the baggage claim with a stuffed cat for Sofia and a chocolate rose for me. I silently handed him *his child,* removed the sling from my aching shoulder, and put it in my suitcase. I did not take it out or even look at it during our entire trip. I had to free my heart of loathing.

DURING THE LAST century, the stroller's reach spread, and in most developed and Western countries it is now a regular accessory for parents of almost any social class. Even among some parents in poorer countries—including Kenya—the stroller has come to symbolize a level of wealth, sophistication, and a move to more modern ways. Very few people use strollers in Nairobi, but their existence has been a touchstone for debate on the Westernization of the nation. A *Washington Post* article on the marketing of strollers in 2002 quoted Kenyans who feared the pram would infringe on the traditions of baby carrying and even breast-feeding.

"There are customs from a hundred years ago that are not relevant today for Africans. Our challenge is to pick the good from the bad," Carol Mandi, managing editor of *Eve*, an East African women's magazine, told the *Post*. "But carrying on your back, well, that is just a wonderful custom that keeps the baby emotionally stable and lets the mother feel bonded. We can't stop being African women just because we are suddenly thrust into the modern world. What next? They will tell us to stop breast feeding in public? No way."

Even in America, there is a small but growing group of stroller naysayers beyond the childless folks who resent being run off the sidewalk by double-wides. Baby wearing is no longer some warm, fuzzy trend by granola parents. More and more mothers and fathers are choosing to wear slings. The Juvenile Products Manufacturers Association reported that sales of industry-certified carriers jumped 43 percent from 2006 to 2008 to $21.5 million, according to the *New York Times*. Just as the demand for strollers resulted in an incredible number of variations, today you can buy slings in every shape and size, inspired by countless cultures from every continent, in tie-dyed colors or lined with pink fur. The rush to profit on baby wearing has led to some massive recalls and bad press. The Consumer Product Safety Commission in early 2009 warned parents that all baby slings could be deadly for kids younger than four years old after three children died of suspected suffocation in Infantino slings. (More than a million of those slings were recalled in North America alone.) The messages are mixed and confusing, and I found it excessive that the media and some parents would conclude a practice that societies have used for decades was unsafe because of one faulty product.

I'm still a big fan of baby wearing. I made peace with my sling shortly after our trip, once the pain in my back faded. Nowadays I try to get my daughter to walk whenever possible. I have to negotiate: "You walk to that corner, and I'll carry you a block." But it keeps her moving and that's good. During our subsequent international trips, we've left the stroller at home.

Still, I'm glad that having one (or two) strollers has been an option for us. This morning I am thinking this as I push Sofia along the one-and-a-half-mile trip to her preschool. Despite the reputation of Buenos Aires as a hip and modern city, most of its sidewalks are a disaster. Some stretches are pure, paved glory, and others are missing crater-sized chunks of cement. I find myself *picking up* the stroller regularly, trying to traverse the rubble. My daughter takes it well, barely even noticing the fairly violent jostling she gets every time we go for a walk in the neighborhood. Behind her, I'm often grunting as I pop wheelies over exposed water pipes and railroad tracks. The wheels on the ole Maclaren are just about kaput, and the sponge handles are shredded, probably from my gripping them so tightly. But it has served us well.

On a day like today, when the sky is deep blue, and the morning sunshine cuts the autumnal chill just enough, the damaged streets don't seem so damaged. My Sofia sings with abandon some made-up song in Spanglish, and people smile. The day opens, and we lean back and enjoy the ride.

Ingenious Products

Perusing the children's section of a Japanese department store, one could find an endless supply of unorthodox baby products, ranging from genius to ridiculous. A pink baby shampoo hat, a foam disk that sits on the baby's head like a visor, keeps shampoo suds out of baby's eyes. Sticky cotton swabs get at the hard-to-get dry bits in your baby's ears and nose. Japanese children often use training seats with handlebars that prevent them from falling off while helping them "push." Babies can chew on teething rings that double as toothbrushes and suck on pacifiers that act as thermometers. Handy underarm ice packs help lower a feverish baby's body temperature. Forget "Twinkle, Twinkle Little Star." Special Minnie and Mickey womb dolls simulate noises that a baby might hear in utero, such as a heartbeat and the sound of blood flowing.

The Pigeon Corporation, a leader in baby products, makes highly effective Japanese-style nasal aspirators. Instead of squeezing a bulb at the end of a tube to remove snot, parents control the suction power by using their own breath. (A container captures the snot before you inhale it.) Interested parents can get the product from Amazon, where it has received top ratings from the few users who have tried it. Pigeon's other products include a soft weaning bottle with a spoon instead of a nipple to help baby transition from milk to other foods, sanitized mesh napkins to wash your baby's teeth, baby powder in a makeup compact case, and a bath-water thermometer disguised as pink seal.

There are dozens of cool tools to make a child's bento lunch more fun, including rice molds that produce Hello Kitty–shaped rice balls and special punches for nori, so moms can put faces and other designs on their kiddie's lunchtime *maki*. Children usually walk home from school in groups, but parents worry so much about their well being that they put GPS devices and loud safety buzzers on their backpacks, to be pushed if approached by strangers.

❧ 4 ❧

How the Chinese
Potty Train Early

Potty time had come.

My daughter was about twenty-one months old, and my friends thought I was nuts. Sofia's too young, they said.

"Wait four or five months, for summer," they told me, "when she's ready."

Yet I was determined. I'd purchased the plastic, colorful baby toilet and a Sesame Street seat adapter. We ordered special training pants that many Chinese use, with a split up the butt. Rolling up our rugs, we mentally prepared ourselves to clean pee off our hardwood floor.

If the Chinese can do it, so can we, I said, inspired, even if I was far less sure than I sounded.

From Sofia's birth, we'd used disposable diapers without much thought. Changing them had become a mindless task my husband and I could complete while more than half asleep—in the black of night, in the backseat of a car, or on a tiny bathroom counter in a restaurant. It was no big deal, simply a rite of parenthood.

Still, there were plenty of moments—like when I was cleaning up a poop that had exploded clear up the back of my daughter's Christmas pajamas upon boarding an international flight—that I thought of the bare-bottomed tot I'd seen in China a decade earlier. In 1999, I joined a tour group that crisscrossed back and forth across the Mainland—from Hong Kong to Xishuang-banna to Beijing. At one of our stops in central China, we saw a boy playing contentedly in a puddle. He looked like so many other children we'd seen on our odyssey through rural areas: face smudged with dirt but so cheerful you couldn't help but smile back. But what grabbed our attention was the sight of his pallid little bum sticking out of the split in his pants.

Some people in my tour group nudged each other and snickered. *The Chinese can be so strange!* I admit, I giggled a little, too, and felt the same confused mix of fascination, admiration, and shame that I'd experienced several times on that tour, observing how things are done in my ancestral homeland. Our guide explained to us that the child was wearing *kaidangku,* trousers made to gape open along the butt seam when a child squats. That way, he can relieve himself anywhere, quickly with no mess, and parents don't have to race to remove pants and underwear. It was a practice most often done in the countryside, but it could be seen in the cities, too.

The boy, who was probably about a year and a half old, splashed in the water, oblivious to our gawking. My friend asked his mother if she could take a picture, and the woman nodded, amused that this group of foreigners found something so normal to be so interesting.

When I became a mom, that Chinese woman seemed like a genius, a spirit untethered by the leaden diapers that stunk up our trash cans. As Sofia grew older, I began asking around, quizzing Chinese relatives and friends, parents and pediatricians. Turns out, many Chinese parents have their children potty trained to some degree before the age of eighteen months, if not much sooner. Some babies go diaperless as soon as they can walk or even sit; I heard about twelve-month-olds who were trained in three days. Moms can control their baby's bladders by making a *shhh* sound, and preschool teachers can make fifteen three-year-olds go on command.

I was astonished. Don't the experts say that most toddlers aren't ready to be trained until at least around two years old? Most mothers and fathers I knew were waiting until their kids were emotionally prepared to do away with their diapers; they let their kids decide when the time was right. I was on that track, too, until I began to run the numbers in my head. When Sofia was born, she averaged thirteen diapers each day. She had slowed considerably at a year and a half, but she still went through about six diapers during a twenty-four-hour period. If we averaged the number of diapers during her short lifetime to about nine a day, we'd probably used a whooping 4,923 diapers. My green heart shuddered with shame, and I turned to China for inspiration.

. . .

MY PRIMARY POTTY guide was Ivy Wang, a woman I'd discovered while cruising the Internet for information on training. Wang had written a short and witty account of her experience in Beijing for a parenting blog in California. I looked her up and we exchanged long e-mails. In no time, it seemed as if we'd been friends for ages, as she shared the lessons learned training her own two children.

Wang had been born in Heilongjian village in northeastern China, close to the border of Russia. Her parents were poor and used rags cut from old clothing for diapers. When Wang was able to sit up, her mother would wake her up and hold her over the chamber pot. Soon after, thanks to patient repetition, Wang learned to pee when prompted by her mother's low whistle and gentle coaxing. This was just the way people did things, she told me. The Mainland is developing at a breathless pace. Urban homes and businesses have flushing, Western-style toilets, and more parents are using diapers longer. But for many families, especially those in and from rural areas, the disposable diaper is still an impractical extravagance that is used briefly, if at all.

Many grandparents helping to raise their grandchildren in the Shun Yi district, northeast of Beijing, still do things the old-school way. Shun Yi is home to the regional international airport, and a place where wealthy city folks go to escape the capital smog, but most of the residents consider themselves peasants with roots in the countryside. They tend to work in factories, own their own shops, or live off agriculture—the farms here reportedly produce 80 percent of the duck consumed in Beijing. Multiple generations often live together in compact concrete homes with small yards. While parents are away at work, grandparents will care for the kiddies, passing on the traditions of baby care that have been practiced for generations. It works like this: Babies might use cloth or disposable diapers up until six months, as in Wang's case, but then adults start letting the child go in the yard or hovering them over a toilet or other receptacle. Little ones are squatted about every two or three hours, depending on how much they ate or drank or when they show signs of having to go: a wiggle, a noise, a funny face. When the child goes, the caregiver makes a whistling noise. Soon, like Pavlov's dog, the child instinctively starts to pee or poop when he or she hears that sound.

That seems early, even for Ying-Huan Huang, a health care worker who works at a local hospital. She usually advises families to wait a little longer to "squat" their children—maybe somewhere between twelve and eighteen months—when bladders are more mature and the toddlers can better comprehend what they are doing. But often, she acknowledged, that is not really practical advice.

"When it comes to potty training, it's not that easy to convince every young mom or their 'experienced' parents," she said.

"Most of the families consider diapers not cheap and not comfortable," she added. "It's okay when the weather is cool and dry, but in summer in southern China, I know diapers always are a nightmare for moms."

In other words, waiting until a child is ready can be an expensive, if not an absurd, notion. The average monthly salary is the equivalent of about three hundred U.S. dollars, so spending eight dollars on a forty-pack of diapers would be unheard of. Even if they could afford diapers, many families choose not to use them for long.

Kelly Dombroski, a mom from New Zealand, heard this a lot from the more than fifty mothers, fathers, and grandparents she interviewed in the western Chinese city of Xining. I ran across Dombroski's story on a website dedicated to "gentle parenting" options, including elimination communication (early potty training) and co-sleeping. She'd spent nine months talking potty training with families for her PhD thesis and was, in the meantime, training her own toddler.

It was pretty easy to do in Xining, one of those mammoth Chinese cities (1.3 million urban population) that most people have never heard of. Best known for being the key entry point for people traveling to Tibet, it is a maze of buildings nestled in a valley on the Huangshui River on the Qinghai-Tibet plateau. Xining is one of the most diverse cities in China, with a large population of ethnic minority peoples, including Tibetans, Mongolians, and Hui. Most residents migrated from villages and still pickle cabbage on their balconies and dress their training tots in split-crotch pants. Life isn't conducive to diapering. Roads are dusty and dirty, and animals like chickens and goats often share courtyards with humans.

"There are definitely no nappy-changing spaces," Dombroski explained. "It would be ridiculous even to try to bring the diapers, the diaper bag, changing mat, and the wipes."

From the time they are born, babies often wear split pants. Underneath, a long cloth tucked into the waistband covers the genitals. The cloth is changed when the child wets or poops, Dombroski said. Around three months or a hundred days, when the baby has more head and neck control, he is held over a basin when he has to go. Adults wrap their babies in blankets and clothing that are easily rinsed and dried and don't make a fuss if they get peed on. An entire household and even community share in the responsibility of training. If a child looks like he has to go, it's just as likely that a brother, sister, neighbor, or friend will squat him—whoever is closest. What's happening, Dombroski said, is not considered "training," as we might define it, but "communication"; there usually is no set goal for when a child must be trained. Still, starting early has become part of the lore of parenting in many Chinese families. Just as we Americans might think it's bad for kids to be trained early, parents there would say it is unhealthy for kids to use diapers too often and too long.

The Chinese "have the idea that [the genital] area needs to breathe," Dombroski said. "It shouldn't get too hot. They will put their children in lots of layers of trousers, but their genitals will be exposed.

"A woman told me, 'Our children can't endure nappies.' They say, 'It's not good for them,' and 'it's not good for the skin.'"

WANG WAS FAMILIAR with all of this. It'd been so simple and intuitive for her parents. Yet despite her upbringing, she hadn't expected to do the same with her own children.

She'd moved to the United States at age twelve, when her father started working for the International Monetary Fund. She attended high school and college in the States and married an American man. They had their first daughter, Kylie, in California while she was earning her master's in business. Wang is Chinese but was inundated by American parenting advice. Books, Internet sites, pediatricians, and fellow parents in the Palo Alto Menlo Park Parents Club told her that her daughter would not be ready, willing, or able to train until well after the age of two, maybe even three. Relieved, Wang diapered her baby and reserved her anxieties for a later date.

When she returned to China, she told me, she was rudely awakened. Wang finished grad school in 2006, and she and her husband decided to move back to Beijing with Kylie and their newborn son, Kaelin, to be closer to Wang's parents. She took a management-consulting job and enrolled her twenty-two-month-old daughter in the preschool at their housing complex.

During the introduction interview, Wang asked the teacher in charge, "What about diapers and potty training?"

All children are potty trained when they enter preschool, the woman said coolly. It was not a requirement: simply the truth, "as inarguable as that Mr. Mao was once the chairman of China," Wang wrote in her blog. On the walk back to her apartment, she despondently ticked off a mental checklist of Kylie's "readiness," according to the many articles she'd read.

Could take own clothes off? No.
Could put own clothes on? No.

Diaper usually dry after nap? No.

Interest in sitting on potty? No.

Bothered by wet diaper? Not really.

Adequate attention span? Definitely no.

She and her husband had a month to work miracles, and they began in earnest. Guided by their Chinese nanny, the first thing they did was let their daughter run around the house bottomless or in split-crotch pants. Chinese homes rarely have carpeting— even wealthy families have tiled or marble floors—so when Kylie peed, it was no big deal. Every time she had an accident, her mom, dad, the nanny, or anyone who was around would correct her and clean it up.

When the family went out, they put Kylie in a pair of panties and helped her go whenever and wherever she felt the need, whether it be on the playground, on a dirt road in the countryside, or even on the edge of an expensive piece of Beijing real estate. *No one minded.* Wang regularly watched parents suspend their children over trash cans in stores or malls, and once she saw a mom holding her son over a plastic bag on a busy subway train. Kids ran around wearing split-crotch pants, and no one except the tourists did a double take. When Kylie went out, Wang and her husband carried extra plastic bags instead of extra diapers.

In less than a month, her daughter was trained and never wore a diaper during the day again. A year later, with much more confidence, Wang started letting her fifteen-month-old son, Kaelin, run diaper-free and had him day-trained by the time he was eighteen months old.

"Everything you read in the United States tells you not to train too early and that kids don't have the muscles, but how do you explain the fact that both my children were able to not only express when they had to go but also actually hold it in when they were told they couldn't yet?" Wang told me. "I can assure you that while they are smarties, they are not beyond the range of normal children. Also, they are fairly average compared to other Chinese children. All kids above the age of [one and a half years] or even earlier are trained to some degree. There aren't even potty-training books here. I really attribute it to the fact that people are just more forgiving about children's bodily functions in China."

The key, she told me, is being relaxed about nudity, body waste, and accidents.

Hmmm, I thought. *Laid-back about poop on the floor?* That, for me, would be a challenge.

I'D HEARD OF groups of American parents who were training their newborn babies, and at first I thought they might be insane. I gasped aloud as I read an essay in the literary parent magazine *Brain, Child* about one mom's experience with what many parents call elimination communication, or early training. The woman described constantly running the baby to the toilet, dangling her over sinks in houses and restaurants, guessing at when the pee or poop would come. "Your whole life will revolve around your child's urination! You'll drive yourself insane!" was her plaintive cry. Even though that mother did make it work for herself and her daughter, I told my husband that these people had too much time on their hands. It seemed an awful lot of pressure to put on baby and parent.

But talking to Wang, other moms from and in China, and some advocates of early training, I began to understand a little of the history and the logic behind they were doing. I figured we didn't have to do it in an all-out way, but we could adapt the techniques to our lives. There are ways to do it part-time, and waiting a while is okay, too, said Laurie Boucke, author of the book *Infant Potty Training: A Gentle and Primeval Method Adapted to Modern Living.* She learned about early training from a friend from India and began training her third son at three months old. I'd contacted her looking for some advice on how to get started.

"Most parents do it part-time in that they potty at the times when they are home and able to. It's okay to use diapers the rest of the times, as long as you are fairly consistent," she told me.

The possibility that we could have Sofia out of her diapers before two began to seem very doable. Even if I couldn't let Sofia pee on my neighbor's doorstep, I was convinced that we could adapt some of the Chinese ideas to our reality.

When Sofia was nineteen months old, I advised our nanny that we would be training Sofia full-time soon, and she gave me a funny look. She'd been raising children for two decades, and she had not known a parent to train their child before the age of two.

"Shouldn't you talk to your pediatrician first?" she asked me in a critical yet polite way. I hadn't, and I suspected that my own pediatrician, as laid-back as he was, would caution against training too early, that not only might it be a futile and frustrating process, but it could damage her self-esteem, something like forcing your kid to walk prematurely. But I followed my own intuition.

"She's ready," I said. The nanny smiled and kept any further doubts to herself. I was convinced that Sofia wasn't too young; in fact, she was old by Chinese standards. And unlike Wang's daughter, Sofia had exhibited readiness. She wasn't telling us she wanted to go, but she had been voluntarily sitting on her potty for a while now. She'd used the toilet successfully several times when we spotted that undeniable watery-eyed look that says, "Poop's a-comin'" and whisked her up and deposited her on the pot. I felt as if I had no more excuses except my own reticence.

The first challenge was to locate a pair of split-crotch pants or an equivalent piece of clothing. I visited Buenos Aires's tiny Chinatown and searched among the rice cookers and bulk packages of chopsticks. No luck. I inquired with local Chinese people, and they said they didn't use them or they brought them from China. I briefly entertained the fantasy that I would sew a pair. Instructions were available on the Internet and seemed relatively simple. After a couple weeks of this task sitting stagnant on my to-do list, I decided to nix the idea. I had neither a sewing machine nor sewing talent; my skills were limited to button replacement and crooked hems. If I waited until I made the pants with my own hands, Sofia would still be using diapers at five years old. So I found and ordered a pair of wool split-crotch pants, made by Ann Anderson, a mom in Columbus, Ohio, who began "training" the youngest of her three sons at the wee age of four months old. Much more talented and resourceful than I'd ever be, Anderson decided after seeing another mom with a pair of split-crotch pants that she would make them herself and began to sell them in a small home-based venture called Wooligans.

I felt giddy and giggly when Anderson's creation arrived, all bright green and white, looking like a wooly pair of chaps for babies. I showed them to my husband, who shook his head, and to the nanny, who furrowed her brow. There was no turning back. I gave myself a week to ponder (and put off) what we were getting into, but time was wasting. In August, I'd be traveling alone with Sofia on the long flight back to the States, and I wanted to get a head start before the trip. I glanced at my calendar and noticed with great irony the Saturday we had chosen to begin: Independence Day.

July 4, 2009

8:20 a.m. Rolled up carpets. Put SC (split-crotch) pants on Sofia. She looks between her legs, looks at me, and grins.

8:26 a.m. Pees not two feet from the potty in living room next to her little plastic chair. I explain to her where she is supposed to go. She looks at me like I'm crazy. I get mop from back room and clean up pee.

8:29 a.m. I come back into room. Monte points at floor by the couch where a large puddle is slowly expanding. I say to Sofia, "We pee-pee in the toilet," pointing to the small yellow and green toilet. (Little did I know how often I'd repeat phrase over the next week.)

8:40 a.m. Sofia passes gas, and it is a startling and funny experience for her, as she is bare-bottomed, pushing her stroller with her doll Mimi, oblivious. I'm thinking it must be a relief to be free from diapers. *(How the heck will I do this at night?)* Monte spots her *Five Little Monkeys* book, which is sitting on her chair after she stands up. "Were you sitting on that?" he asks. She smiles.

9:09 a.m. She lifts up her shirt and looks at her genitals curiously and then goes back to playing with her puzzle pieces and while counting, *"Uno, dos, cuatro, cinco, seis."* *Why does she skip* tres? I wonder. I remind her to pee in the toilet.

9:15 a.m. I rummage through the drawer looking for a missing puzzle piece and find eight packages of baby wipes I had bought on sale at the local pharmacy. I think about all the waste and feel sick.

9:19 a.m. It occurs to me that my child is playing too contentedly. I walk over and touch behind her butt, and as expected, it is wet. "Sofia," I say, "Look. No. We pee-pee in the potty." I make her stand up so I can clean, but she gets angry and starts yelling, "Chair! Chair!" I wipe down chair and floor with rags.

"It's quite nice out," I observe to my husband. The temperature is around seventy degrees and sunny.

"It was nice yesterday, too," he says. "But I don't know if it's bare-ass warm."

I ask Sofia once a few minutes later: "Do you have to go pee, Sofia?"

"No, Mama!" she snaps.

I fear that she is going to not like sitting on the potty if I keep pushing like this. I know I have reached a low when I find myself also trying to squeeze my own bum atop the potty, to show her how to use it.

10:23 a.m. I just had her on the toilet after she announced, "Poopy." I let her brush her teeth while we waited. She didn't go. So I went instead, and while I am going, she runs out of the bathroom and then back and says, "Poopy!" and points to my bedroom. (Oh Lord!) I go in to see a big puddle spreading in front of the full-length mirror and nearby lies my leather jacket. The sleeve was a little wet. (Note to self: Move beloved objects off floor, out of splash range.)

9:30 p.m. Uggggggghhhhh. Monte and I are beat. Whether it's from our first bare-assed day or because our child is a perpetual, incessant, insistent early riser, I'm dead. Sofia did not once go in the potty. It is worse than normal. The one thing we have managed is to make Sofia conscious of what she is doing and that she should not be doing it. She is conscious of her body waste now. I guess that's progress—I have to think it is or else I'll go nutty.

AMERICAN PARENTS DIDN'T always wait until their kids were two or three to train. In 1947, most children began, if not completed, potty training before they reached eighteen months, according to one study. But gradually, lifestyles changed, and children no longer spent all day in the arms of a caregiver who might have the time to start training early. Both moms and dads were working, and institutionalized child care replaced family care.

Yet the real turning point seems to have been the rise in popularity of the disposable diaper.

The earliest versions of disposable diapers emerged in the 1940s in places such as Japan and Sweden. Marian Donovan, a working mother in Connecticut, invented a waterproof diaper cover in 1946. The following year a man named George Schroder, working for a textile company in Tennessee, was asked to come up with a disposable from a nonwoven fabric, and a Brit mom, Valerie Hunter Gordon, developed a two-piece diaper, according to Richer Investment Consulting, a diaper industry expert. Disposables really took off in the 1970s, as companies such as Procter & Gamble, Kimberly-Clark, and Johnson & Johnson churned out more absorbent and affordable diapers, with better adhesive strips and hourglass shapes. Diaper makers began casting themselves as family heroes. Pampers kept "babies dry and parents happy"; Huggies gave you a "happy baby." Working parents embraced the diaper, and demand exploded into a global market that is expected to reach almost twenty-seven billion dollars in 2012, according to Global Industry Analysts, Inc.

Still, rapid innovation and intensive marketing come with a price, critics say. First, there's the threat to the environment. The average baby goes through five thousand to ten thousand diapers before being trained. The Clean Air Council and the Environmental Protection Agency estimate that Americans throw away forty-nine million diapers a day, and each of those diapers will take about 450 years or more to decompose.

Even so, for many parents—including myself—this disturbing reality is somehow easy to overlook when you simply want your baby to be dry. We love these super-absorbent moisture-wicking miracles with Dry Max, nonwoven, nontoxic fabrics, and Velcro closures; parents as well as their kids are physically and mentally dependent on diapers. The ease and availability remove any practical urgency that might compel us to train.

"Manufacturers of disposable diapers . . . now market large-sized pull-ups, so not being toilet trained at 4 years of age is not a problem," wrote Dr. Barton Schmitt, in the magazine *Contemporary Pediatrics*. Schmitt is a pediatrician and director of the Encopresis-Enuresis Clinic at Children's Hospital in Denver. "In advertisements, children in pull-ups are extremely happy. Delayed toilet training has been legitimized, and that's good for business."

Schmitt's article argued that early or delayed toilet training is a "parental preference, and not developmental limitation." Yet many American pediatricians, child development specialists, and plenty of parents prefer to embrace a "child-centered" approach, arguing that one ought to wait until the child is physically and emotionally ready. The most common advice today is that a child should be trained no earlier than eighteen months and more likely between two and four years of age or older. But,

I wondered, were we keeping diapers on the baby longer for the sake of the baby—or for ourselves?

Well-known pediatrician T. Berry Brazelton strongly believes that waiting is better for the baby. "We have found that later training (when the toddler can control himself and cooperate on the toilet) avoids problems like enuresis, soiling, throwing feces, constipation," he said in an interview. "When we allow the child to master his own training, he will feel 'I did it myself.' It becomes a major source of self-esteem. I don't see our society changing. Earlier training models have not worked, and I don't think they will in the near future."

A study of American children published in 2010 by the Bristol-Myers Squibb Children's Hospital reported that between twenty-four and thirty-two months of age is the most effective time to train and that children who are trained after thirty-two months are more likely to suffer from bed wetting, accidents, and other incontinence issues.

Still, there is a vocal minority who think that training should start much earlier. Linda Sonna, a psychologist, author of several child-care books, thinks starting between the ages of six to twelve months is a good time. But wouldn't that be forcing a child into something he or she is not willing or able to do? I asked her. Sonna offered me this comparison: if it's cold outside and a two-year-old doesn't want to put on his coat, a parent will still make her put it on. Yet with potty training, if a child resists, her parents are afraid to go ahead and tell her she must try—"Like any kind of struggle around the potty is going to scar them for life and create mental problems," she said. It's key, Sonna and other fans of early training say, to differentiate early training with bad training methods, such as forcing a child to sit on the potty or punishing him for accidents. Families in many other developing countries for generations have shown that kids are capable and not permanently damaged if their diapers are removed at a very young age.

Yet more and more, families even in China are choosing to use disposable diapers for longer periods, especially in urban areas. According to a 2004 article in the *China Daily,* "Annual sales for some brands are climbing by 50 percent or more. Upscale stores are no longer carrying split-pants outfits, instead shelf after shelf of diapers. Just about all of the babies who grace China's sleek parenting magazines are wearing diapers."

A journalist in Shanghai, Uma Chu, reacted with dismay over the idea that children might go to the bathroom in the streets. "In big cities, such as Shanghai or Beijing, people feel uncomfortable or even upset not because they see children pee or poop in public, but it's an uncivil act, no matter who you are."

She told me she struggled to find people who trained before two years among her peer group. To them, disposable diapers are progress: they eliminate dirty behavior. Families who have accumulated enough wealth to purchase diapers seem to illustrate a leap from the old ways into modern living.

I ADMIT MY own experiment with the old ways was rocky at times. Frankly, giving up diapers was tougher than I imagined. I found myself constantly cleaning up messes, doing an abundant amount of laundry, and following around my child, asking if she had to go. When Sofia's split-crotch pants were dry-ing, we used leg warmers or BabyLegs, the ingenious and popular invention created by a mom who wanted to keep her baby's legs cozy while diaper-free. At first, Sofia had lots of accidents, and we winced when we stepped in puddles in socked and bare feet. Thankfully, we had only a couple episodes in which number two ended up on the floor, including one that is forever burned in my memory as the 2009 Wimbledon Federer-Roddick poopy inci-dent, in which a string of accidents lasted as long as the final sets of that prolonged match.

The important thing was that Sofia was getting it. In diapers she didn't even notice she was going, but now, without them, she'd exclaim, "Uh-oh!" in mid-pee. At least she knew where she was *not* supposed to go.

All the same, my preoccupation with our daughter's bathroom habits was exhausting, and during those first days, all I wanted was for Sofia to get it and move on. I had to digest an important lesson: Chinese parents don't actually obsess about their child's bowels. As Dombroski put it, many Chinese are *managing waste* rather than *training a child*. It's about learning to read your child and teaching him to communicate needs. It's not a task or even a goal but simply something that is done with gentle patience and persistence. Early training in not necessarily for the modern, busy, milestone-driven parent. One of the only proven negative effects, studies have found, is that children who start younger tend to take longer to pick it up. But Wang told me that most Chinese parents she knows don't put a hard deadline on their kids' training; she and her husband had wanted to train Kylie before preschool started, but usually it's just a gradual process, part of growing up.

"Maybe that in itself is the difference between Eastern and Western cultures," Wang said. "In the East, people tend not to force the issue as much, whereas in the West it's something that's kind of regimented, documented, and written about a lot more. In America there is definitely a more scientific approach to it and people need rules and signs and other ways to gauge how to go about it. Parents always *have* to do it within a certain time frame, like in a week, a month. Maybe you only need a week when potty training a three-year-old, but that child can be trained much, much earlier, if you are willing to stretch out the potty-training period a bit.

"It took a couple months before we really nailed it with my son, and it was okay," Wang said. "Accidents are no big deal and we knew that we had to start slow and that it would take some time. But after [my son] was trained everything was just so much easier and we threw away all the diaper rash creams. I think the entire [American] society needs to be more relaxed about it before parents can take on a different attitude."

Okay, so I had to relax. Around day four, it started getting easier. Training melted into daily life, and soon our nanny pointed out that Sofia didn't like the feeling of wetness in her panties, so we let her use them more often. During the day, we tried to stay away from diapers or pull-up pants, though we did use them in emergency situations (a trip on the bus in which there'd be no bathroom break, for example). I never used a plastic bag to catch pee, but I did squat her a few times at the side of a tree when it was clear we'd never reach a toilet. We always tried to be discreet.

Sofia learned in less than two weeks, when she was one year and ten months old. Nighttime training would take several months longer, though I was shocked that within weeks, we were able to stop using diapers during naps. There were occasional accidents, but mainly when she or we were distracted.

Many of my friends' kids are now reaching the age at which they start to become "ready," around two and a half to three years old. The talk is focused mostly on how their child does or doesn't want to train—"Matt just refuses to go without a diaper." Some people are impressed when I tell them that Sofia has been diaper-free for a year now, though I can tell that others think I was too pushy or hasty. I agree that each family has to decide on its own timing—it takes a lot of patience to go diaperless when children are very young. Perhaps I might have waited three to six months longer had it not been for what I heard from Wang and others, and perhaps Sofia would have learned quicker. Letting her run around in a diaper is definitely easier than steering her bare bum clear of cherished items. However, it is such a relief to have the training long over with, so we can move on to more important things. And I figure we saved around a thousand diapers.

I suspect I'll want to start even sooner with our next child, slowly but surely; we'll read her development first, and see how it goes. It's not unrealistic to imagine that I might let the little one toddle around a bit on our terrace during the summer when she is one, diaper-free and bare-bottomed, child and parent so cheerful you can't help but smile back.

Managing Baby's Bottom

Before I had a baby in Argentina, I changed plenty of dirty diapers during my babysitting years. All I needed was a good changing space, a clean diaper and lots of wipes (the kind that came prepackaged in neat plastic containers).

Yet when Sofia was born in the Swiss Medical Center maternity ward in Buenos Aires and I suggested as much to the nurse attending my baby, she gave me a gentle, corrective look and put in my hand a small bottle of a cream called *óleo calcáreo,* a blend of oils with water and sometimes calcium hydroxide that Argentines have used for a century. Pediatricians recommend this mom recipe–turned–everyday product during the early months because it's a gentle cleaner that keeps a baby's sensitive skin soft while protecting against and treating chafing, dermatitis, burns, and other skin maladies.

"That's all you need," the nurse assured us. "No wipes. Not yet."

No way, I thought. Cotton balls and a bottle of this stuff seemed hardly enough to battle the quantity of poop my gorging newborn produced several times a day. Yet not once did my child suffer from diaper rash in her first three months of life. I'm convinced after hearing my friends' diaper-rash horror stories that the *óleo* made a difference.

Óleo calcáreo is not available in many places outside Argentina, but you can make it yourself. A friend passed me a recipe adapted from one that appeared on the Embarazo y Bebes website. It uses a tablespoon of limewater (available online or at health food stores), a cup of water, and a half cup of sesame, flaxseed, sunflower, or olive oil. Mix the limewater (be extremely careful with it) and the water and let sit for twenty-four hours. Strain the liquid and mix it with the oil. You'll need to shake the mixture each time you use it, because the oil and water will separate. Use a cotton ball to smooth the mixture on the skin after cleaning off your baby's bottom. (*Óleo* is also good for cleaning skin in general.) Important note: each child's skin is different, so be sure to check with your pediatrician before using this recipe.

How Aka Pygmies Are the Best Fathers in the World

Before Sofia was born, my husband and I'd decided that feeding the baby was going to be a team effort. We'd heard the advice on how dad could bond with his new child, and Monte declared that he wanted to do night feedings. I was all for it, imagining the magnificent egalitarian parenting team we'd make.

Yet once our constantly nursing, pooping, and waking bundle-of-joy arrived, reality hit. Doctors and nurses said I wasn't to pump during the first month so that my body would get into the rhythm of producing milk and our baby would continue preferring boob to bottle. At first, I'd feed Sofia, and Monte would change her during the night, but in those hazy nighttime hours I began to reason that it was silly to wake him up every time she needed to eat: *At least one of us should get some sleep and be coherent in the morning.* So Monte rarely participated in the night feedings; he'd wake and offer to help, but I'd hush him back to sleep. After a while, my husband learned to sleep through the baby's minor squeaks and squawks; my senses, on the other hand, became hyper–tuned into them.

Most nights I was okay with this arrangement because I enjoyed the sleepy tender time with Sofia. But sometimes, when I was at my most tired or moody, a growly resentment would lash out, and I'd start keeping score of the minutes spent with our infant, wallowing in mothering martyrdom. My husband, in turn, would feel defensive and unappreciated for his contributions, and we'd boil over at each other. We moved past it, but I'm not sure we reconciled our feelings every time.

Anyway, my *girlfriends* understood me. When we got together, any built-up tension would come out in a cascade of quibble. Still, almost any rant was precluded with the given: we know our guys are outstanding fathers, better and more attentive than most others, especially in generations past. They babysit, change diapers without a complaint, and are cuddly and affectionate with our children.

Yet it was clear to all of us that Babyland was still pretty much the mother's domain, even if some of us started out not knowing much more about parenting than our husbands. There was an assumption among our families, in society, and even in our reluctant psyches, that women should be in charge. Fathers, on the other hand, could get away with distance, since baby was utterly connected to mom's breast day in, day out. As my husband put it, "The idea that there's going to be total equality is one of the hardest things for a new father to deal with, because the fact remains that in the early months it's impossible—and would be a false feat of engineering—to swing a total fifty-fifty thing in terms of physical time with the baby. So the dads, very generally speaking, tend to contribute in other ways that don't depend on immediate, ground-zero baby concerns (working for the salary is the obvious one). It's natural for a woman who's used to fighting for equality in other aspects of life (and not always getting it) to feel the right to demand equal time, and it's natural that any justification for why that wouldn't happen feels like an excuse advocating some convenient status quo tradition."

I suppose you make a good point, I told him. But *grrrr*.

I'd never imagined myself to be the commandeering mom I was turning out to be. My husband had been ready to have children before I was; I'd put it off until almost my midthirties because I wanted to focus on my career, travel, and enjoy our marriage. But once I decided that I was as ready as I'd ever be, I threw myself into it. In short, I took over. Monte was involved in obvious and important ways, but when it came to things like seeking out prenatal classes and ordering baby products, he was content with my being the driver (or he might say that he didn't have a choice). He did everything asked of him and more, even attending breast-feeding classes. (Impressively, almost all the moms were accompanied by their mates). But when it comes down to it, the actual act of breast-feeding is something men can't help much with.

Or can they?

. . .

THE HEADLINE GRABBED me: "Are the Men of the African Aka Tribe the Best Fathers in the World?"

The subhead made me snort out loud: "While the Women Hunt, the Men Look After the Babies—Even Letting Them Suck Their Nipples."

The *Guardian* writer went on to wax ironic as only an English journalist can: "It's a question that has united Aristotle, Darwin and my three-year-old in puzzlement: what exactly are male nipples for? This week, the charity [formerly] Fathers Direct came up with an answer, courtesy of some research it unearthed about a nomadic tribe of African hunter-gatherers. The answer, it seems, is the one my three-year-old (and Darwin, to be fair) suspected all along: male nipples are there as a stand-in for when mum isn't around and there's a squawking bambino in dire need of something to suck."

Male breast-feeding, I thought. *Now those are some dedicated dads.*

Intrigued, I dug up some research on this tribe little known to the public and found the fine work of anthropologist Barry Hewlett, who spent more than thirty-five years living with and studying the Aka. In fact, he wrote a book about them, *Intimate Fathers: The Nature and Context of Aka Pygmy Paternal Infant Care,* and his work has been cited and recited in many cross-cultural discussions of fathers.

The Aka are about thirty thousand strong and live in forests on the border of the Congo and the Central African Republic. They are shorter than most Pygmies, with an average height of five feet, about an inch shorter than the Pygmies in Western Central Africa and nearly four inches less than the average non-Pygmy. They are among the last true hunter-gathering people on earth. Men and women collect fruit and nuts and hunt red hog and elephant with spears. They worship forest spirits, and they go to their *nganga* (traditional healer) for ailments ranging from malaria to lovesickness. Like so many indigenous people, the tribe struggles with survival as so-called modern civilization creeps ever more into their lives.

What has made the Aka famous—and infinitely interesting to me—is their devotion to fatherhood. When Hewlett began his ethnographic work with the Aka in 1973, he had no idea how unique this devotion was. During the more than ten years he spent living with them, he observed that fathers were "exceptionally close" to their children, but it didn't seem so remarkable because everyone in the camp was close. What made him really take note was when he started reading Western scholars who characterized the "nature" of fathers, which didn't jibe with what he was seeing in the Aka community.

So Hewlett set out to document in qualitative and quantitative scientific terms, the Aka father-child relationship. What he discovered was that from birth, Aka children spend almost as much time with their fathers as their mothers, during times of work and play. Aka dads harness their babies in infant slings and take them on hunts, babysit when moms need to set up camp, and bring them along when they let off steam with the guys at a palm-wine happy hour. Aka men take care of their babies 47 percent of the time—a current record, according to the advocacy group formerly known as Fathers Direct, now the Fatherhood Institute. Only Sweden—where fathers handle 45 percent of the child care on average—comes close.

Forty-seven percent! I thought about how those numbers might translate in my family's life. That would've been a couple more hours a day for dozing, writing, a trip to the gym. When I recalled the sleepless nights spent with my baby while my husband was traveling for work, I thought moving to the jungle didn't sound so bad.

Hewlett told me that Aka women are still the primary caregivers in their tribe, but that "there's a level of flexibility that's virtually unknown in our society. Aka dads care for children while moms hunt, and cook while moms set up camp, and vice versa. Aka fathers will slip into roles usually occupied by mothers without a second thought and without, more importantly, any loss of status."

When I spoke to Hewlett, from his office at Washington State University, he told me that the Aka make a strong case that fathers are perfectly capable of being much more engaged with babies immediately with the right attitude and support from family and society.

"There's a big sense in our society that dads can't always be around and that you have to give up a lot of time with your child, but that you can put that right by having quality time with them instead," he told the *Guardian*. "But after living with the Aka, I've begun to doubt the wisdom of that line. It seems to me that what fathers need is a lot more time with their children, and they need to hold them close a lot more than they do at the moment. There are lots of positive contributions fathers can make to bringing up their children, but we shouldn't underestimate the importance of touch and cuddles."

The Aka have become living proof that fathers can and do participate evenly in child care, if called upon, if expected, and if given the right circumstances and support. At a time when everybody tries to pin down universals on a father's nature, the Aka break the rules.

HEWLETT OBSERVED THIS scene: Kakao reclines with his daughter Bambiti in his lap. Even though the baby's mother is mere meters away, Kakao wants to bond with his daughter before heading into the jungle to hunt. He lovingly feeds her water from a gourd, encouraging her with coos and kisses. His daughter smiles and grabs his ear. It's getting late, so both father and mother stand to leave. Kakao puts on a makeshift infant sling, gently places his baby inside, pulls his spear out of the ground, and walks into the jungle. His wife follows, carrying her basket. Kakao asks for help once during this hike, when he hands the woman his spear while he wipes his daughter's nose.

A group of men gather around a campfire, talking trash, sipping palm wine, and holding their infants in their arms. If a dad tries to get his baby to suckle on his nipple to calm her while the mother is away foraging for the day's meal, the other guys don't bat an eye.

The scenes are tender, and they are notable to me because they challenge our stereotypes about where, when, and how a father interacts with his children.

The reasons behind the Aka's closeness begin with biology and environment, scientists say. Mothers and fathers hunt as a family team. They've got a cooperative strategy: the man puts out the net and chases the animal; the woman hides near the net and when the prey runs by, she scares the animal into the net and kills it. Their baby isn't able to stay home, because there aren't a lot of grandmas around to babysit (they are usually pretty young and have babies themselves). The baby is also pretty heavy; adult Aka are smaller than your average non-Pygmy, but their babies are about the size of an average non-Pygmy baby. So if somebody's got to carry the baby, it makes sense that the stronger partner—the man—would do it.

"That very fact breeds inter-dependence between father and infant," said Adrienne Burgess, research manager for the Fatherhood Institute, the group that in 2005 named the Aka "the greatest fathers in the world." Burgess, author of a book called *Fatherhood Reclaimed: The Making of a Modern Father*, spoke to me from her office in Marlborough, a town in England.

"The baby reaches for the father—not necessarily out of preference or a lot more than the mother, but because the fathers are carrying babies. They are *used* to the father carrying them, it's a practical thing."

. . .

AMONG HUMANS, THE variation in fathering styles is vast and extreme. The Aka's jungle neighbors, the Ngandu, are absentee fathers; mothers and female kin do all the caring and carrying. In America, we see every degree of involvement, from dead-beat dads and men who see their kids once a week to dads who stay at home to care for their kids while their wives work.

Michael Lamb, professor of psychology at Cambridge University and a leading academic expert on fatherhood, said in a Fatherhood Institute press release, "Internationally, over the past 20 years, we have seen fathers who live with their children spending more time with them and doing more diverse activities not just in Britain but in every known society. However, we are also seeing another trend—increasing numbers of children who are fatherless for much of the time because of factors such as migrant labor, fragile relationships and divorce."

No other primate on earth varies so much in its parenting styles, said anthropologist and primatologist Sarah Hrdy, author of two books about the role of mothers, fathers, and other caretakers. Baby titi monkeys are in the arms of their fathers for as much as 90 percent of daylight hours. Golden lion tamarin males carry their infants most of the time. Red howler monkey fathers barely tolerate their offspring, though their presence ensures that other monkeys don't kill them. But at least these species are *consistent*. Human fathers are all over the map.

Why? I wondered.

Countless scholars have dissected fatherhood in every different way, attempting to determine what factors influence and characterize fatherhood participation, from economics to the relationship between the parents. Anthropologist Margaret Mead argued that tribes and nations that expect their men to go to war tend not to let their men get too close to their young.

"The theory was if they go and get attached to their babies, they wouldn't go out and do their thing," said Burgess. The Aka are an example of a nonwarring tribe, she pointed out. They have their own small region and are looked down upon by surrounding tribes.

"They are not on the make, so the fathers don't need to be distant," she said. "What you end up with is a tribe of men who are very proud of being close to their children. "

In a chapter written for the book *The Role of the Father in Child Development,* Lamb and his coauthor, Charlie Lewis, pointed out, "As a rule, men seem to spend more time with children in societies that are less differentiated on the basis of age, gender, wealth, or status. Economic factors also affect fathers' involvement in the family. In many parts of the world, particularly in southern Africa and Asia, men work several hundreds of miles away from their homes in order to provide sufficient income for their families. Many other men have to work long hours, often in two jobs, in order to keep their families afloat. Under such circumstances, hands-on involvement with children is impossible. By the same token, as indicated above, much of the increase in men's domestic involvement has been the result of shifting labour force patterns that include a massive expansion of the female labour force and increasing opportunities that allow both mothers and fathers to be active as carers and breadwinners."

Hrdy dug even deeper into our evolutionary past to try to answer the question of why fatherhood should vary so much among humans. She wrote in her book *Mothers and Others: The Evolutionary Origins of Mutual Understanding* that human fathers have the luxury of being so inconsistent because we evolved as cooperative breeders. To survive, human babies needed not only their mothers but also a tribe of support that included the father, and grandparents, siblings, aunts, and other relatives and friends. She argued that with all that backup, the role of the father *could* vary.

"If our ancestors had evolved in a social context where no child could survive without a committed father, fathers in the human species would all behave like Mrs. Doubtfire," she told me. "But we didn't."

Human moms can be every which way, too. Hrdy, in another book, *Mother Nature: Maternal Instincts and How They Shape the Human Species,* argued against the dominating social mantra that mothering is automatic and natural to women. Men and women respond to babies and the enticing cues that babies emit, such as gurgling, smiling, whimpering. New moms, thanks to the endocrinological changes that come with pregnancy and birth, are more sensitive to those cues. But men also respond physically to the intimate proximity of a new baby, she told me. They have similar hormonal responses as women during the "critical survival period" of birth and early infancy. Dads have an elevated level of prolactin, a hormone usually abundant in lactating moms, at the end of their partner's pregnancy. But like women, men have to be around, holding their babies a lot, for these chemical changes to take place and simply to learn the ropes of interacting with the child. Experience plays a big role. For example, a big brother who spends a lot of time babysitting his younger siblings is more likely to be more responsive to a baby than a man who declines to hold babies out of fear or inexperience.

"The point is that both sexes have a tremendous nurturing potential," she said, "albeit a potential not always tapped or encouraged by circumstances to be expressed."

It was a simple realization that struck me hard: *biology (birth and breast-feeding) often puts the babies in the arms of the mother more, but culture and societal norms—and pure habit—often keep them there.* The Fatherhood Institute reported a study of 156 cultures showed that only 20 percent of those cultures encouraged a close relationship between fathers and their babies, and only 5 percent helped fathers be closer with their little kids. Research showing how children benefit from a good relationship with their dads seems indisputable. Kids who spend more time with their fathers are more sociable, adaptable, and tend to have healthier relationships in the long run. They perform better in school. Boys with more positively involved, present fathers have fewer behavioral problems and girls have fewer psychological issues.

Yet despite knowing all this, we in our families and society at large sometimes fail to trigger those instincts that would help men be more engaged. I realized I might have been undermining my husband's own instincts when I'd reach for our newborn every night. Historically, in American culture, men didn't cuddle babies or kids much in public—it would seem strange, un-macho, or even creepy. When I moved to Argentina, I was surprised when men—perfect strangers—would talk to my small baby, even reach down to touch her face and hands. Despite having an affectionate father, I realized that I had my own deep-seated perceptions about men and their relationships with children. After I got past my initial alarm and slight discomfort with this effusive affection, I liked it. It caused me to confront my own perceptions and stereotypes.

Expectations feed the way we behave. If we assume that men shouldn't be affectionate with children, they won't be. If we assume they'll be the lesser parent, that's what they become. Lamb and Lewis wrote that many fatherhood researchers survey fathers using measures that inevitably put them in a bad light when compared to mothers. Researchers tend to observe how much dads engage in activities that are more mother-centric rather than activities that are traditionally paternal in many cultures, such as play.

Women also can take the blame for assuming we know how to do things better. For example, we often complain that our partners can't multitask, and that, Burgess said, is a flat-out mistake.

She pointed out that guys actually multitask really well. She described the quick thinking of a bartender: "The bartender is talking to someone, taking orders, slipping a little extra into his pocket, thinking of three or four drinks at once," she said. Computer engineers might be working on four different programs on different screens while tracking the scores of two or three different baseball games. What we have is not a multitasking problem. More accurately put, she said, women tend to multitask more in the domestic sphere. And whether you argue that society, husbands, or the women themselves dictate that role, the end is the same.

"The mother often sees herself as the manager and the father as the helper," Burgess said, and added, "It is pernicious, the belief that men can't multitask. And then what that morphs into is the idea that men can't be good parents, that women are more sensitive. If you hold these beliefs as kind of a given, then there's something immutable. What that means is you give up on gender equity."

To their credit, dads everywhere are spending more time with their kids, especially in societies that have been more stable in recent centuries. Burgess said, "American men are actually very close to their children, and Scandinavian fathers provide very high levels of care."

My husband *really* is a great dad, and so are his and my brothers, and many of the dads we hang out with. They attend prenatal classes, rally at mom's side during the birth of their children (something that was rare only thirty years ago). If they are divorced, they fight for custody and want to care for their child regularly. I can't help but smile when I see dads pushing their kids in swings or walking hand in hand with their sons and daughters during weekend mornings. Guys carrying their infants in Baby-Björns are a common sight in many big cities.

Hewlett agreed that Western fathers are doing more, yet he says they still spend significantly less time with their kids than the Aka. He pointed out to me that most fatherhood researchers focus on how fathers interact with their children, how involved or what they are doing when they are together. Aka fathers, even today, are doing everything: "They are holding, they are educating, they are providing, they are protecting. They are with them more than just strategic times of the day. They are doing so many kinds of things right . . . It's again, this physical proximity and closeness."

Simply put, what sets the Aka apart is *constant, consistent time spent with their children.*

When I asked Hewlett how being around the Aka has impacted him as the father of seven children, he told me he learned to "make time."

Because of the harried way we live, families tend to emphasize quality of time over quantity of time spent. But for moms and dads alike *all* time is important, whether you are completely engaged with your child or not. The Aka relationship is special, Hewlett argues, not because of how a father interacts or plays with his child but because father and child know each other exceptionally well because of the time they share together.

"We have these busy lives with both husband and wife working and can't be around the kids, and the kids are going to school," he said. It's about being open to having kids around at work or when we're socializing with other adults. "You don't have to pay total attention, just have an intimate knowledge of where they're at . . . Work we see as work, and work means no kids. I teach classes, and students ask, 'Can I bring my kids to the classes?' I say, 'Of course you can.' Of course, you can't do it in particular jobs, but in particular classes you can."

Or during what might be adult parties or dinners. Or just going out and doing errands or hanging out with the guys (or girls). Or co-sleeping.

Americans "have this idea in terms of separate spheres and things that are categorically for adults and for kids," Hewlett said. "If we don't have our kids around more of the day, how can we act in a responsive way or sensitive way if we don't know them?"

My husband and I negotiate daily over who has to take care of Sofia, so that the other can get more done; we are lucky that we work at home and are able to do this. Perhaps we ought to be arguing over how we can spend more time with her. Yet that seems easier said than done when we're trying to manage our busy days.

"Our value of children has to increase," Hewlett said. "Pretty much, here [in the Unites States], children are seen as a burden — we want to reduce the burden on us, so let's spend quality time and not real time."

I ADMIT THAT as much as I liked the idea that babies should spend as much time with dad as they do mom, it seemed unreasonable. I accepted that it would not be so, and I contributed greatly to its nonfruition. I'd bought a book about fatherhood for Monte (hinting, hinting) that had lots of practical, good advice, such as how to prepare our home for the new baby and how to hold preemies. But even I thought a lot of the stuff was too touchy-feely. (The author suggested buying his-and-hers YES SIR, THAT'S MY BABY T-shirts, for instance).

From the day of Sofia's birth, I commanded a slow and steady takeover of her life. I'd interact with the nanny daily, plan out the baby's diet and do our daughter's hair. *It's easier,* I reasoned. I tended to dominate Sofia's time during her first two years. To be fair, there were plenty of good reasons for this. First, when she was a newborn, Monte was busier because as a foreign correspondent he was traveling a lot chasing earthquakes and covering elections. He hated leaving us, and did it tearfully sometimes, but we had to pay the bills. Before becoming pregnant, I used to take plane trips almost monthly, too. But once I became a mother, I rarely traveled, save for visits home to see family. The arrangement seemed to make sense.

Plus, I'm much more of a socialite than Monte, constantly organizing outings and gatherings. (My husband tends to be more comfortable at home, hanging out with just us or with close friends.) I'd take Sofia out a lot to spend time with other moms with babies. She'd even come along when my girlfriends and I would get together for a happy hour, if we met at a fairly kid-friendly place where Sofia could sleep in her stroller or on the lap of a willing friend. When she was one, Sofia and I started taking a mom-baby play class weekly. Once in a while a dad would tag along—usually on the child's first day—but mostly it was a mom thing. Only once during the entire year did the daddies come alone with their kids.

I often wondered why baby playgroups seemed to be a chick thing. The most common answer was work. Among most of the friends we had in Buenos Aires, the dads were still the main breadwinners. They did manage to organize occasional outings "with the guys," but they rarely suggested getting together with the guys *and* the kids. At one point, I thought that Monte and his friends should round up a daddy playgroup. My mom friends loved the idea.

"No planning or help from us!" one of them exclaimed. She knew as well as I did that it would be easy for them to ask us to shop for the snacks, set up the living room, suggest the activities, give the directives, and even dress the kids for the occasion. And we knew, as well, that we were just as guilty for taking it upon ourselves to do all of the above, not just because we wanted to help but because we assumed that our husbands wouldn't do it right. But we liked the idea of letting go and having the dads walk in our shoes and empathize with our daily experience. We harbored some hope, I think, that they'd end up loving it, and say, with genuine enthusiasm, "Let's do it again."

But even though Monte and the other daddies agreed to the idea (albeit halfheartedly), it was never to be. I'd nag, and the time was never made. When I confronted my husband, he told me that it didn't feel right. The guys rarely got together, and if they did, it was usually to get some drinks in a bar, hardly a kid-friendly environment. Most of the men we knew preferred to spend their time with their kids in a more intimate setting, either one on one or with their wives. I grumbled that playgroups and dates weren't necessarily a natural thing for women either, given that often we got together with moms with whom we had little in common so our children could have playmates.

He explained that it was more comfortable and natural for him to do smaller outings with other dads and their kids. He invited a friend who liked bird watching to take our girls on a nature walk. Monte and Sofia went with another dad and his son on a train trip to a town outside of Buenos Aires named Tigre. Sofia could be with her daddy and a friend, and I could have a couple hours on a Saturday to myself.

In the end, we figured out that we'd both have to put in some effort to achieve a more balanced parenting life. I'd have to let go, and Monte would have to take more initiative. His contributions couldn't be counted diaper for diaper, playdate for playdate. His own way of interacting with Sofia is unique from my role as a mother, and I need to appreciate the special relationship they have.

Monte told me that despite his contention that the outings would be no big deal, he did learn something. Most of the time, he said, new fathers want to project an image of the "fun" parent, the laid-back dad (versus the uptight mom) or maybe the "realist" (what my husband thought he was), a father who believes today's parents are way too careful and don't let them explore on their own. Spending more time with Sofia, away from me, my husband realized that he's actually a hoverer and a worrier, and that's okay. He has come to know his own tendencies and capabilities as a father more intimately, and his relationship with our daughter grows deeper every day.

As Sofia has gotten older, she is sleeping only slightly better than she did in her early years. At three she still has nights in which she wakes up every few hours, and now Monte tends to our daughter as much—or more—than I do. Lately, she prefers that he come to her room to check on her. I admit to feeling some poetic justice when I hear, "Daddy! Daddy! Come here!" in the middle of the night.

Paternal Leave

Slowly but surely more countries around the globe are introducing paternal leave. Sweden did it first in 1993, requiring that one of the thirteen months of generously paid leave given to each family be exclusively reserved for fathers; if daddy didn't take it, the family would lose it. Now that requirement is up to two months, and the result is that eight out of ten dads take paternal leave when their child is born. "From trendy central Stockholm to this village in the rugged forest south of the Arctic Circle, 85 percent of Swedish fathers take parental leave," wrote *New York Times* reporter Katrin Bennhold in June 2010. "Those who don't face questions from family, friends and colleagues. As other countries still tinker with maternity leave and women's rights, Sweden may be a glimpse of the future." Portugal, Iceland, and Germany are now among several countries that have implemented leave for dads, though the idea hasn't quite taken off in places like Japan (only 1.2 percent of dads took the available benefits in 2008) where most men still work long hours and don't take an active role in child care or domestic chores.

The United States is one of the stingiest of the world's wealthy countries when it comes to any kind of parental leave. An analysis of twenty-one countries by the Center for Economic Policy and Research in 2008 showed that Sweden and Germany are among the most generous overall with paid leave for new parents, requiring employers to allow forty-seven weeks of paid leave per couple. The United States placed last with zero weeks of paid leave required by law and twelve weeks of unpaid leave only for employees of firms with more than fifty employees.

~ 6 ~

How Lebanese Americans Keep Their Families Close

Raising our daughter in another country has had its perks. In Argentina, we can afford to pay a part-time nanny and a weekly housekeeper—luxuries that would be unimaginable on a free-lance writer's salary in any big U.S. city—and we're able to buy into a comprehensive private health care plan with no deduct-ibles that costs about half of what it would in the States. By law, any medication needed by a pregnant woman and every vaccina-tion during a child's first year of life is insured 100 percent. Latin America tends to be very kid-friendly; if you've got a little one in your arms, you are urged to the front of the line at the bank, given a seat on the train. Our child speaks Spanish and English and has dual nationality.

Yet the major downside is how far we live from our families. Sofia sees her grandparents, aunts, and uncles during our visits home two or three times a year and talks to them on the phone, but it isn't nearly the same as real time spent together.

When I'm feeling guilty, I rationalize that we weren't visiting family a whole lot more when we lived in the United States, and even if we did move back, my husband and I would be unlikely to resettle in or near either of our hometowns because we couldn't get the jobs we'd want. I also tell myself that we're not alone in our thinking. Even though we've traveled farther than most, many of our friends are raising their children far from family. Most of us love and miss our kin, and scurry back home when we can, cramming airports and highways during the holidays. Yet I've gone months without seeing my brothers, with nary a phone call or e-mail, even though we consider ourselves close, and years without visiting cousins.

In sharp contrast, in many cultures close is a requirement—not an option—and often it's at a level that might make the average privacy-loving American squirm. In some villages in Nepal and Nigeria, for example, a bride moves in with her husband's family after they marry. In Kazakhstan, traditionally the youngest son is expected to stay in the family home to take care of his parents until they die. Children in these families grow up with a network of caretakers who are far more intensely involved in their upbringing than I could imagine. Not only moms and dads but extended family, too, participate in everyday decisions, meals, and activities. Sometimes everyone is living together—if not constantly visiting one another—sharing each other's things, nosing around in each other's business.

It would be easy for an independent person like me to judge that kind of environment as stifling, but I realize there are also advantages to having kin so close and closely involved with your kids. I wondered: What is the real impact of these relationships and the expectations on children? How do you teach them to have a good relationship with their kin?

As I pondered this question, I thought of some of the Arab American families I'd known in my youth. My hometown bordered Dearborn, the city with the largest percentage of Arabs (about a third) in the nation. Drive down stretches of Warren and Michigan avenues in that city, and you'll see that every business from hair salons to boxy corner pharmacies advertise in English and Arabic. Most of the kids at the summer camp I attended during my teenage years were Lebanese Americans, who were there with their many cousins. Their families seemed almost packlike: grandparents, parents, kids, uncles, and aunts living as neighbors or sometimes in the same home, going on errands and trips, doing business together. While I admired their intimacy, to some outsiders, their unity was unsettling and foreign. Not infrequently, their kinship made local headlines in accusations of nepotism or tense relations at high schools when clans clashed.

Such "strong" family networks are "not a by-product of 'family values' or the idea that 'kinship is important,' vague notions to which most Americans subscribe," wrote University of Michigan anthropologist Andrew Shryock in *Arab Detroit: From Margin to Mainstream*. "What sets Arab Detroit apart from the larger society is the extent to which Arab immigrants use kinship to accomplish things, and the extent to which things cannot be accomplished—cars and houses cannot be bought, businesses cannot be run, mosques cannot be established, political connections cannot be held together—without resort to kinship ties."

For more than a century, thousands of families from places such as Lebanon, Yemen, Iraq, and Palestine immigrated to metro Detroit to get jobs on Henry Ford's assembly lines, escape wars, and seek a better economic future for their families and villages alike. In the Detroit area, the community was able to create a kind of cultural refuge where they could hold on a bit tighter to their language, traditions, and religion. The fierce dedication to the extended family network that was so crucial for survival in the Old Country continued and evolved in their new environment.

My friend Tammy Audi, whose Palestine-born parents immigrated to the United States from Lebanon, and who worked as a journalist in Detroit, explained her own expansive definition of family: "My extended family includes my grandparents, aunts and uncles, and cousins and my father's cousins and their children. My grandparents' cousins and their children's children. My great-aunts and -uncles and their children and grandchildren. Even people who weren't actually related to us but became very close family friends in Palestine or Lebanon. Their children were just always considered our cousins. In fact, I only found out a few years ago that my 'cousin' Tanya is actually Armenian and not related to us at all. So it's a very, very large group."

That didn't sound so different from other American families, I said.

"Well, I know in my husband's family, the attitude about

sharing and extended family is different," said Audi, who was raised in Boston and is married to a non-Arab from suburban Detroit. "They obviously love each other, but they don't move as a giant group. Like, if someone wants to go to the mall, they go [alone]. If someone else wants to go to dinner, they go. In my family, we all go together. So that means thirty or forty people going to dinner at once. Nobody will make a move without the group. This often leads to chaos, since it's really hard to get that many people to agree on one activity. I'm not saying it's the best way to do things. But that's how we do it. It feels unnatural to leave someone behind, or separate. So the group sticks together, even if half of it is miserable."

Audi's description intrigued me. So, hoping to understand how this plays out in one family over generations, I drove to Ron Amen's house in suburban Detroit. I'd met Amen in the fall of 2009 when he was working as the facilities manager at the Arab American National Museum in Dearborn, the first museum dedicated to Arab American history. He was sixty-five, a big man with a shock of white hair, broad shoulders, and a hearty handshake. When I explained to him that I wanted to write about the role of extended families, he invited me to hang out one evening with him, his wife, his daughter Melinda Farhat and her son and daughter, and Amen's brother Alan and his two children.

From the outside, Amen's home in suburban Detroit looks like any other in his neighborhood, a colonial with white columns and a perfectly groomed lawn. But inside, he and his wife, Mona, have created a decor that is distinctively Arab and American. A framed Egyptian pharaonic scene hand-painted on reed paper hangs in the family room, next to a color print of a photograph of the Holy Kaaba in Mecca showing over one million people praying in the courtyard of the mosque during the Hajj pilgrimage. Over his fireplace hang about thirty ceramic faces from various parts of the Middle East. An end table with a glass case contains a very old copy of the Qur'an in Arabic. Off the family room in an unheated space used mainly during the summer months, Ron keeps Middle Eastern pottery and a large hookah. On the wall over the door is a full-size replica of Zulfikar, the shield and sword of Imam Ali, the successor of the prophet Muhammad. An English translated version of the Qur'an sits on another end table. Prayer rugs hang on the walls. According to Islamic custom, no depictions of the Prophet or his family are displayed.

Amen is a fourth-generation American. His great-grandmother settled in Highland Park, Michigan, in about 1910, but his life has been deeply shaped by Lebanese and Muslim customs and beliefs. One of the most important, instilled in him from the time he was born, was that family is the core around which his life must revolve.

Amen lived in Dearborn with his parents, his mother's mother, two aunts and two uncles, and his brother Alan until he was about five years old. His aunts and uncles are only about six or seven years older, so he called them by their first names, as if they were older siblings; they taught him to play basketball, ride a bike, mow the lawn, and talk to girls. (Later, when he started dating, he'd borrow their cars.) Amen's *sitti,* great-grandmother, helped his parents buy a three-bedroom home on Holly Street and stayed with them until she died at ninety-three years old. Amen learned to speak Arabic from his *sitti,* and to respect his elders. If he or his siblings would misbehave, she'd give them a whack with her slipper, sometimes throwing it at them. A devout Muslim, she urged Amen to marry a woman with the same background and faith, which he did. They never hired babysitters; *sitti* or another relative would always care for the kids. Relatives regularly dropped by one another's homes unannounced and were invited to stay and eat. Amen lived within walking distance from his parents and grandparents until he was married, and even then he stayed in Dearborn. (He moved to Livonia, a nearby town, much later, when he was a grandfather.)

As the eldest son in his family, Amen was told by his parents that he was to be the patriarch and that he'd be emotionally and financially responsible for the members of his family (especially for his two younger brothers and one sister) all of his life. The kids were to share everything: clothing, toys, and later cars. If one brother got into a fight, all were punished because each child had to take responsibility not only for his own behavior but for that of his siblings. When Amen was thirteen years old, and his mother was pregnant with his younger sister, his parents charged him with much of the housework: pressing shirts, pants, and the lace doilies that were the rage back then. Once his sister was born, he'd change her diapers and bathe her, and he'd dress and prepare his brothers for school.

Even today, Amen feels directly responsible for his siblings, even though they are all more than fifty years old, successful, with jobs and families of their own. When we met, he told me he'd just been arranging to send his sister his extra car, a 2003 Mercury Grand Marquis that he'd kept at his home since his parents' death.

"When my siblings need money, anything, it's not like they ask," he said. "They tell me, 'This is what I need.'"

These seem like heavy expectations, especially for a kid, but Amen said the connections—while sometimes overwhelming—are also immensely grounding.

"When I sit down and think about it, I don't have that many 'friends,'" he told me. "Most of the people I associate with are family. If we go out to dinner, we go out with cousins. We have a few friends, but our social circle is almost exclusively family."

Amen wanted to pass this close-knit experience down to his own kids. His children were always in and out of their relatives' homes, gathering almost without fail on weekends for a massive Sunday dinner. Amen also impressed on his oldest daughter, Melinda Farhat, her responsibility to take care of her sister, who was five years younger, and her thirteen-month-old cousin, whom the Amens took in when Farhat was fourteen years old.

"My dad sat me down and said to me that if we adopt this little girl most of the work would be on me," Farhat recalled to me. "At the time I said, 'Okay, I will do it because she is my cousin and I'm not going to let some stranger raise her.' Then my life was over but in a good way."

After school, Farhat, who carried the house key around her neck on a string, would pick up her sister from class, and then they'd walk two blocks to get their cousin from day care. Then they waited for their parents to come home from work. Her sister, Farhat said, had a lot of friends and would head out the door to play as soon as mom or dad came home, but Farhat was expected to be home helping with dinner, laundry, cleaning the house, and taking care of their younger cousin. Sometimes she hated the obligations, but she knew it was for the best.

"It's not that I resent it or anything, but I feel like I missed out on a lot," she said. "Mom and dad were fair with me . . . When I would ask to go somewhere they would always say yes. I understand what I went through. I think it made me a better mom to my kids."

SCHOLARS SAY THAT historically Arab communities have had lots of reasons to stick with family, having endured invasions by outsiders and rulers that disappointed, betrayed, and oppressed them. Governments didn't work and often made their lives harder. People came to believe that they could only rely on those they knew best, those who were related to them. Traversing the branches of the family tree seemed the most reliable route to reach success.

"Multifamily involvement comes with the expectation that 'we care of each other because that's all we have,'" explained Suad Joseph, an anthropologist who has researched Lebanese families for more than thirty-five years. There is a lingering expectation among many families that despite the scattering impacts of war, natural disasters, and the global economy, "you will grow up together, and raise your families together and die together," she said. "If you have this expectation, this formulates your ideas on your rights and responsibilities to each other."

If you believe you will be living with your extended family members all of your life—in the literal and metaphorical sense—it makes sense that they would be your top priority. Without a doubt, you'd help your third cousin move into his new house even if you thought he was kind of a jerk, you'd take care of your dying, distant uncle, and you'd loan—or give—your little sister money without a second thought. It also means you might choose to move to a city or a home to be near your sisters and brothers—even if you had better employment opportunities elsewhere—so that you can raise your kids together. Actions and decisions are made not only for the good of an individual but for the group.

This kind of thinking is not exclusive to Arab families—it's seen cross-culturally in families of all different classes, on every continent. Anthropologist Sarah Hrdy believes that intense family kinship and communal-type child care dates back to the Pleistocene era, more than two hundred thousand years ago. In her book *Mothers and Others,* she suggested that humans naturally evolved as a "cooperative breeding" species, because youngsters needed members other than the parents to survive in an environment characterized by famine and populated with roving predators. They needed their mothers but also fathers, grandmothers, siblings, aunts, uncles, cousins, and others. According to Hrdy, this is a major reason that humans evolved into the perceptive, engaging, empathizing species that we are: we needed those networks to survive.

Even today, the belief that it takes a village to raise a child resonates from tribes in Africa to the barrios of East Los Angeles. In Mexico, large Zinacantan Mayan extended families lived together in the same housing compounds. One in five Czech families live with other families, in part thanks to a housing shortage but also because having a relative around allows women to work and get educated. And among three hundred families surveyed in two South African cities, nine out of every ten elders lived in a multigenerational setting, a 2003–2004 report on Africa for the United Nations said.

When I met my birth family in Taiwan for the first time back in 1997, I was touched, overwhelmed, and irritated by their assumed relationship with me. Despite the fact that we really didn't know each other, family members had no qualms about telling me how to wear my hair and spend my money and they thought it was perfectly normal to suggest that their children should study in the United States—and live with me while doing so. During one visit to my parents' home, I was expected to sleep on the same mattress as my sister, her husband, and two boys. And I did—no questions asked.

Close-knit extended families are rather prevalent in many U.S. communities, too, especially in smaller towns and rural areas and among recent immigrant groups. A childhood friend of mine whose parents emigrated from Macedonia had to include a dozen of her cousins in her bridal party, some of whom she didn't know. Later, when she had kids, her parents bought a house and moved in a few doors down from her, so they could spend time—lots and lots of time—with their daughter and grandkids daily. My husband, who is from central Illinois, pointed out that where he is from, traditionally people stuck around, and there was no question that you'd end up living near (but probably not with) your family.

Still, in the United States throughout the last century, nuclear families tend to be the norm; while Americans cherish their families, they also passionately value their privacy and independence. Most of my friends were expected—and in turn expect their own children—to get a job and start their own lives as soon as possible following their schooling (in contrast to, for example, Confucian societies in which elder sons were expected to return home to take care of the family). Some historians believe that the American tendency originated in northwestern European countries such as England and France, where children also moved out of their homes when they married and created their own households. Yet many experts believe it was the industrialization of America that took our ability and need to detach to a whole new level. A famous sociologist in the post–World War II era, Talcott Parsons, argued that Americans came to favor the nuclear family to fit the needs of a competitive, capitalist society. Free of the constraining bonds and expectations of extended family, the tighter unit of husband, wife, and kids could move freely and go where the jobs and opportunities were.

In our society, "you must learn to detach," Suad Joseph told me. "You must learn to let go in order to create a viable life."

Joseph sometimes asks the students in some of her Middle East studies classes at the Davis campus of University of California, how many of them expect to go back and live in the places they grew up. Predictably, most of them don't. They are from all over the United States and will be further dispersed when they graduate in order to have the careers and lives they want. Many of them have been preparing to leave home their entire lives. While many Arab families, out of love, might insist that their children grow up cultivating lasting and essential relationships within the family, many American parents, out of love, encourage their children to reach for the stars, even if it means that they will never come back to stay. Many of us begin teaching this to our kids from the first day they are born. I want my two-year-old to fall asleep in her own bed in her own room, to get along without me, without a tear, in her new preschool classroom. If she decides to go away to college after high school and follow the path she desires, I'll be behind her. Americans tend to want our kids to be successful, independent grown-ups; we want our kids to need us but not too much.

Even the neighborhoods we choose reinforce our family structures, according to the Pew Research Center. Shortly after World War I, when families began moving away from traditional clustered housing or their immigrant neighborhoods and bought bigger dream homes in the distant suburbs, life became centered on the nuclear family, and kids played with neighbors instead of cousins. Now, many retirees choose to relocate to warmer climes, even if it's far from their children. They like the grandkids to visit, but they don't want that visit to be too imposing or long. This doesn't mean that Americans care for each other less, but it does illustrate different values in our society and the tendency for us to put our individual interests first.

I'm a product of this mentality. My American family was structured like many other nuclear families. My parents and two younger brothers and I were close, spending most of our time outside of school and work together. We grew up in the same town where my father was born, raised, and made his career as a teacher and union leader. My mother was from a town an hour north, outside of Flint. We lived in two houses during our child-hood, moving only once, three doors down. We visited Granny, my father's mother, at her apartment about a mile away regularly and saw my mom's parents who lived an hour and a half north once every other week. A couple times a week we'd hang out with our aunt Alice (my mom's sister) and her husband, Jim, and their kids. We saw most of our other aunts and uncles and cousins far less often.

After they graduated from college, my brothers chose to re-main in Michigan, within a couple miles of our parents' home. The younger one moved away to Florida only later, during the financial crisis of 2008, because Detroit's economy tanked and he lost his job. I left home early and hardly looked back. At age sixteen I went away to college in Missouri, living in my parents' home again only during summer breaks and briefly before I got married. My parents and grandparents would have liked for me to settle closer to them, but they encouraged me to study and live where I wanted, to follow my dreams wherever they took me. To succeed and move up quickly in journalism, you need to go where the better opportunities are. So I traveled, enthusiastically, with my parents' blessing. My husband was the same way. He worked as a journalist in Egypt and Kuwait before we met in St. Louis and began our meandering life together.

We lived in St. Louis, metro Detroit, and Washington, D.C., before Monte got an offer to work in Buenos Aires. We jumped at the chance because both of us had dreamed of working abroad. No matter that it was several thousand miles away from his hometown and mine—it was an adventure and the career move of a lifetime. I love our families with every inch of my soul. Yet I appreciate that our parents never made us feel bad about leaving and encouraged us to find success and happiness wherever we could. Today, I talk and e-mail with my mother at least weekly (my father died in 2002). My brothers and I exchange occasional e-mails every few months, but we try to visit whenever we travel home—a task that is more difficult now that my younger brother lives in Florida. I track my aunts and uncles and cousins on Facebook, but we rarely see each other.

Having a kid makes you feel the absence of your kin, I think, especially your parents. It was sad for me that Sofia's grandparents couldn't be with us when she was born; my mom came a few months later to visit after we had a handle on what we were doing. And we can't just drop in so Sofia can see her grandma and grandpa on a whim; nor can we ask them to watch her in a pinch.

Beyond the obvious babysitting advantages, research suggests that having lots of relatives consistently and positively involved with a child's life can be very good for the health and development of a child, and for the sanity of his parents.

A study of ten thousand families in Australia released in 2008 showed that children three to nineteen months had higher learning scores if they were cared for by family and friends (including grandparents) as well as their parents. The Baltimore-based Interactive Autism Network published preliminary research in 2010 that showed from financial support to caregiving, grandparents play a significant role in the lives of grandchildren diagnosed with autism spectrum disorders. A 1985 University of Alabama article on southern African American families found that people who perceived their kin to be more supportive reported fewer symptoms of depression.

Scholar Robert Milardo interviewed more than one hundred aunts, uncles, nephews, and nieces for his book *The Forgotten Kin: Aunts and Uncles* and concluded that while their role is often overlooked, aunt and uncles (whether blood related or not) can offer important extra support to parents while being mentors and special confidants for children. "Aunts and uncles complement parents by providing experiences that parents cannot provide," Milardo wrote for a parenting website in Australia.

Najah Bazzy, a third-generation Lebanese American and native of Dearborn, told me that she's been greatly impacted by those benefits. Bazzy, like Amen, was close to first, second, third, and fourth cousins, plus aunts and uncles. When she was growing up, relatives who were immigrating to the United States often stayed with her family until they could get established. Her home was always full of family. In addition, her mother worked hard at forging interdependence among Bazzy and her five siblings, saying things like, "You all shared my womb and your children are an extension of my womb. You have to take care of each other. You have to be part of everything that each other does."

"It builds within you as a child a very extraordinary level of confidence of belonging," Bazzy told me. "It's not just belonging to your immediate family; it's belonging to something bigger than that. For me it's a feeling of deep rootedness and security. No matter what I do, where I go, and what I need, in happiness or in grief, there is an authentic love, concern, and sincerity about what happens to me and my children and my family."

The impact of those values became clear when I asked her what she had done with her family that day.

"Hmmm," she said, pausing to think. "Okay, so I put in a call to my mom: just a 'How's your day? I'm doing nothing.' I have a brother with muscular dystrophy and we set up our schedule. I told her that I'd be back to feed Sammy at noontime and later in the evening. My son will be there at eleven p.m. to tuck him in."

Then Bazzy's brother called from Texas to check in, as he did regularly, and so did another sister-in-law who has a mother in

Syria who is ill. Bazzy spoke with one of two aunts in Lebanon, because she is trying to help them sell some family land. Later, she'd have to call her mother-in-law and pick up her kids from school. In the evening she planned to attend a fund-raiser for a cousin who was running for state representative.

"Wow," she said, realizing how overwhelming this list of connections might sound. "I've never even thought about it. It's just so natural."

I wondered if having the attention of this many adults would spoil the children. Maybe, some parents said, but more often than not, having so many adults around makes it less likely that kids will act up because someone is always there to catch or correct them. In fact, the Amens, Audi, and Bazzy all agreed, that is one of the challenges involved with having such a large and involved family. Nosy relatives are sure to report any alleged bad behavior. Kids or parents can't get away with much and are taught to be especially conscious of their actions because everyone is going to know if your child misbehaved or got a bad grade.

And individual possessions and desires? Not so important. In some families, it means you are taught that you co-own (as opposed to merely share) your toys with not only your siblings but also your cousins and neighbors and anyone else who might come over and break them. Audi recalled that her father once explained to her that she owned nothing and that her favorite crayons were not actually hers but belonged to the entire household. Moreover, small and big decisions such as what you wear, and what and where you will study, and who you will date are not yours to make alone—the whole family will have opinions. When you marry someone, that person will become part of the family, so it's important that the existing family members approve.

"The worst part," Audi told me, "is that the group can be judgmental and weigh in on your life choices when you don't want them to. You also don't have much freedom to go your own way and do your own thing. And you get sucked into activities (helping someone move or paint or going to your aunt's cousin's daughter's baby shower) that you don't want to do.

"On the other hand, I wouldn't have it any other way," she said. "You have a huge network of people to tap into for all kinds of help and advice on jobs, college, travel, moving, children, car and house buying, etcetera. And I absolutely know this massive group of people would drop everything to help me if and when I needed it."

There are people who don't like or can't adapt to the constant imposition of family. Feelings of suffocation lead some teens to rebel and reject their relatives as they get older, especially when the expectations of their families clash with their own dreams and desires. Critics have accused more insular and secretive networks in some cultures of sheltering domestic abuse and oppression of its family members—particularly girls and women, though research also has shown that having strong networks can protect victims. Bazzy founded a nonprofit that has created a program for battered, widowed, divorced, and single mothers, which helps them build networks that model the support a tight extended family might give.

THE ROLE OF kin is constantly changing with the globalization of economies and the spread of Western education
and political models. Many families in places such as Lebanon
and China, where extended family networks have dominated
for centuries, are moving toward more compact, nuclear families. At the same time, the global financial crisis in the late 2000s
has made multigenerational living more common in the United
States and England; thirty-year-olds living with their parents are
no longer mocked for not having "launched." In 2008, the Brit-
ish Skipton Building Society predicted that cohabitation would
be a growing trend and that the number of "extended financial
families" would triple in Britain over the next twenty years from
seventy-five thousand to two hundred thousand. In 2008, an estimated forty-nine million Americans lived in a multigenerational
household, according to a survey by the Pew Research Center.
That's a small percentage of the population (about 16 percent) but
a huge increase over the 1980s, when twenty-eight million adults
lived with their parents, stepparents, or grandparents. Part of the
reason for this jump is because people are getting married and
moving out of their parents' homes later, but others are moving
back in with their elderly parents who need care. The increase
also reflects gains in Latino and Asian immigrant populations
that are more likely to live with extended family.

Other people live with their parents because it is cheaper. An
analysis of census data by *USA Today* found that multigenerational households tended to have bigger homes and more income.

Scholars have pointed out that the definition of extended

family is constantly evolving. Children with divorced parents are being raised by not only their mom and dad but also by their stepfamilies. Same-sex couples are adopting children or pitching in on the care of their friends' children. Adopted children are establishing relationships with their biological families.

In lieu of biological extended families, many American parents have created their own networks (dubbed fictive family by some scientists) that, handpicked from friends in the neighborhood, playgroups, and local schools, are no less significant in their children's life. That's what Monte and I have done in Argentina, because instinctively we knew that we would need some kind of network to survive. We have good friends in Buenos Aires who are regular fixtures in Sofia's life; they babysit, teach, discipline, and dote, and Sofia adores them in turn. They are, in effect, her representative aunties and uncles, and their kids are her cousins. They mean a lot to us, but it's hard to predict honestly how lasting those connections will be, especially given our impermanence, and how they will impact our daughter in the long run. For now, they are key. I realize that, just as with family, these relationships take some effort and commitment to establish and maintain.

The Amens work hard at keeping their family close because they sense inevitable change. With every generation, their family is becoming busier and more dispersed. While Alan and Ron and their families live in metro Detroit, their sister lives in Virginia and their other brother is in Florida. Two of Ron Amen's daughters live in Florida. They lament not being able to see each other more, but they often speak to one another. At least a few times a day, each of them is on the phone with a relative outside their immediate family. The young Amen cousins who live in the Detroit area see each other regularly, borrow each other's clothing, stay overnight in each other's homes. Family, the teenagers told me, is still their top priority.

This kind of coherence made an impression. I find myself not only urging Sofia to share but reminding her that what is hers is ours and what's ours is hers. I want her to feel a sense of responsibility to her siblings and connectedness to her relatives. I've been inspired to follow the pull I'd already been feeling since we had Sofia. Perhaps it is instinctual to want to be more connected to your family and your roots when you become a parent. Until now, my husband and I had bounced about fairly carelessly, thinking mostly about our careers or our personal adventure and growth. But now I'm thinking differently.

The next time we move, I told my husband over dinner recently, I no longer want to go where the wind takes us. We need a family, whether literally related to us or not. We need to visit our parents more often or at least for longer periods. Our connections should hold more weight than an interesting place or a fun job. It is a big emotional shift, one that I'm not sure my husband has quite bought into. I still will tell Sofia that the universe is her oyster, but I'm reminded, too, that she should feel grounded before she conquers the moon.

On Adoption

As an adoptee, I've found that many people think of adoption as a novelty at best and something to hide at worst, even if is fairly prevalent in the United States these days. Loving adoptive parents fret over how (or whether) to tell a child she is adopted and how he or she might process that fact later, because the way their family came to be is considered by many to be outside the norm. Even with the changing definition of family these days, our society still tends to put great importance on the biological relationship between parent and child.

Yet in some cultures, adopting and fostering children are so commonplace that a lack of actual genetic ties is no big deal. In Botswana, Tswana relatives flat-out request to raise a child, and parents often acquiesce. Erdmute Alber observed that among the Baatombu in West African Benin "fosterage is not the exception, but the norm." Alber reported that only 2 of 150 adults she interviewed while visiting the tribe said they grew up with their biological parents. In other African communities, children are fluidly circulated between co-wives. Chinese migrant workers will for years leave their children to be raised by relatives or neighbors while they live in faraway cities to earn a living. Among the Zumbagua people in the highlands of Ecuador, sex and pregnancy can bond two adults, but the adults who feed a child over an extended period of time can adopt a child into their family, according to Northwestern University anthropologist Mary Weismantel. Care trumps biology, and everyone seems to have lots of parents and children.

Signe Howell offered some of these examples in *The Kinning of Foreigners: Transnational Adoption in a Global Perspective.* "In societies where there is an institutionalised practice of bringing up the children of others as if they are one's own," she wrote, "children become kinned to those given responsibility for their care, and the relationship is expressed in conventional kinship terms." These practices, she argued, "challenge western-centric notions of what kinship is all about—namely relatedness constituted through flesh and blood."

~ 7 ~

How Tibetans Cherish Pregnancy

As I stared down at the positive result that appeared on my pregnancy test, I felt despondent.

It's happening again. I'm miscarrying.

Officially, we'd been trying for our second child only a few months, but I'd spent a miserable year trying to prepare my body. Almost all of my life, my cycle had been as regular as a heartbeat, but post-child it had fallen apart into an unpredictable mess of early, late, barely at all, and most recently and maddeningly, two straight weeks of steady flow. It'd been a couple years since I'd given birth to Sofia and a year since I stopped breast-feeding, so I couldn't figure out why. My only theory was that my body had internalized the stress of the year: parenthood, the publication of my first book, touring, traveling, and incessant worrying. Finally, my gynecologist concluded that I wasn't ovulating and prescribed a drug to get the eggs moving again.

My system appeared to be getting back on track, when I really started bleeding, more than a week before my period was supposed to come. The symptoms were just like those I'd suffered when I'd had an early miscarriage almost four years before. I called my doctor, who told me to take a pregnancy test. Immediately, the result that should have made me so happy appeared. Yes, we'd managed to get pregnant, but it was clear that it was ending as quickly as it had happened.

My doctor instructed me to come in for tests the next day. Logically, we agreed that this was a good sign of my potential fertility. Trying to stay positive, I thought of Sofia and how she'd turned out so perfectly. *Steady, girl,* I told myself. Cool as a cucumber, I picked up the phone to call my husband. But when I heard his voice, I collapsed into sobs, barely able to speak. Insisting that I was *fine,* I urged him and Sofia not to run home from breakfast at a friend's house to be at my side; I wanted time to steady my shocked heart, alone. In that moment, I was caught off guard by the return of the emptiness I'd felt that time before, the intense sense of loss for something that I couldn't have even known was happening.

That night as I lay in my bed cursing the painful cramps and feelings of utter helplessness, I thought of Tibet.

After my first miscarriage, I'd done some research on birth practices in Tibet. I was wounded, looking for ways to regroup, and when I read that Tibetan Buddhists put great emphasis on the mental and spiritual state of a mother-to-be, I was intrigued. It was not something I'd considered, having been so focused on the science of what I wanted to happen: when I was supposed to ovulate, what to eat and drink, which vitamins to take. For Tibetans, pregnancy can be a highly spiritual time, laden with tradition and ritual. Women are urged to constantly meditate and pray, think positive thoughts, and do good deeds. They seek blessings from Buddhist teachers, who will prescribe special prayers and even give the child a name.

Norbu Samphell, a Tibetan American father, explained it to me this way: "For an unborn baby, everything is connected to his or her mother. He or she feels everything through her, physically, emotionally, and intellectually. Therefore, for the all-around development of the unborn baby, we need to provide the pregnant mother with a congenial atmosphere, where she is not stressed out mentally and emotionally. She should be happy and joyous. She should not worry about anything."

There is a direct link, he and other Tibetan Buddhist parents said, between the mental and spiritual state of a mother and her child's health and personality.

"Physicians during the Buddha's time were encouraged to look after not only the physical but the mental aspects of the fetus during pregnancy," according to a professional newsletter advising fellow doctors in Australia. "Just as we now understand that maternal blood sugar level control is important for neonatal health in women with diabetes, it is believed that the consciousness of the fetus may be conditioned by encouraging the pregnant mother to live in a peaceful meditative state."

This had seemed like just what the doctor ordered. My shrink—who is not Tibetan but quite spiritual—had told me I needed to relax, reminding me that my mental health had a direct impact on my ability to have a baby. So I chilled, refocusing my mind on positive thoughts (*We will be great parents someday, somehow*) and actions (meditating, taking time for myself, dancing). A couple months later I was pregnant. Yet once I had Sofia and moved on to breast-feeding and potty training, I'd forgotten the lesson I'd learned. Suddenly, in the throes of another miscarriage, it all came back to me.

Stillness, I told myself that May night in 2010 after my second miscarriage started, as the painkillers failed to alleviate the pain that pulsed in my right side. The next day, my doctor determined that I'd had an ectopic pregnancy in which a fertilized egg lodges itself outside the uterus. Mine was in my right-side fallopian tube. I might have had to get surgery within two days because ectopic pregnancies can bust open organs and cause internal bleeding.

"Let's wait until Wednesday," the doctor told me. If the level of pregnancy hormones in my blood dropped, the embryo might expel itself. We'd have to be vigilant and patient. For the past several months, I'd been so focused on the problems of my body. Now experience was reminding me that I needed to clean house emotionally and spiritually.

THE TRADITIONAL STATE of Amdo, on the northeast plateau of Tibet, is a place of expansive rolling grasslands where farmers harvest wheat and barley, and nomad families roam with their yak and sheep, living in temporary yak-hair tents and mudbrick houses. The Amnye Machen is one of many sacred mountains that frame the landscape; each summer, hundreds of Tibetan families—sometimes entire villages—make the eighty-two-mile pilgrimage, or *kora,* around the mountain hoping to gain karma. Amdo is home to many important monasteries and has produced prominent spiritual leaders. Tenzin Gyatso was born in the region before being declared, at age two, the incarnation of the Dalai Lama.

Tenma Tsering spent the first seventeen years of her life in a village in Amdo. Now a mother of two sons living in the suburbs of Chicago, she remembers that many women would pray for years to Buddhist gods for the blessing of pregnancy. Tsering's aunt, who for years had struggled with miscarriages and infertility, was so grateful when she eventually became pregnant four times that she named all four children *shou,* after a deity. Expectant mothers, Tsering said, would eat only natural foods, sometimes choosing special diets that prohibited eating animals with claws, such as chickens. Parents would pray constantly and make pilgrimages for miles on foot to local monasteries to make offerings hoping for a healthy pregnancy and baby.

Tsering, like many other Tibetan Buddhist parents, believes in an essential truth: birth is not merely an isolated and special occasion but part of the cycle of birth, death, and the state between life and death, called *bardo.* A baby is not conceived but is invited into the womb, and the karma of the mother, father, and assuming spirit must be in harmony.

"To give birth and be blessed with a possibility of human life is incredibly important," explained Dartmouth University anthropologist Sienna Craig, who has been studying and working with ethnic Tibetan families in Nepal, India, and Tibet since 1993. "It means that you have accrued enough karma to get this chance.

"If this is your belief from the onset, before conception, you have a spiritual connection and obligation that is different than how we might say 'birth is a miracle' or 'each birth is a gift.'"

Buddhists believe that everything in the universe is composed of subtle forms of five elements: earth, wind, fire, water, and space. The human body is not merely cells, blood, vital organs, and muscle; it is also composed of these elements, which impact the function (or malfunction) of the body. In Tibetan medicine, a healthy body is one in which the elements are in sync inside and outside.

Buddha and his disciple Ananda were explicit about the "sutra of conception," explained Dr. Pasang Arya, founder of a center on Tibetan medicine based in Switzerland. It has been lyrically detailed in texts such as the expansive academic book called *Religion, Medicine and the Human Embryo in Tibet,* by Frances Garrett, a scholar in Buddhist studies at the University of Toronto, and in a handy layperson-parent guide called The *Tibetan Art of Parenting,* by Anne Maiden Brown, Edie Farwell, and Dickey Nverongsha. The conception and birth process is explained in detail on Arya's website, which aims to demystify Tibetan medicine for Westerners. The *bardo* consciousness is responsible for the union of the mother and the father, and once it enters the womb, the five elements start transforming the embryo into a physical being. During the first day of the first week of pregnancy, "the mixed sperm and ovum is like a drop of yeast mixed with milk. A subtle wind, called *Myonmongpei-yid-srog-rLung-A,* manifests from the mind consciousness (*Srog-rlung-A*). During the next weeks, winds are going to manifest from this wind. It harmonizes the elements and energies of the parents to develop the [baby's] body."

Arya told me, "According to the Tibetan Buddhism and medicine concept, if the consciousness of the child is in harmony and healthy emotion during the conception, the mind and emotion of the child will be more peaceful and tranquil after the birth, which is essential to the basic psychology of the person. A mother's healthy emotions also greatly influence the child's mental state during the conception and fetus development." A meditative mother, too, is a more receptive vessel and is more likely to get pregnant and give birth to a happy and healthy child.

Arya's language might seem pretty touchy-feely, but it made some sense even to my skeptical mind, especially given that we know that the converse is true. Scientists have demonstrated that stress hormones—called glucocorticoids—inhibit the body's main sex hormone, gonadotropin-releasing hormone (GnRH) and subsequently suppress sperm count, ovulation, and sexual activity. Many couples can testify that when they are tired or worried or depressed, they simply are less likely to be in the mood. A Slovenian study of 1,076 couples published in 2008 found that women who had a harder time coping with the stress of infertility were more likely to suffer a miscarriage during the first trimester.

Depression can have a devastating impact on women's and men's fertility. A study of eighty Turkish couples published in 2009 found that women reporting high depression had fewer immature egg cells.

So it seems reasonable to assume that good emotional and mental health can improve the conditions for conception and pregnancy—at least it can't hurt.

In the Tibetan Buddhist lexicon, that often translates into being spiritually connected and, once pregnant, protecting a fetus or newborn from potential harm, ranging from disease to ghosts and demons, contamination (garbage, blood, feces), and malicious emotions. Much of this protection revolves around ritual. Sienna Craig, during her many years traveling in Tibet talking to women and studying medical traditions, witnessed many of these practices in action. She said women often consult with *amchi* (spiritual guides) who will analyze the health of mother and child through pulse diagnosis and prescribe both dietary advice and medicines made from plants, minerals, and animals. Pregnant women tend to stick to unprocessed foods—if they can afford them—and even seek special, spiritually charged nutrients.

"Some eat the small fish that swim in Lake Manosarovar in western Tibet, at the base of sacred Mt. Kailash," Craig wrote for a book called *Childbirth across Cultures: Ideas and Practices of Pregnancy, Childbirth and the Postpartum*. "One of the most pervasive such rituals is the creation of a fish out of butter that is then ritually imbued with *mantra*. Tibetan medical treatises also enumerate specially formulated medicines to help speed and aid delivery. Likewise, before a newborn nurses for the first time, he or she often has a small bit of butter mixed with honey, saffron water, and musk water to give the child the power of wise speech and to protect the child from harm by a variety of earth spirits."

Religion is infused into every step of the process, from pre-conception to after a child is born. Craig said that if a baby is frequently ill,

> parents might give the child a new name—that of a black-smith, for instance, or others whom Tibetans consider to be of low birth—as a way of tricking malevolent forces into leaving the child alone. A mother, spent from delivery, might have her abdomen massaged with oil—a means of quelling the pains of childbirth and helping her uterus con-tract. When a child is anywhere from a few days to a few weeks old, the new member of the community is honored with elaborate life welcoming (*bang tsol*) and long life (*tshe dbang*) ceremonies. At this time, many women offer a first feeding of a mixture of butter and barley flour: the staples of life on the Tibetan Plateau. This act not only grounds the infant in this world but also ties the child to its home and lineage, endowing this new life with the strength of generations.

Arya noted that after delivery an herbal pill can help clean the uterus and expel the placenta. The mother should rest with the comfort and moral support of her family, and she isn't allowed to take a cold bath or touch cold cement to prevent her from coming down with any illnesses, from respiratory problems to osteoporosis. He added, "After the birth, the child should be given a name chosen by the family, and brought up with love and care."

The ideas were enchanting, but Craig cautioned me not to romanticize "the Tibetan way." Craig, along with other health professionals, and government officials, and nonprofits, has been working for years to help Tibetan families balance their customs with the benefits of modern science. There are some real health concerns in the region. For a long time, rural Tibetans did not have access to contemporary medical care. Even today, the Tibetan fear of spiritual contamination may cause an especially superstitious woman to avoid going to a hospital for necessary prenatal care or even delivery, out of fear of spirits associated with sickness and death. Historically, families in especially the poorest regions have struggled with infant mortality, though deaths have declined dramatically in recent decades.

Still, Craig agreed that spending time with parents in Tibet deeply affected her own views as a mother-to-be. She spent the first six months of her pregnancy there and told me that it was "wonderful to be in a culture that did not medicalize birth as much as our own. I really did get to enjoy the sense of natural rhythm of pregnancy and the sense that birth was part of what women do, even in the midst of working very hard or just living life."

TENMA TSERING'S MOTHER bore eleven children in Amdo, via natural childbirth with no painkillers, with only her husband attending to her. As the eldest, Tenma remembers many of those births vividly, how everyone worried about the birthing woman, because it seemed that her health was most at risk. Babies were resilient, people believed, and would survive. If there were complications, instead of rushing the mother to the hospital, a cleric would be brought to the home to pray. Perhaps this was not the most effective treatment from a Western medical perspective, but it was the way they lived. They felt in their mind, body, and spirit the full intensity of the experience, before, during, and after their pregnancies.

More than thirty years later, Tsering's birth experience in the United States was drastically different. She'd come to the United States, after crossing the Himalayas by foot to settle in Dharamshala, India (home of the Dalai Lama and the Tibetan government in exile). Heeding the wishes of her dead father, she hoped to get an education and save money so she could support her siblings. While attending school, she won an immigration lottery and moved to the Chicago region in 1992. She met and married a Tibetan man, and they settled in Skokie.

When she became pregnant with her first child, Tsering knew that her prenatal care should entail keeping her body and mind pure. In Tibet, she'd never seen a chemical in her house—no shampoo, cleaners, or artificially processed food. She used a yellow butter from a Tibetan plant to make her hair clean and shiny. She ate fresh fruits and meats from her father's farms.

In 2002, she had her first son, an experience she recalls with awe, for its significance and for how completely different it was from anything she'd known. Even the littlest of things felt strange. Tsering couldn't believe that American women drank Diet Coke, for instance. She wouldn't allow herself anything but natural foods and beverages, not even tea. "Whatever is natural, that helps me more than a doctor," Tsering said. But in her new country, fertilizers touched even the freshest produce at the grocery store.

She'd watch pregnant American women shuttle off to monthly doctor appointments. In Tibet, "we don't go to the doctor," she said. "We pray to God." And she did pray, every day, all the time. She prayed for the health of her child and that she could follow the example of her own parents. "It was very peaceful," she said.

Tsering marveled at how other parents-to-be searched for baby names in books and on the Internet. Back in her homeland, she would've waited until a month after the baby was born and then would have taken him or her to a cleric to get a proper name. In the States, she knew the doctors and nurses would ask for a name immediately, and she worried about how to reconcile her beliefs with those in her new home. Three months into her pregnancy, the solution found her. She heard that the Dalai Lama would be visiting nearby Madison, Wisconsin, about 150 miles from where she lived. She, her husband, sister, and brother packed their SUV and made the two-and-a-half hour drive north, to give an offering of a white scarf and ask for blessings and peace during her pregnancy. They spent the day worshipping at the altar, and when Tsering was able to speak with one of the Dalai Lama's assistants, she presented the scarf and asked for a name for her child. He promised to get back to her by mail.

Two months later, an envelope from the Dalai Lama's office arrived. The certificate inside was graced with both the signature of His Holiness and the full name for her son: Tenzin Chosang.

Three years later Tsering had another son, and by this time she had become well versed in the rules that American parents followed: Go to your prenatal appointments. Get an ultrasound. Buy your layette. Get your shots. Later, in order to go to school, her boys—now five and eight years old—had to get vaccinated, a practice Tsering wished she could have avoided. While she appreciated some of those norms, she often felt like she was a fish out of water, in a place where people looked outside themselves for answers rather than within.

She recounted this one Sunday afternoon as she sat with other Tibetan mothers in an abandoned store space in Evanston, Illinois; on weekends it became a gathering place for Tibetans who live in the area. Her sons were studying Tibetan language and culture in the next room. Streamers left over from a birthday party held by a member of the Tibetan community hung limply from the ceilings and walls. A large rice cooker spat steam and a starchy smell pervaded the room. Nearby, three men stirred chicken curry and noodles with broccoli in cast-iron pots.

Tsering considers the moment in which she began to surrender to the Western way to be the day she gave birth to her son Tenzin. In the delivery room of Northwestern Hospital, Tsering was terrified, but she didn't want an epidural to help her get through labor.

Are you sure? the doctor asked her. It's common here. It won't hurt your child. There are complications only 5 percent of the time.

She hesitated, thinking of her mother, who'd never used any drugs to survive birth. But blinded by pain, she relented.

After the baby was born, she watched in awe as the doctors and nurses handed her child back and forth, checking his vitals. For ten minutes, they fussed over the baby, paying no attention to her. "They forgot me," she said, something she thought would never have happened in Tibet.

The important thing, she knows, is that Tenzin was healthy. The modern ways of America have their advantages; for example, she marvels at how her sons are already so technologically advanced and know how to use a computer. Her family has resources here she couldn't have dreamed of in Tibet. Still, there are plenty of times that she feels completely different from the mothers around her.

Tsering shared a final story about a walk she took last year, with an American friend and mother.

The two women used to stroll together regularly, chatting about their lives and families and getting a bit of exercise. One day, they spotted a parade of ants on the road. Tsering kneeled down to observe them marching, working, carrying leaves and sticks. Suddenly, her friend started stomping on the ants.

Tsering gasped. Why would she do that? The ants had a right to be there—it was their nature. She imagined that her friend, by killing the ants, was ruining her karma and putting her own children's health at risk. For days, Tsering was haunted by this image.

"My friend is a mother of a three daughters; she has no reason to kill," she said. Tsering said she would always think twice before hurting another living thing, because she believed it would be paid back in other ways. "I think, I have two boys to raise in this world and I could never do that."

I DON'T CONSIDER MYSELF a particularly spiritual person—or rather, I don't follow any organized religion. My parents grew up going to church but abandoned it and never passed those beliefs to us, encouraging us instead to choose our own paths. When I was young and people would ask me if I was Christian, I'd say yes because that's what I thought they wanted me to say. I didn't know what it really *meant*. Around all the people who went to church each Sunday, I felt embarrassed to be something different. Now that I'm an adult, I feel more comfortable saying that while I have great respect for many faiths, I pray to a god without a name.

I was praying to that god on the bus as I headed to the doctor's office that Wednesday for another round of tests that would determine the course of my week and quite possibly my future fertility. People around me ignored each other on their own journeys to work and school. I felt ghostly, as if I were dreaming my way to the appointment. I didn't ask God to save the pregnancy; rather, I asked for strength and a heart filled with peace (I also mentioned that I'd prefer not to get cut). Even if my doctor wanted to avoid the operating room, he'd prepared me for that real possibility because if the pregnancy was advancing, then it posed a risk to my fallopian tubes and perhaps my life. He'd gone ahead and scheduled me for a noontime surgery and sent me to get a blood scan and EKG in preparation. It would be a laparoscopy, in which he'd make one incision through my navel to insert a camera and another somewhere in my abdomen to remove the aborting embryo. I'd have to be put under general anesthesia and would deal with the usual recovery issues faced by people whose internal organs have been cut into, including increased difficulty in getting pregnant again.

All of this was riding on the outcome of a hormone test and an ultrasound that I'd have later that morning. I chilled, looking for a steady emotional center from which all the rest of me could function. *Think of the good things in your life. Breathe.* At 10:00 a.m., my doctor and the technician took an ultrasound and saw that the embryo was still there, with a significant clot around it, no bigger and no smaller than two days before. We'd have to wait for my blood results to see what to do next. So I waited, immobilizing my thoughts and worries, resigned that whatever was to happen was already happening. By 11:15 a.m., there were still no results.

Finally, at 11:35 a.m., my doctor emerged from his office and gave me the thumbs-up. It seemed as if the failed pregnancy was clearing out on its own. I'd have to take it easy, but we'd avoided the operating room. I was relieved and grateful.

PREGNANCY AND BIRTH are occasions celebrated and protected in unique ways. Christians baptize their children.

Some Jewish women chant psalms or go to *mikveh*. The Sha-hadah, a declaration of devotion to Allah and his messenger Muhammad, is the first sound many Muslim babies hear when they are born. An expectant Navajo mother might have a bless-ing gathering, where other women pamper her by brushing her hair, massaging her feet with blue corn, and offering her symbolic gifts (an apple for health, a coin for wealth) and emotional sup-port. Hmong shamans will use tools such as a gong, bells, and the horns of a water buffalo to protect a woman's unborn child.

Even if I'm not a superstitious person, I'm fascinated by the taboos and myths associated with pregnancy, some arguably based on real medical concerns and others not so much. Like Tibetans, Guatemalans believe pregnant women are susceptible to evil spirits and ill will, and many choose to have their chil-dren at home, according to a report on cross-cultural maternal health by the American Public Health Association. That report also noted that in some Latin American cultures, not meeting a mother's cravings can be dangerous; the baby could be born with physical or personality defects. My husband stayed with an indigenous tribe in Brazil that named their children after the first animal seen in the fathers' dreams. A 2009 *African Press Inter-national* article described some amusing beliefs among Kenyan tribes: pregnant Akamba are not to view dead bodies to avoid physical and spiritual contamination, and Luo mothers are not supposed to eat hippo meat because the baby will grow up to be one who "snores like a hippo." My sisters in Taiwan had a long list of dos and don'ts for me following my miscarriage, including not drinking cold beverages, which could prevent my body from healing (a view held in many cultures from Asia to Africa). The mother-in-law of one of my sisters insisted that she not bathe or wash her hair for at least a week after her first child was born. The idea behind this was that water could enter her body and cause swelling, headaches, and other maladies. (After a few days, my sister couldn't stand it anymore and took a shower.)

No matter the customs or traditions that govern their childbirth experiences, many mothers have observed that, by its nature, pregnancy makes you turn inward, to the incredible process, the miracle, the blessing—whatever you decide to call it—that is happening in your body.

At the same time, I agreed with Tsering that in modern times, there are so many external voices that your internal voice can get drowned out. You can spend countless hours reading posts on miscarriage and weight gain. While some of this mass commiseration can be comforting, it also can leave you unnecessarily worried. I've found medical technology a mixed blessing, too. While I'm mostly very grateful for the doctors, ultrasounds, and high-tech tests, if not careful I could worry myself to pieces about the correct level of human chorionic gonadotropin in my blood and other things I can't control and thereby overlook the magic of the experience.

I was curious about the advice Anne Maiden Brown's Tibetan sources might impart on healing after a miscarriage within in a modern Western setting. She told me because miscarriage, like birth, is a result of karma, the advice would likely be something along the lines of "give to the needy, feed birds and children, and give service to others."

She continued, "I am thinking of Laura Huxley's Los Angeles–based Project Caress, in which women give time (and love) to holding premature newborns in hospitals. Spiritual practices like meditation and blessings would also be suggested, and you can make up your own, like the practice of writing seven things you are grateful for each day."

A Tibetan doctor might suggest massage, moderate exercise, and without a doubt, lots of prayer. He might warn against bad thoughts, words, and emotions such as anger. My sister in Taiwan, whose spirituality, like the rest of my biological family's, is heavily influenced by Buddhist and Taoist traditions, made one thousand tiny cranes and stars during her first pregnancy. I thought it was a bit of a crazy superstition at the time, but I realized that it served not only as a wishful appeal for a healthy baby but also as a kind of meditation. She was forced to slow down so she could concentrate on those two-inch pieces of paper and lose herself in repetition. You don't have to fumble around with excruciatingly small origami to find peace, of course. You could simply take ten minutes to practice breathing deeply in a quiet space. Yoga is another easy alternative these days, given that there seems to be a prenatal yoga class offered in every city and town and even on the Internet. And the benefits of the right class aren't just mental or spiritual, according to some research. A study published in 2005 of 335 pregnant women conducted by the Vivekananda Yoga Research Foundation at the Gunasheela Surgical and Maternity

Hospital in Bangalore, India, found that women who enrolled in a yoga program that included physical postures, breathing, and meditation at eighteen to twenty weeks of pregnancy were significantly less likely to go into preterm labor and were more likely to have heavier babies. They also were less likely to suffer such complications as hypertension. In 2010, the National Institutes of Health and the University of Oxford found that women trying to conceive who had high levels of stress hormones in their blood were 12 percent less likely to conceive during their peak fertility period in a month. Lead researcher to that study, Germaine Buck Louis, of the Eunice Kennedy Shriver National Institute of Child Health and Human Development, told the health website Med Guru: "Stress-reduction techniques can improve pregnancy rates in couples who use in vitro fertilization and related methods."

It can't hurt for women hoping to conceive to try to relax, using whatever approach works for them (except, of course, alcohol or cigarettes). The beauty is it's such a low-tech solution.

After my first miscarriage in 2006, I tried to focus on renewing my positive energy. I slowed down. I meditated. I reflected on the good parents I'd been given and focused on the positive idea that my husband and I would be good parents (through birth or adoption) rather than worrying that we'd never get pregnant. Throughout my eventual pregnancy with Sofia, I felt surprisingly calm, almost Zen-like in the face of whatever outcome might come. Even my husband was surprised by my composure, given my tendency to fret. It was as if I'd been inside of one of those souvenir snow domes that had been shaken up violently. Now the shaking had stopped, and the snow was flittering about, and everything seemed quiet, falling into place.

This is the feeling I'm going for now, some days more successfully than others. I've got to believe that inner peace and acceptance of the incredible abilities and the limitations of your body have got to be good for you and your baby, no matter your religion or spiritual center. It is redeeming, renewing to shift your focus to giving, appreciating, and accepting. I remind myself how thankful I am for my child and my own family. I'm not going to become Buddhist, but I like the idea of polishing my karma. I'm trying to absorb the mystery of the process rather than just trying to dominate it. My inner dialogue has calmed, and I'm asking my doctor to relax, too. I'm praying and believing again, trying to wait as patiently as I can for what may—or may not—come.

A Prenatal Paradise

W hen it comes to empowering expectant and new parents, Sweden has long been one of the countries to emulate. The Scandinavian nation has a worldwide reputation for its progressive laws and policies. In as early as 1910, Sweden established its first voluntary child wellness clinics for new babies. Today, rather incredibly, more than 99 percent of parents receive prenatal and postnatal care. Almost every baby visits taxpayer-subsidized child wellness centers, where they are weighed, measured, and thoroughly assessed for physical and even mental problems. Nurses counsel parents on health concerns and parenting techniques—spending an average of thirty minutes per visit. Services are free, so no parent would ever refuse a test or treatment for lack of money. Critics may knock the high taxes and intrusive standards that support this system, but it gets results. During the last half century, Sweden has managed to drastically reduce the deaths of its babies. In 2010, the Central Intelligence Agency's *World Fact Book* ranked Sweden's infant mortality rate (an estimated 2.74 deaths per 1,000 live births in 2011) fourth best in the world, only behind Monaco, the republic of Singapore, and the island of Bermuda. The United States ranked forty-seventh with an estimated 6.06 deaths per 1,000 births, and the African country of Angola ranked the worst with 175.9 deaths per 1,000 births.

"The Swedish success in infant mortality is a success of good antenatal maternity care service and good infant health care [well-baby clinics]," said Stefan Johansson, consulting neonatologist at

Karolinska University Hospital. In-country experts say there are still plenty of improvements to be made, but over and over measures of child welfare show Scandinavian children to be some of the healthiest in the world. Sweden was the only nation to meet UNICEF's ten recommended benchmarks for children in 2008, from the quality of preschools and funding for child care to the frequency of child poverty.

～8～

How the Japanese
Let Their Children Fight

Sofia wakes from her afternoon nap, wide-eyed and raring to go.

"Matias is coming over," I tell her, and a toothy grin breaks across her face. She claps her hands together once, her signature expression of joy.

Three months younger than Sofia, Matias is the son of a Chinese Brazilian mother and an Uruguayan father. He caught my eye one Saturday at the playground we visit. I recognized immediately the Eurasian curve of his eyes, the tint of his skin, and the lankiness of his body; this boy looked as if he could be Sofia's brother. We eventually became close with his parents and got together every now and then for a playdate.

The weather is hot and sticky, so I set up a kiddie pool on our rooftop terrace. The two toddlers immediately jump in, alternately splashing water out of the pool and at each other. They ride Sofia's plastic car or kick a ball and then return to the water: harmless summer fun. Then the pushing starts.

Sofia begins nudging Matias's shoulders from the front. She repeats the motion in quick succession, harder each time, like a bully from a bad kids' movie. Matias doesn't push back; he just steps backward, trying to keep his balance.

"We don't push," I explain in English and Spanish. "You can hurt your friend and he might not want to come over to play with you."

She stares at me, with a smirk on her face.

"Do you understand, Sofia?"

Nothing.

"Do you understand, Sofia?"

"Sí," she says. I tell her to apologize and give Matias a kiss, and she runs over to where Matias and his mother are standing, though it seems primarily to escape me and not because she is feeling any regret. Most days, our kids get along swimmingly, but there are times when one or the other picks a fight. This time, lucky me, my daughter is the naughty one.

Five minutes later, Sofia is at it again. Once again, I take her aside, a little more forcefully this time, demanding that she look me in the eye. She says she understands and that she won't do it again. Yet another ten minutes later, when the children are fully dried and dressed, in a series of rapid-fire movements too quick for me to catch, Sofia nudges and then pushes Matias. He falls back, butt first into the little pool.

Lucy and I swoop in quickly. Matias is unhurt, just wet and startled; he doesn't even cry. I, on the other hand, am angry. I walk Sofia to the other end of the terrace, holding her tightly by the arm.

"We don't push," I tell her again. "You got Matias all wet, and you could have hurt your friend." I make her stand there until she tells me (again) she understands but still my daughter shows little remorse, which annoys me even more. Matias's mother is gracious and quickly reassures the kids (and me), "It's over, let's do something else." I run downstairs to get Matias a new diaper and a change of pants, mortified.

I can be a tough-cookie mom, especially in the presence of other kids and parents; I have a hawklike sensitivity to Sofia's misbehavior. My instinct is to jump in at the first sign of trouble to quickly defuse, correct, and punish before conflict even has a chance to blossom. So it was fascinating to hear about school in Japan, where parents and educators think that fights between children can be *good*.

A FRIEND SENT me a DVD of a research project spearheaded by Arizona State University professor Joseph Tobin that compared preschools in three different cultures.

"You have to see this," she told me.

In 1985, Tobin and Professors David Wu and Dana Davidson documented through video and later in a book a day in the life of preschools in Kyoto, Japan; Kunming, China; and Honolulu, Hawaii. They dispassionately observed and recorded the children's arrival, their facilities, and their routine and activities at each school. Then researchers showed those videos to educators in the three countries and documented their reactions. From his office in Tempe, Tobin enthusiastically explained the motivation and the lessons of this compelling work.

"Preschools are sites not for children to grow up and learn, but to grow up and learn to be part of a particular culture," Tobin said. "They try to produce citizens that are going to be able to succeed." The goal of the project was to compare and discuss how the schools reflect and affect philosophies of child rearing, education, and larger social patterns. I got a kick out of seeing the different schools, witnessing different rituals and kid activities: origami in the Japanese school, blocks at the Chinese school, and role-playing at the American school. But the scenes that most mesmerized me were those that featured a little boy named Hiroki.

Hiroki was an adorable, smart, and very ill-behaved four-year-old who attended the Komatsudani preschool, located on the grounds of a three-hundred-year-old Buddhist temple on the east side of Kyoto. He started his school day by pulling out his penis and waving it at the class during the morning welcome song. Often the first to complete his work, he yelled responses out of turn, sang aloud when everyone was quietly completing their workbook exercises, and imitated cartoon characters. Hiroki went on to use crayons to illustrate that he had a blue, a green, then a black penis. (The irreverent authors did note that four-year-olds in all three countries liked to joke about their genitals and their butts. "The only noticeable difference was that such humor was most openly exhibited in Japan, where the teachers generally said nothing and sometimes even smiled, whereas American teachers tended to say something like 'We'd rather not hear that kind of talk during group time.'")

Hiroki pushed and poked the boy in front of him when he was waiting in line to get his work checked. He spent the rest of his day making wisecracks, throwing around classroom supplies, and hitting, punching, stepping on, and wrestling his male classmates. But his behavior wasn't what unsettled me—I'd been around plenty of naughty children. What bothered me most—and apparently many of the American and Chinese observers who watched this footage—was that the teacher didn't intervene; she seemed to ignore him and his outbursts. The boy got a brief, quiet talking to by the principal, but he kept being bad, bad, bad.

His teacher and other administrators later explained that this was a deliberate strategy for dealing with Hiroki's behavior that they'd developed after many meetings and "trial and error." It was working, they claimed. Hiroki was behaving *better* than he had the year before. Most of the time, educators at the school didn't isolate a disruptive child from the group by punishing or excluding him. Researchers noted that the teacher "scrupulously avoided confronting or censuring Hiroki, even when he was most provocative. (Indeed, she remained composed even during those moments when it was all we could do not to drop our camera and our posture of scholarly neutrality and tell Hiroki to cut it out.)"

The teacher did encourage the other children to take responsibility for Hiroki's actions. When a little girl tried to tattle on

Hiroki for throwing cards over a railing, the teacher told her to go back and teach him not to do it. The adults seemed to have more tolerance for "childlike" behavior, fighting, acting up and out: it wasn't unusual for four-year-olds to joke about their genitals, and it was normal for little boys to fight. Overall, "the staff of Komatsudani believes that children best learn to control their behavior when the impetus to change comes spontaneously through interactions with their peers rather than from above." It wasn't that adults didn't intervene. If a child's health was in danger, teachers would jump right in—it was just that they often chose not to for smaller skirmishes.

More than twenty years later, I wondered if the philosophy had changed given the surge in youth violence globally and increasing concern about *ijime,* or bullying, in Japan. Yet when Tobin and another group of researchers returned to the three schools in 2002, they found that nonintervention was still a legitimate approach to dealing with behavior problems. Once again, they focused on many aspects of school life, from teaching philosophies and changes in economics to societal values and testing requirements, and they published the results in a video and a book called *Culture in Three Preschools Revisited: China, Japan, and the United States.* At modern-day Komatsudani, Tobin didn't find a kid that rivaled Hiroki. (They did ask what became of him; the principal—who was still working at the school—was amused with their interest in a child the staff didn't find remarkable and said he'd heard Hiroki was living a normal life.)

This time, researchers did witness a notable scuffle between girls. The youngest in the class struggled with three older girls over a bear, a battle that happened frequently according to their teacher. The kids pulled and tugged at the teddy bear until they fell into a pile of battling limbs. The teacher called to them to cut it out and stood nearby but otherwise didn't run over to break up the fight. Eventually, the conflict dissipated and the bigger girls convinced the smaller girl to share, pronounced they would be friends, and moved on.

Again, researchers showed this footage to teachers and parents in Japan, China, and the United States. And again, many Japanese educators generally approved of the teacher's approach, though some did have specific criticisms: the teacher should have intervened sooner, for example, or she should have actively helped the children learn from the conflict (and find different ways to solve it). Educators at a Christian school in Japan said that the nonintervention was "an example of what's wrong with Japanese education and with Japanese society," and that it leads to the blind following of the group's will.

Still researchers pointed out that the Japanese criticism largely focused on the *way* she intervened. When Chinese and American viewers saw the footage, they believed the teacher showed "a failure or a lack; a failure to protect the children from harming each other and a lack of awareness of what is going on in her classroom, of concern for the children's well-being, and of attention to their social development."

Tobin and his fellow authors politely disagreed with this assessment. "We suggest that her appearance of indifference to the girls' fighting was a performance intended to encourage the girls to relate to each other and solve their own problems rather then turn to her," they wrote. "Knowing the girls well enough to anticipate when and where a situation has the potential to become dangerous or spin out of control, Morita-sensei [the teacher] can give them time and space to work issues out on their own, rather than adopting the strategy favored by preschool teachers in the US and (at least until recently) in China of preemptive intervention to head off disputes before they have a chance to develop."

Nonintervention was not a policy but a tool. The teacher did stop the girls' tussling when they approached the corner of a piano, and she reprimanded the youngest girl for swinging her arms out of frustration and hurting another child. She told the researchers: "If I think a fight such as this one in the video is unlikely to result in anybody getting hurt, I stay back and wait and observe. I want the children to learn to be strong enough to handle such small quarrels. I want them to have the power to endure. If it's not dangerous, I welcome their fighting."

THE ISSUE OF child discipline can be touchy and highly personal to parents, determined by a number of different factors, including the personalities of the caregiver and child, upbringing, class, education, religion, and culture. Everyone in even the tiniest village may not discipline exactly the same way, but societal norms usually have a profound impact on the way parents attempt to shape their child's behavior.

It starts with our core values, including how our society regards children, wrote Meredith Small, in her book *Kids: How Biology and Culture Shape the Way We Raise Young Children.* She pointed out that Westerners traditionally adopted the Roman and Greek view that children are "moldable" and the Puritan notion that they are brimming with original sin and need to be disciplined. So for a long time, many people believed that kids had to be controlled. This contrasts greatly with how, for example, the Utku people believed "a child's mind, his mental faculties, and understanding grow only gradually, so there is no point in trying to discipline a small child; he is incapable of learning or remembering," according to anthropologist Jean Briggs, who observed Inuit cultures for more than forty-five years.

Caretakers fill their arsenal with techniques that can range from praise and overindulgence to shame and mental and physical punishment. Despite being banned in about twenty-four countries (most of them in Europe), corporal punishment is still common albeit controversial. The degree and form varies, but even in Sweden where corporal punishment was first outlawed in 1979, an estimated 10 percent of parents still believe it is a legitimate way to correct kids. The University of North Carolina's Injury Prevention Research Center in 2010 reported that nearly 80 percent of preschoolers in the United States have been spanked. In countries as diverse as Singapore, Bangladesh, and Nigeria, children are caned (sometimes publicly) and in Afghanistan, they are lashed. Child development experts have widely condemned hitting as an inhumane and even ineffective form of correction. However, many parents still believe that if you "spare the rod, you spoil the child." Social worker Susan Schmidt, in a report on Liberian refugees, said that among Liberians, "corporal punishment is an accepted, even expected, form of discipline for children, and is seen as an indication of good parenting. A rattan switch, or belt, might be typical items used to punish a child, often called 'beating.' A beating that leaves a mark on a child is not necessarily considered excessive, as it would be by child welfare standards in the U.S." She wrote that another traditional form of discipline, reportedly used by the Kru, Bassa, and Grebo ethnic groups, is the use of ground hot peppers placed on sensitive parts of a child's body, which burns and will "ensure that a child does not misbehave again." (Ground peppers are also placed on the lips of women during labor and put in a baby's nostrils during the first week of life to make them strong.)

At the other extreme, some societies tend to be more permissive and focus on shaping rather than correcting children, especially in their earliest years. It might be hard to swallow, but there are people who believe that mentally wrestling their kids into submission is a bad thing. Ruth Benedict, who is regarded as one of the pioneers of cultural anthropology, wrote, "Many American Indian tribes are especially explicit in rejecting the ideal of a child's submissive or obedient behavior. Prince Maximilian von Wied, who visited the Crow Indians over a hundred years ago, describes a father's boasting about his young son's intractability even when it was the father himself who was flouted; 'He will be a man,' his father said. He would have been baffled at the idea that his child should show behavior that would obviously make him appear a poor creature in the eyes of his fellows if he used it as an adult."

Scholar Julie Sprott, author of the book *Raising Young Children in an Alaskan Iñupiaq Village: The Family, Cultural, and Village Environment of Rearing* wrote that the traditional Native discipline style of reasoning and explanation can be mistakenly cast as noncontrol, when actually those methods—"along with a high degree of warmth toward children are strengths in the rearing system that should be amplified." She titled an essay criticizing the ethnocentric views about parental control "One Person's 'Spoiling' Is Another's Freedom to Become."

In America, parents put a lot of thought into the issue of discipline; hundreds of books, television programs, and blogs have been devoted to figuring out how to raise a well-behaved child. In schools, the paddle—a punishment my seventh-grade science and math teachers used almost daily—is rarely pulled out, and educators have zero-tolerance policies for fighting or violence, even for the youngest of children. At home, many parents use a kind of rules, rewards, and punishment system and prefer positive reinforcement and time-outs rather than hitting. Meanwhile, we watch shows like *Nanny 911* with gritted teeth as rowdy children overrun their homes, convinced weary and inept parents need to take a harder line.

Part of the reason that the whole idea of nonintervention in the Japanese classroom threw me for a loop is because I'd thought that parents should correct conflict or bad behavior before it blossoms into full-scale warfare. Plus, this technique seemed a little out of sync with what I knew about Japan. When I traveled to Tokyo I'd been impressed by the order, how people politely moved about their city, waiting in line to board trains and elevators; they seemed to go out of their way to avoid conflict. Despite some notable rebellion, Confucian ideas about duty and obedience, the greater good over that of the individual, and a deep respect for elders (including parents and teachers) influence the way Japanese society molds its children.

Tobin explained that Japanese are having fewer and fewer children, so the preschool experience is fashioned to help children *value* the pleasure and the pain of being a member of a community. Surviving a fight or putting up with a character like Hiroki was just a greater lesson about group harmony. The principal of Komatsudani preschool in 1984 told researchers that dealing with Hiroki was "hard on [the teacher], but I wouldn't say it's hard on the other children. By having to learn to deal with a child like Hiroki, they learn to be more complete human beings." I imagined some American parents would likely demand, "Get that kid out of the class! He's disrupting my kid's learning." Instead Komatsudani educators said children need to learn to deal with annoying characters (who will always be part of life and society), so the experience is actually *good* for them.

Tobin further explained the educators' rationale to me in this way: "If you don't have this experience, you will always need someone else more powerful to step in and make things better. We have a responsibility in our social world. We have to be responsible for not always yelling for teacher or mom. In American schools, the teacher is extension of mother. In Japanese schools, there is more emphasis on the kids' relationship to each other."

American Suzanne Kamata remembers vividly the surprise she felt witnessing this philosophy in action a couple years after she moved to Japan in 1989, when she was teaching English once a week in a rural community on the island of Shikoku. A local veteran teacher oversaw the class of about a dozen kindergarteners in a quaint building next to an elementary school. There was a fenced-in playground, a study area with tables and chairs, and a rhythm room with a stage and space where the kids could run around.

One snowy morning, a couple of boys began hitting and kicking each other in the study room. Instead of breaking them up, the teacher told them to take their fight into the rhythm room. She gathered up the other kids and told them to come into that room and watch. The fight ended shortly after. Kamata figured maybe the boys became self-conscious, or the fight had run its course.

"The teacher had a talk with the boys afterwards to find out what they were fighting about and try to get them to see the error of their ways," she told me. "I was appalled." Given that she was a foreigner, however, she didn't feel it was her place to bring it up.

After living in Japan for more than twenty-two years, marrying a Japanese man and raising her children in Tokushima City, Kamata now has a better understanding of the teacher's approach.

Her daughter is hearing impaired, so she and her brother fight a lot because of communication problems.

"I try not to jump in right away," she said. "Instead of pulling them apart immediately, I encourage them to talk to each other."

She added, "I am concerned, however, that [Japanese] teachers sometimes look away when they shouldn't. Kids don't always manage to work things out by themselves. I think that the Japanese tend to be nonconfrontational and that may be another reason why teachers are reluctant to get involved. They may not have the skills to deal with the situation."

In recent years, bullying has made headlines following high-profile suicides and attempts by kids who had been harassed and viciously picked on. Japan's Ministry of Education has tried to raise awareness of the problem, and some teachers have tried to put emphasis on caring about the feelings of others, directly addressing the problem and reading folk tales that illustrate how someone feels when he or she gets bullied.

THE ONLY PERSON I ever punched is my brother, and the last time we duked it out, I was about seven years old (when I was still bigger than he was). My two brothers fought a lot more often, up until their preteen years. My parents taught us that physical fighting was bad, though I can't remember those exact words being said. They didn't believe in corporal punishment and never threatened to spank us. The disciplinary details of my childhood are blurry when viewed through the fog of selective memory, but our dad yelled at us more than our mom, and we got sent to our rooms when we were naughty. Most of the time, my parents corrected our behavior through stern discussion. My mom was principal at a school with a lot of troubled kids and parents, so when we were in the hot seat, she spoke to us as if we were one of her students.

Mom told me thirty years ago, when she was teaching, that letting kids work out conflicts on their own was more acceptable in the United States than it is now. Today schools fear legal ramifications if fights and conflicts aren't broken up early enough and someone gets hurt. There have been many cases nationwide of parents who have sued school districts for failing to protect their children from harassment or fights. The infamous Columbine shootings and other violent incidents at schools have scared everyone, and most schools have implemented some kind of no-tolerance fighting and violence policies. Even so, serious bullying problems still exist in American schools.

I tend to have my own no-tolerance attitude with my child. When Sofia was merely a year old, I would pull her aside when she took away another kid's toy. At first, she'd look at me with her big brown eyes that said, *I don't know what the heck you are talking about lady, but gosh, aren't I cute.* She seemed to think standing in that corner was fun. As she got older, smarter, and slyer, I found myself taking a harder stance. I'd intervene before conflicts arose between her and her friends. (A preemptive strike seemed to save all parties a lot of headache.) When the kids would begin to scuffle over the play broom that every child who comes to our house seems to love, I'd quickly remove it from the scene.

No broom, no problem. I'd try to explain why it was good to share ("You like it when other children let you use their toys") or why one should not hit ("You don't like it when someone hits you"). But I'd also find myself raising my voice and threatening punishment a lot. Sofia was and is a good kid, but she is strong-willed, and I thought it was important to tame those tendencies.

Hearing about discipline philosophies in other cultures made me think more about how I was treating my daughter and what she might be or might not be learning, despite my intentions. That's when I found the fascinating work of George Bear, an expert in discipline and self-regulation at the University of Delaware, who published a study in 2006 comparing the moral reasoning of Japanese and American fourth- and fifth-graders. His researchers surveyed 132 kids in the Mid-Atlantic region of the United States and seventy-five students from similar-sized towns in the Hyogo prefecture, outside of Osaka. Each student was given scenarios that commonly occurred in school: hitting, fighting, saying mean things, and spreading rumors. After each scenario, the children were asked to talk about why one should not commit those aggressive acts.

Almost all of the American kids—92 percent—told researchers that one of the reasons one should not do bad things is they might get caught and punished. In stark contrast, 90 percent of Japanese students never mentioned getting caught or punished as a reason *not* to do something bad. They were more likely to say that doing something bad would hurt other children or cause them to feel shame or guilt. To the Americans' credit, they, like the Japanese, did often express concern for the feelings of other children, but fear of punishment played a prominent role in their decision making. Japanese children focused more on the "intrinsic, rather than extrinsic, reasons for not transgressing against others," Bear and his coauthors noted. They were more likely to think that they had to follow the rules of society rather than just the rules of the classroom.

Bear and his colleagues attributed this difference in response to social values and styles, especially the way that Japanese mothers dealt with behavior and conflict problems. They found that Japanese tended to use indirect and psychological methods rather than coercive ones to manage their kids' behavior. In particular, they often used moral reasoning, encouraging children to conform to the rules of the group, appealing to their children's feelings and goals, and asking them to consider how their behavior looks to others. They encouraged their kids to play rock-paper-scissors when they couldn't agree on something.

Japanese adults were more likely to manipulate through guilt, anxiety, and shame. For example, they might tell a child that he or she should not embarrass himself, his family, his class, or his school by behaving badly. Bear suggested that shame might be considered something very deeply negative—even sexual, because of Freud—in the Western world, but it's not *always* a bad thing. Sure, we don't want to make them feel so bad they end up in therapy for years to come, but it's also a bad thing if a child feels no guilt, shame, or remorse when he hurts someone.

Kahori Mori, a mother of a ten-year-old and a seven-year-old son in Nara, a city in western Japan, recalled a time when one of her sons was fooling around with a friend, and somehow that son stepped on his friend's back.

"I first listened to both sides and it was clear that my son did it just as a joke. So I scolded my son, telling [him] it's not right to step on anyone's back. 'No matter how much fun for you, it will hurt your friends. You would not like to be stepped on, either,' etcetera. Later, my son called his friend and said 'I'm sorry.' I apologized to his mother, too."

The Japanese tendency to emphasize autoexamination related directly back to the value of maintaining group harmony. Critics argue that conformity in Japan can be stifling and cripples creativity and freedom of expression—important values in American culture, which tends to stress individualism. Some also argue that what is going on in Japan is "group" regulation—rather than self-regulation—and that the pressure to fit in and a lack of intervention from adults have contributed to bullying.

On the other hand, Bear said that in the United States parents and teachers might assert their authority too much. (I hear my own voice now, telling Sofia, "You will listen to your mother" and "I am your boss, so you will do what I say.") We liberally dole out punishment (me, often, to Sofia: "Do you want a time-out?"), rewards ("You can have dessert if you eat all your soup"), and anger (I've perfected a pretty menacing look of disapproval). But these techniques alone don't necessarily stop kids from acting up.

"In America, there's just way too much external discipline," Bear told me. "You're always told to watch the kids, watch the kids." He pointed out that in the schools where he has worked, teachers send bad kids to the principal for punishment. Japanese school principals told him that a teacher should never send a child to the office. It is the teacher's responsibility to foster a relationship with the student so that bad behavior *doesn't* happen.

Nonintervention probably wouldn't work with kids who have extreme behavioral problems, yet I learned something. Bear argued that we need to not only focus on the punishment but also on the relationship and on respecting norms. The most effective teachers and parents blend lessons and punishment, a style known as authoritative parenting or teaching. I should be teaching and explaining the moral reasons why something bad should not be done, in addition to punishing bad behavior and rewarding good behavior.

"I don't think it should be one or the other," said Bear. "Just make sure you get the message across that explains 'this is why it's bad."

SOFIA STILL LOOKS to me with puppy dog eyes when another kid is doing something she doesn't like, waiting for my godlike word to save her day. Because she is now three, I can urge her and her buddies to try to work out the problems with words. It's a good thing that she is learning to get over the fleeting disappointments of life. More often than not, my daughter and her friends seem to move past conflicts quickly and pleasantly, in a ways that many adults cannot.

I've noted that South American parents, too, seem to have

a higher threshold for "kidlike" behavior and bickering. At Matias's second birthday party, for instance, he and a friend got into a squabble over a toy and started slapping at each other. I tattled to their fathers, who are Uruguayan and Columbian, respectively. They turned, looked at the boys, saw that they weren't inflicting mortal damage, and went back to their sandwiches. "Let them work it out," one said, and the other agreed with a shrug. Indeed, after a few more shoves, the toy was forgotten and the boys moved on.

Personally, I'll probably always lean toward intervention and discipline, but I'm trying to be more patient, to give Sofia a strong framework, and to trust more that she can take it from there.

Last week when I dropped off Sofia at her preschool class, she walked right up to a smaller boy named Pedro, looked him in the eye defiantly, and took the giant blue block he was holding. The boy stared back, teetering somewhere between lashing out and crying. He reached down and picked up a red block. Sofia took that from him, too. My narrowing eyes stayed glued to my naughty daughter. Part of me was ready to walk over, take her hand, and sternly correct her. Instead, I held back, allowing time for the scene to play out. After a few seconds, Sofia picked up a yellow block and handed it to the boy. His face lit with a smile, and they began to play together, absorbed in toddler babble. I recognized that they'd found a way to get along. I left thinking—at least this time—that I did right by staying out of it.

Scaring Kids Straight

Even if some child psychologists might frown on the practice, people from all walks of life and classes have invented stories of bad guys, ghosts, and monsters to amuse and scare their kids into behaving. These tall tales go well beyond the innocuous threat that Santa might leave coal in their stockings.

In the United States, we've got the bogeyman (a word that may have originated in Scotland or was perhaps derived from Bugi pirates in Indonesia), but one of the most pervasive legends that haunt children in countries as varied as Armenia, Haiti, Chile, and parts of India is the specter of a sack or bag man that threatens to kidnap naughty children. In Lebanon, he is known as Abu Kees (Father of the Sack). The Brazilian *homem do saco* is portrayed as a vagrant adult male who carries a sack on his back and collects mean children to sell. (*O bicho papão*—the eating beast—is the representative nighttime monster for kids who refuse to sleep.)

David Lancy, in *The Anthropology of Childhood: Cherubs, Chattel, Changelings,* mined these legends from fellow social scientists: Navajo children hear that if they are bad, the big gray Yeibichai will kidnap and eat them, and Bena-Bena boys and girls in Papua New Guinea, when they are threatened—albeit in jest—with axes, run shrieking in mock terror. "Children in Punam Bah village on Sarawak are threatened by various evil beings, including penjamun, creatures that abduct and sacrifice children, and by Europeans bearing injections," he wrote.

After listening to some of these scary stories, a Filipina American friend of mine laughed and told me, "I imagine many American parents wouldn't dare tell their kid a monster is going to eat them; mine brought it up once a day." Happily, she reports no long-term damage from such torment; she's happy and is as close to her parents as anyone I know.

How Polynesians Play
without Parents

When Sofia was eighteen months old, I enrolled us in a mom-baby class called Planeta Juego (Play Planet) "where play is a serious matter." A willowy brunette named Natalia, who sang most everything she spoke, led us in several organized activities during the hour-long session. She'd bang her tambourine and call us to the circle, where we'd clap while our little ones banged and gnawed on plastic instruments. We rolled our babies on Pilates balls and helped them cross obstacle courses. The idea at Planeta Juego was similar to the philosophy of many parent-child play classes: parents can use these activities to bond with their babies and also educate and socialize them. Sofia seemed to enjoy every moment: the bunny song, the switches and levers that they'd installed at baby level on the wall, the endless supply of toys, the parents and the other children.

From the time she was born, play has been an important way in which my husband and I interact with our daughter. We've danced, sung, peekabooed, and built sand castles for countless cumulative hours. We do it mostly because we enjoy it, though many psychologists, doctors, child development specialists, and parenting gurus say that parent-child play is not merely rewarding but crucial to the bonding process and to child development.

Yet if you dig around a little bit, you'll find that the playground is another one of those socialization spaces that belongs almost exclusively to children in many other cultures. In fact, it is only recently that adults in the West not only wholly assumed the caregiver role but felt compelled to become the star entertainment, too. Traditionally in many places from the Polynesian islands and Kipsigis farms in Kenya to *villaggios* in Italy, diversion—as well as teaching and discipline—is a responsibility that belongs to other children.

A VIVID EXAMPLE of this can be found in the Polynesian Islands, where the idea of *whānau,* or wider family care, prevails. In those intimate communities, everyone—including extended family and neighbors—pitches in to help care for children, but there is a heavy reliance on siblings and peers for socialization and play.

University of Hawaii professor Mary Martini made some dramatic observations of dynamics among children in the Marquesas Islands, an archipelago in French Polynesia nestled in the Pacific Ocean about nine hundred miles northeast of Tahiti and 3,000 miles from the western coast of Mexico. The locals call their home Te Henua Enana, the Land of Men (they themselves

are "the men"). During the fourteenth century, these dozen islands were a humming center of Polynesian life, where warring
chieftains oversaw a population estimated at around one hundred
thousand. But following their "discovery" and renaming by Europeans in the late 1500s, the population was decimated by disease,
war, and out-migration, leaving only about two thousand people
alive in the early 1900s. Throughout the last century the population has slowly recovered. In 2007, almost eighty-seven hundred
people lived on the island chain in small villages and homes em-
bedded in the rocky terrain. To get there, most travelers end up
taking the infrequent cargo-tourism ships that stop there about
fifteen times a year. The people of the Marquesas are not cut off,
especially with the advent of satellite television and the Internet,
but because of their relative isolation, many of their traditions
and values have stayed intact.

Martini observed at close range a group of about thirteen
children between the ages of two and five on Ua Pou, the third-
largest island in the Marquesas, daily for four months and less
frequently for another two months in 1976. Their families lived
in a settlement built into the steep slopes of a valley. Men and
older boys fished from outrigger canoes and women minded the
home, cooked, and cleaned. Adults held, coddled, entertained,
and slept with their children when they were babies, but as soon
as a child learned to walk, his mother turned him over to the
care of other children, a group that adults distantly oversaw
but little ones governed. Preschool-aged children learned to
calm babies, and toddlers became self-reliant because they were

taught that that was the only way they could hang out with the big kids.

In their peer group, Martini observed, kids rarely hung out alone. Together, they played "ship" and "fishing" and "hunting." They pretended to drive, dock, and anchor boats, and load on and off the dried coconut that was used as currency. They hunted goats and prepared and "ate" mud meals. Sometimes they played games, or sat and talked and told stories. They also fought, teased, hazed, and competed for status. Some of the scenarios sounded pretty harsh; children threw lemons, stones, and mud at each other (usually missing, Martini noted). They shamed one another for hurting or endangering themselves, accidentally hurting others, making mistakes, and being too bossy.

In "Peer Interactions in Polynesian," Martini writes,

A plane flies overhead and children jump up and down, yelling "avion, avion" [plane, plane]. Stephanie (2.5) falls off a wall in excitement. Children stop yelling and watch silently until Stephanie sits up and begins to cry. At this point they begin to point, laugh and chant "Ste-pha-nie! Ste-pha-nie!" Her older sister climbs down, yanks her into a standing position and slaps her. Her 4-year-old brother picks up a rock and threatens to heave it at her. She cries louder and tries to crouch. Her sister makes her stand and says, with disgust, "tuitui" ("too much noise"). She takes her home.

"Typically no one clearly wins or loses status conflicts. Rather children turn them into games or jokes, dissipating the group tension," Martini observed. She wrote that the children often expressed compassion, comforted and helped each other, shared food, groomed each other, stood up to bullying together, and included each other in play. Life was rough and tumble, but Martini argued kids learned to survive in a way that Western children do not.

> American children's concern with the sanctity of self makes them vulnerable to the vagaries of social life. The everyday social hazing that Marquesan four-year-olds learn to handle with poise and humor would devastate most American preschoolers and would be considered emotional abuse by our courts. The Marquesan children learn not to take these events personally and not to assume that others' attacks are aimed directly against their persons. They learn to define their selves as something more stable than their (frustrated) plans of the moment and as something more worthy than how they are portrayed by their tormenters.

A husband and wife team of anthropologists, Jane and James Ritchie, observed similar child-on-child care during three decades of research in New Zealand and other Polynesian islands. In *Growing Up in Polynesia,* they wrote, "Indeed in Western societies, the degree of child caretaking that seems to apply in most of Polynesia would probably be regarded as child neglect and viewed with some horror. There are two reasons for this. One is the extreme danger to young children that has been created by the environment of Western technology and the other is the Western theory of human nature, which implies that children are not to be trusted—and certainly not with the total care of other children. Western society still believes that children are imperfect adults. In Polynesia, children are children, and so there is no reason at all not to trust older children with the care of younger."

I traded e-mails with Jane Ritchie and she told me that today "one of the major influences on the functioning of peer groups has been the introduction of formal schooling, which takes up a lot of the time that children would otherwise spend in peer groups. But even with the requirements of schooling, older children in Polynesian families still have a lot of responsibility for looking after younger children. This would happen in cultures where large families are still the norm."

I asked her if this was something worth mimicking in everyday American life, and Ritchie reminded me that on a Polynesian island, which is a relatively safe environment, "children have the freedom to roam in the company of their peers, in ways that would simply not be possible or desirable in a contemporary Western urban setting." Still, she stands by some pretty provocative statements in her book, such as this one: "If we were to rewrite Western manuals of child care, we would put in strong advice to the world in general and the Western world in particular. Sibling caretaking should be recognised, promoted and valued; it develops some valuable human attributes."

IN MANY COMMUNITIES in many countries, children are not merely playmates but are charged with passing down "knowing," as anthropologist Patricia Zukow-Goldring put it.

Zukow-Goldring, a University of California at Los Angeles professor who studied sibling relationships in tiny villages outside Guanajuato, Mexico, explained that in traditional and/or rural agrarian cultures, children played many of the roles that we might today assume should be reserved for adults. These are societies that need the mother out in the field. "There is an economic pressure for the mother and anyone who is healthy and has a strong back to be out working," she told me. In Guanajuato, Zukow-Goldring observed that while parents were away, grandparents or other adults might oversee the operation of the household, but the nitty-gritty day-to-day child care and interaction was led mostly by kids ranging in age from seven to eleven. The relationships went well beyond babysitting for a couple hours; children were changing, bathing, and potty training babies and preparing food for and feeding them. They were teaching the little ones to play and comforting them when they were hurt or sick.

Kid socialization is a messier, clumsier, and harsher process. As seen in the Marquesas, kids tend not to worry much about hurting feelings. Directives are to the point: "No. That's not how you do it. You do it like this." It might not be, as Zukow-Goldring put it, the "polite middle-class way," but the job gets done. And there are benefits for all parties. For instance, it frees up adults, allowing them to work, and gives children valuable skills.

"It teaches responsibility to the older [child]," she said. "It teaches them to put the needs of this dependent child before their own. These children learn this at a very young age, and it certainly helps them in the transition to becoming an adult."

Kid caregivers develop their perceptual-cognitive and communication skills trying to figure out what the younger child does and does not know, and then they knowingly or "accidentally" implement what that child-novice needs to know to engage in ongoing events. Meanwhile, babies learn the developmental skills they need.

"Is it better than what [babies] would get from adults? I doubt it," she said. "But it does seem to be just as good." She even suggested, in light of the child care crisis in the United States, that siblings and cousins could be organized to help watch the little ones (with adults supervising) when afterschool care is lacking. "It'd be a whole lot cheaper and a whole lot more effective" than other forms of child care, she said.

Historically in the United States, children lived and played with much more freedom in many communities, from farming towns to immigrant neighborhoods. When they weren't working or at school, kids roamed the streets, alleys, and country roads, commanding and constructing their own reality. A century ago, they cared and took responsibility for each other at a level that is rare today.

This began to change as America became more industrial and urban. In his book *Children at Play: An American History,* Brown University historian Howard Chudacoff charted an adult takeover of child time and play. During the early twentieth century, he reported, adults started to view childhood as something that needed protection, and compulsory schooling, plus labor and curfew laws, began to restrict the movement and role of children; older siblings and others were less available to care for the littlest among them. Meanwhile, extended families began to break up, and households began to get smaller and scatter into the suburbs. Still, Chudacoff called that period the "golden age of play," a time when the boom in domestically manufactured toys began—bringing us Erector sets, Patsy dolls, Lincoln Logs, Tinkertoys, and board games. But children still were trusted to amuse themselves.

During a speech to the Brown Club of Oregon in 2008 Chudacoff said that, for him, a watershed moment—when children's playtime began to be defined by adults—was when the *Mickey Mouse Club* first aired on ABC in 1955. It was the first daily program for children, starring children, and most significantly, the Mattel toy company was the sponsor.

"This was the first time that a toy company had tried to market its goods to children every day of the week, every day of the year, not just at Christmas time," he said. From there, toy companies grew ever more creative, aggressive, and shrewd. Play became synonymous with toys. In the 1970s, electronic gadgets that moved, beeped, and spoke entered the market, just as children were starting to play in smaller groups, indoors. More families were building separate playrooms and limiting outdoor play in urban areas to playgrounds (always in the company of an adult). Parents began to try to enhance their kids' development even before they exited the womb, streaming Mozart into pregnant bellies and choosing videos and toys that promised leaps forward in development.

At the same time, parents became more anxious for their children's well-being. While rates of child abduction haven't changed much over the last century, parents kept their kids at home to keep them safe. Parents even feared baby products and toys and expected the government, the Consumer Product Safety Commission, and other watchdog agencies, to keep their kids from harm, and if they failed, lawsuits followed. Though some sibling care still goes on today, children seem safest under their parents' close watch.

Chudacoff has theorized that parents in their goal to enrich and protect began structuring their children's time more often than ever before, filling what once was free playtime with play groups, baseball leagues, and afterschool programs. *New York Times* writer Dominique Browning suggested a final factor that has intensified parental control of play: "Baby boomers constitute the first generation to have both the desire and the means to remain children themselves; they have been known to take over the Xbox altogether, or to up the stakes so that their toys become their kids' toys (the iPod, for example)."

Study after study has measured mother and/or father and baby interactions in laboratories, linking play with brain development, intelligence, responsiveness, and cognitive abilities. There are countless books, websites, and special play institutes that instruct parents to play and teach, using blocks, games, songs, and toys. Some experts try to help parents integrate teaching and playing into daily life, even explicitly suggesting the dialogue and scenarios that you can act out with your kid. The National Association of Child Care Resource and Referral Agency has a nifty tool on its website whereby you select the age of your child and a suggestion for play pops up.

However, as I began to delve into the vast amount of historical, anthropological, psychological, and educational literature on play in other parts of the world, I was surprised at the number of cultures in which mom and dad don't play much—if at all—with their children.

Harvard professor Robert LeVine, who spent many years studying the Gusii people in southwestern Kenya, observed that while Gusii mothers are super responsive to their infant's cries (picking them up, feeding on demand), they tend not to talk to their babies. "Mothers rarely looked at or spoke to their infants and toddlers, even when they were holding and breastfeeding them . . . The Gusii mothers in our sample expected their infants and toddlers to comply with their wishes, and they could be harsh (by American standards) in exerting control over them. They rarely praised their infants or asked them questions but tended to issue commands and threats in communicating with them," he wrote. Because they were so worried about their children's survival, Gusii parents did not explicitly strive to foster cognitive, social, and emotional development, he said. These needs were not neglected, because once they left their mom's arms, they got what they needed socially from the other children who ended up being their caregivers and playmates. "The Gusii people didn't talk to their babies, and babies talked just as well," anthropologist Meredith Small pointed out to me. (If the Gusii way seems

neglectful or odd to us, their parents feel likewise about our behavior; when LeVine showed Gusii mothers videotapes of American mothers tending their children, they were upset that women
would allow their babies to cry for so long without picking them
up. And they couldn't comprehend how parents could put baby
to sleep in a separate bed.)

In Civita Fantera, a small north central town in Italy, thirty
miles south of Rome, mothers were hands down the most important caregivers for babies, but they didn't believe it was their role
to play with them. Rebecca New, a teacher and cultural psychologist who visited the town frequently during the 1980s and 1990s,
observed that that moms often indulged their babies by always
holding them, responding instantly to cries and frets and sleeping
in the same room until their tots were two years old.

"While enjoying an occasional game of peek-a-boo, sample
mothers rarely engaged their infants in the kind of one-on-one
play sessions that have been observed in American mother-infant
dyads, focusing instead on infant care tasks such as feeding and
grooming and including the infant in domestic routines as well
as social encounters," she wrote in a book she coedited called *Anthropology and Child Development: A Cross-Cultural Reader*. "At
no point did any mother suggest that play was an important con-
tributor to infant development."

New further reported, "When asked to 'play with your children any way that you choose,' several mothers declared, 'I never
play with him. I don't know what to do.'" Fathers didn't play
much with infants either, feeling clumsy and fearing they might

hurt the babies. When toddlerhood came around, parents recognized that children wanted and needed to play more. "While
mothers did not relinquish their predominant role as caregivers,
they became much more likely to share the supervision of the
thirty-month-old toddler with others, including the mixed-age
play groups of siblings," New noted. Little ones who lived in the
centro storico (the historic downtown), for example, hung out
with other kids in the cobblestone streets chasing balls and avoid-
ing passing cars.

It wasn't that mothers didn't appreciate the importance of
play, but rather they figured play would occur regardless of their
involvement. Toddlers mostly played with older kids and with
other adults. "The two- to three-year-old child might be observed
on the floorboard of a teenager's moped, cruising up and down
the street; on the shoulders of an uncle or grandfather as he took
a stroll; or in the grasp of a female neighbor or relative at the
market."

New observed, "What seemed most important to all concerned—the toddler included—was that he or she had left the
confines of the infant care environment and was rapidly becoming a willing observer and active participant of the community
at large."

Plenty of research seems to show that human children learn
the skills of socialization and the rules of their culture through
some kind of play or variants of play, and that parent-child play
can be beneficial. (The parents in Italy I spoke to said that today
more and more moms and dads are involved with their children's

play.) The problem, some cultural scientists say, is when the so-called experts start prescribing parent-child play as the best way to bond for *every* family.

David Lancy is an anthropologist and professor at the Utah State University and the author of an extensive survey of scholarly research on parenting in distinct cultures called *The Anthropology of Childhood: Cherubs, Chattel and Changelings*. In a scathing critique in the *Boston Globe,* Lancy said that parent-child play is a feature of wealthy developed nations, a behavior we've only recently invented and not necessarily for the better. In many, if not most cultures, he argued, "adults think it's silly to play with children."

Intrigued, I felt compelled to ask him personally, What've you got against play? So I rang him in his office in Logan, catching him between lectures on cross-culture child development.

Lancy said that he took interest in the topic of play after listening to a well-known developmental psychologist speak at a conference in St. Louis. The man described how parents can and should introduce block play. Lancy raised his hand and told the speaker that he ought to be careful about generalizing about such recommendations because parents' playing—and even teaching children—was something only a tiny fragment of the human population did. The psychologist, he recalled, was "incredulous." He "refused to believe all parents (unless they were flawed in some way) wouldn't engage in block play with infants if the materials were available."

Lancy said, "There are no toys for the most part in most

cultures of the world and parents don't get on the floor and play with kids. For one thing they don't let kids get on floor because it's dirty and there are bugs, snakes and things that could hurt them."

After that conference, Lancy started reading the advice for parents on play.

> The crusaders seemed all on board with the idea that mother-child play, and to some extent father-child play, was natural, necessary, and essential to the attachment and to development of the relationship between a mother (or father) and a child . . . And it followed if that was absent there was something wrong with the parents and the child would be harmed.
>
> I knew it couldn't possibly be true in a general sense. Yes, it happens in contemporary middle-class European, American, Asian, and East Asian families, but I was really upset at others casting aspersions at parents who didn't play with their children.

So Lancy started speaking up and wrote an essay for *American Anthropologist* that caught the attention of the national media. He offered a litany of examples of cultures in which parent-child play is not common. For example, in a tribe in Africa, parents put their smallest children on "the Mother Ground" (the title of one of his books) where children play, fight and entertain one another, and parents monitor only from a distance. That said, Lancy told me that he personally knows and understands the value and joy of play between parent and child—he played with his two daughters all the time when they were little. But he and some other cultural anthropologists bristle at the argument that a certain kind or amount of parent-child play and learning is essential for bonding and development for *anyone and everyone*. Lancy argues that some child development specialists are too zealous about pushing an interventionist parenting style. His motto when speaking to professionals and parents these days has become "Don't turn nurture into nature."

"The problem is when the predominant, trendsetting, fashion-setting culture convert their practices into generalizations, and what they do becomes considered natural, biological, and genetic," he said.

I THINK MY daughter, if she could describe me, would say I'm pretty fun, but I admit to having mixed feelings about parent-child play. Frankly, when I'm not in the mood, it can be a drag. There are lots of things I can do with Sofia for long periods of time (read, visit friends, go for walks), but I only enjoy intensely *playing* with her for so long. My husband is a more creative, interesting playmate; he will strum the guitar and sing with her and invent creative games, such as hunting butterflies or making a book with drawings. He imagines spotting animals in exotic settlings while we sit at the dining room table. I tend to get tired somewhere around the forty-five-minute mark and suggest going out. I enjoyed Planeta Juego, but for me, the mother-daughter interaction wasn't the most fulfilling part. (I love spending time with my baby, but as a mom who works from home, I do that all the time.) I was more intrigued with the group dynamic, the fact that we'd created an artificial tribe of sorts. While we mothers shared our stories, anxieties, and secrets, the babies-going-on-toddlers laughed, examined, and amused one another. Sofia and I both delight when other children divert her attention.

Feeling a bit guilty about these feelings, I asked random parents on Facebook how they felt about play, and the first answer from one mom seemed typical: "I love playing with my boys. Both are autistic, 15 and 4. We have a blast running around playing, swimming, or just watching movies. How could anyone not enjoy spending quality time with your kids? You're their teacher, friend, and playmate." Despite many other parents' more complicated, conflicted thoughts about play, this woman's indignation with the question seemed to sum up how lots of middle-class parents think they should feel nowadays.

It was a relief to think that quality time doesn't always have to be play. But the very attractive idea of having a natural and diverse child playmate (and caregiver) pool is more complicated when you have one child and live a continent away from your already-dispersed extended family. Fortunately, even though Monte and I had our first child relatively late—he was thirty-six and I was thirty-four—lots of people we know are in the same boat. Many of my friends delayed having children for different reasons, including careers and desire to travel. When we can get together, our kiddies can bond. While most of the bigger kids we know aren't Sofia's caregivers, I appreciate the time she spends with them. They always encourage her to participate just by their presence and make her laugh more heartily than she ever does with us. The prospect of seeing her friends Henry or Morena (who are a year older) can compel her to behave or put on shoes she initially refused to wear. These little rascals might expose her to bad words—poop is a favorite—and bad habits, such as refusing to eat healthy food or throwing that same food on the floor, but these are trade-offs that I'm happy to make. At the same time, Sofia seems to express an affinity for babies. Our close friends in Argentina had a boy named Adrian a couple months after Sofia turned two, and she adores him. Sofia wants to bathe and feed him, behaviors I once thought might be a little girl thing. But I've realized that she's more nurturing because she is around him and other babies regularly, sees how we treat them, and can practice to some degree. The exposure is already turning her into a more conscientious and helpful little person, and that's great—especially because we were expecting her little sister in May.

Nevertheless, real quality kid-on-kid time takes at least some parental intervention to gin up: identifying kids and families that are appealing to all of us, finding an amenable place to meet, and coordinating work and nap schedules. As much as I don't want to be a mom who commands her child's time, it can be hard to avoid a takeover. When Sofia was merely two years old, we enrolled her in preschool and in an art class, because she enjoys coloring and drawing (and there are older kids in the class). We briefly tried dance class because she loves dancing, though we quit when we saw that her time was getting too scheduled out. In recent years, child development experts in the United States have begun to push once again for giving kids unobstructed free playtime. Activists are protesting cuts in recess, and parents are buzzing about the Vygotsky way and the importance of learning and developing self-control through imaginative play. There are programs, institutes, and camps dedicated to free play (which, Chudacoff notes with some irony, are organized and guided by adults). As often as possible, we try to give Sofia the unrestricted time with kids she craves. She savors the attention of her cousins, who range in age from one to twenty-two. Sofia's dad and I are thrilled that she's old enough to wander with her buddies into another room or to the other side of the playground, to play, discover, bicker, and resolve. We might orchestrate these encounters, but the children define them, and that's what makes them special.

All the same, my husband and I still play with Sofia with pleasure, because her youth is already escaping us. She is only three, but it feels like she's going on eighteen. So we reserve plenty of evenings when our time is all hers. We read books, Sofia makes us imaginary soup in her tiny kitchen, we practice the alphabet, and she and Monte draw people with mustaches on the DoodlePro. We fade in and out of her games, and she interrupts our conversation. The day will come—too quickly I'm sure—when she will close herself in her room, preferring to be the phone with her girlfriends or boyfriends. So even if I'm tired or not in the mood, I dance with her to Michael Jackson (even if her favorite song happens to be "Bad"). We play until the hands on the clock and her heavy eyes remind us that the next day is not far away.

Historic Toys

DOLLS: From prehistoric times, humans have fashioned dolls and images of themselves or deities from materials such as sticks, mud, and fur. A fragment of an alabaster doll with movable arms from the Babylonian period was unearthed. Dolls made of painted wood dating back to 3000 to 2000 BCE have been found in the tombs of wealthy Egyptian families, as well as in the graves of Greek and Roman children.

KITES: The exact origin of the kite is unknown, but some legends say that a Chinese farmer tied string to his hat to keep it from being blown by the wind. Around 200 BCE, General Han Hsin of the Han Dynasty flew a kite over the walls of a city he was attacking, according to the American Kitefliers Association. The kite, which has been used by adults for everything ranging from carrying bait out to sea in Micronesia to flying military banners and studying weather, remains a popular toy in many countries and cultures today.

MARBLES: Historians believe that this toy dates back to the Harappan civilization in the western part of South Asia (which flourished around 2500 BCE and is one of the earliest-known civilizations); stone marbles were found in an excavation site near Mohenjo-Daro. In ancient Greece and Rome, children played games with round nuts, and Jewish children played games with filberts at Passover, according to iMarbles.com.

BOOMERANGS: Historians can't pinpoint the exact origin of the first boomerang, but the sporty folks at boomerang.com believe that, most likely, a hunter trying to perfect his (or her) hunting stick discovered it accidentally. Australian aboriginal boomerangs date tens of thousands of years old, but older hunting sticks have been discovered throughout Europe. King Tutankhamen of Egypt collected boomerangs. While aficionados insist that it is a sports article, not a toy, children have amused themselves with variations of the boomerang for centuries.

⟋ 10 ⟍

How Mayan Villagers
Put Their Kids to Work

I've decided to find my daughter a job.

Yes, you read me right. And yes, she is only going on three years old. And I get if you, kind reader, along with my friends, say "Oh, Mei-Ling, childhood is a fleeting joy. There'll be plenty of time later for work." But I'm not talking about starting my daughter on some shift at a thimble-making factory. I'm simply suggesting a little chore, a real job she can call her own.

My child spends almost all of her life playing, but she is at an age at which she *likes* manual labor. I see great promise in this delicious naiveté and would like to start rotating her into the flow and function of the household.

There are lots of places—often in rural, nonindustrialized areas—where children are integrated into the needs of the household early on, and chores and play are blended fluidly. I'd heard this from parents in the mountain villages of Juarez, Peru, and have seen it in my own birth sisters who worked in the fields side by side with our parents in southern Taiwan. Children help their parents in essential ways, doing anything from feeding the chickens and taking care of their siblings to earning wages. This contribution is essential and expected by everyone involved. Kids might complain, but there is rarely a battle over chores or work because it is just understood that full household participation is key to family survival. I'm not trying to romanticize poverty, but I'm impressed by this sense of responsibility and contribution that some children seem to have from a very young age— something that many middle-class kids lack these days. I hear parents so often complaining that they have to bribe their kids to wash the dishes or take out the trash. How many college freshmen show up at school not knowing how to wash a load of laundry? How did we end up so educated and well rounded in so many ways yet lazy in others?

Recently, during a preschool parent-teacher conference, Sofia's teacher told me that cleaning up was something that my daughter and her little classmates had some trouble with. All of the parents seemed to be trying to change this, invoking songs and incentives, but it was not easy. How did other families in other places compel their children to want to participate, and why did our children resist?

THE TINY TOWN of Petac in the Mexican Yucatán lies half an hour south of the five-hundred-year-old Spanish colonial city of Merida. It's "a step back in time," said Colleen Casey Leonard, manager of a converted seventeenth-century estate in the town, who put me in touch with some of her staff and their families. About two hundred residents live in the pueblo of Petac; most people live with extended family in communities of traditional oval-shaped thatched huts called *palapas* or *chozas,* one-room homes made from stone or sticks and mud, covered with limestone and roofed with tar paper. (The traditional Mayan palm-thatched roofs are too expensive and labor intensive.) Everyone sleeps in hammocks. Cooking and eating are done outside, usually in the shade of a mango or avocado tree. Outhouses are set up somewhere in the backyard, and while running water is still a luxury, most people have their own wells. Chickens peck the ground hoping to kick up a morsel, and turkeys roam the streets. Most people have a variety of fruit trees such as lime, mango, *guanabana, ciricote, ciruela,* banana, avocado, and sour orange. Every household has a couple of habañero pepper plants and one or two green *chaya* bushes.

Crescencia Dzul May, who is sixty-five and has lived in Petac all but two years of her life, said that being the eldest of four daughters, she was expected to work, period.

"I had no brothers to help my father cut *penca* [the Mayan word for henequen, an agave plant]," she said. "So when I was little, about four, I had to start working in the fields and *monte* [an area where people hunt] with him." They got up while the moon was still in the sky and headed to work.

"Once a snake chased me and I ran screaming after my father. He got mad at me and told me to leave the snake alone!" She laughed deeply revealing a mouth full of shiny gold teeth. As a child, May chopped the henequen leaves, bundled them, and hauled them to spots to be picked up later and sent to the hacienda and made into rope. She also helped to collect firewood. Chopping the henequen and wood didn't fetch much money. "But it was something," she said. Every bit helped, and she was proud of her contribution.

When she and her father returned from the fields, he would rest in the hammock until the meal was served, and she would help her mother. She ground corn and made the masa, or dough, for the tortillas that were prepared on a flat griddle called a *comal* over the wood fire. The family always ate together. When her sisters were old enough to help in the fields, her father took them along as well.

Did she ever play?

"No. We always worked. There was no other way. We were very poor." So poor that she remembers times eating only chopped-up rinds of limes mixed with sliced raw red onions in tortillas. There was a little school in her town, but because her father needed her help, she was not allowed to attend.

It seems like this would be a tough childhood, and it was. But was her family happy? Was she? When asked these questions, May didn't have an answer—it really was not something that she thought about.

Life was a little different when she raised her own nine children. May said that her husband worked at the local hacienda until it closed in the 1970s, and then he hunted and labored in his own fields growing most of their food. He collected firewood to sell, and sometimes he bought oranges from a nearby citrus farm and took them to market in Merida. The boys accompanied their father everywhere. They attended school through sixth grade but still started working for wages when they were around seven. The girls regularly helped cook tortillas when they were about the same age, and they washed their own clothing once they were a few years older. The youngest daughter, Marlene, started babysitting her younger brother, Will, when she was about five, a responsibility that she enjoyed. The family didn't distinguish between work and play—they simply did what had to be done. If it was difficult, they didn't complain.

Leonard said that among the young families who work at her resort, the standard seems to be changing as schooling becomes more important. María del Socorro, who is thirty and works as Hacienda Petac's assistant day cook, hopes her sons go on to have more professional and educated lives. Socorro quit school at a young age and can't read but is proud that her oldest son, Juan José, is getting good grades and wants to be a teacher. Still, she and her husband, Gustavo, insist that their children work, and they've integrated their boys from a young age into their daily routine. Socorro always asks Juan José, who is ten, to help sweep, pick up trash, weed the yard, and do other tasks. His brothers, Alexander, five, and Eliazar, three, eagerly follow his example; Eliazar takes pride in having his own special small bucket to help fetch the water that his mother uses for cooking and cleaning.

Recently, the family purchased a small piece of land, about ten by thirty meters, in town to plant fruit trees, chiles, and other vegetables. When Gustavo goes out to chop, the two little boys insist on tagging along. (Juan José is usually at school or helping his grandmother, who lives in a nearby town.) Even though the boys are quite young, Gustavo lets them use old *koas,* curved, bladed knife tools that the locals use to chop and weed. The boys actually only work for a few minutes and then dawdle around before working again for a few more minutes, but being at Gustavo's side, watching and keeping him company while he works, ensures that they are learning what he is doing.

Socorro said, "They need to learn how to take care of their own houses someday." If they help while they are young, "they will be able to achieve all the things they want to."

THIS SORT OF commitment to the value of work is something that Suzanne Gaskins, a psychologist at Northeastern Illinois University, has documented extensively in another small Mayan village in the eastern Yucatán. Since 1978, Gaskins has traveled there at least once a year. She even built her own small home, learned Yucatec, and is considered a regular if unorthodox resident.

Gaskins admitted that much has changed in her village (which she declines to name to keep tourists from dropping by). Back when she first visited there, it was primarily agrarian, with almost every man in the village working as a corn farmer. They left home early most mornings to clear forests, burn fields, plant crops, weed, and harvest. The women's lives revolved around corn, too;

a good chunk of their day was spent cleaning, boiling and grind-
ing the corn, and preparing it to eat.

The village and region as a whole has evolved dramatically,
propelled by the popularity of nearby Cancún as a vacation desti-
nation. Families went from primarily depending on corn to traveling to the spring break town to sell their goods or earn wages in
the tourist trade. Improved roads made getting around easier, and
the village now has television and some limited Internet access.

Yet one thing has not changed: families place great importance on the value of real work. A child of two or three will start
feeding chickens or washing clothes. Children as young as five
help take care of their siblings, bathing, feeding, and watching
over them when they are not at school. Little girls will help their
mothers do laundry and make tortillas, and little boys will help
their fathers purchase goods that they will take to larger towns
to sell. Almost all of them may go to school, but they still have to
help at home.

Work not only serves the function of helping, Gaskin said,
but it also enables children to learn that they must grow up and
be motivated workers. The kind of social skills that Western
children learn through play—such as how to get along, problem
solve or negotiate gender roles—the families in this village have
historically learned through work. While work might not promote creativity as much as play, it makes children feel competent,
useful, and important while teaching them the skills they need
to survive.

In a piece she wrote for *The Child: An Encyclopedic Companion,*

Gaskins described children at work in her village:

> Two Yucatec Maya sisters (Mar, age 8, and Chula, age 9)
> were interviewed about what they did every day after school.
> They both quickly answered that most days they did laun-
> dry (scrubbing the clothes by hand in a wash basin). With
> great enthusiasm, they explained that not only were they
> allowed to wash all their own clothes, but they also washed
> the clothes of their younger siblings, and Chula added with
> pride—and a touch of superiority—that she sometimes
> got to wash her older brother's clothes, too. When asked if
> they minded having to work after school instead of being
> allowed to play, they answered no, because they felt good
> about being able to help their mother. They added that
> some days, if they got their work done early enough, they
> did play house or store with their younger siblings. How-
> ever, if needed, they might instead help with the cooking or
> cleaning, and, with an air of importance, they announced
> that they were learning to embroider, too. The time and
> energy required for these children's daily chores far exceed
> those of children in many industrialized cultures—as does
> their enthusiasm for doing them.

Gaskins was told that play was an afterthought, rather than a
priority, even in the children's eyes.

Kids in the village feel so strongly about their role that they
ask for *more* work, which was surprising to me. Gaskins offered
a few explanations. First, kids are around, observing in settings

where adult work is done, and the tasks are repetitive and simple enough for them to participate. Chores are age appropriate and closely supervised. A three-year-old might take care of the baby, but mom is nearby watching and explaining what needs to be done. Gaskins said that the only structure that parents impose on a kids' schedule has to do with work.

This idea might strike us as a little harsh, especially at a time when our society is so preoccupied with the importance of how and how much our children play, and when most people believe that the best path to a successful life is to get an education. In reading and writing about work and children, I find myself feeling as if I'm walking a fine line between glamorizing child labor and trying to understand the real work that children do. I asked Gaskins about this, and she responded this way:

> Participating in daily family work is very different than doing wage labor as a child—it is not usually harsh, exploitative, or unpleasant for the child. They often seek to do more than they are asked to do in the village where I work. And they enjoy the feelings of competence and belonging when engaged in work. There are undoubtedly both advantages and disadvantages to too much work and to too much play, I think, as well as too much school. From my point of view, most middle-class American children may have too little work and responsibility to help them become competent. We protect our children from work but not from school. Learning though everyday experience is a different kind of learning with its own advantages, and the ideal, I

think, should be to have a balance. Think of someone learning to cook by helping in the kitchen, or someone learning to fix cars by hanging around a garage.

Then she added, "Children in many cultures, where they participate in adult daily life, seem to be more grounded and more settled. I think it is not what they are shouldering, but rather that they feel like they belong and that they are useful and competent at something important to adults."

Tufts University professor Marian Zeitlin, in her writings on Yoruba parental practices in Nigeria, contrasted the Western view that chores might be preparation for exploitative child labor with the Yoruba view that manual work was good for parent and child, a sort of "on-the-job training" for real life. The main type of early stimulation activity in Nigeria was the errand—at age two, for example, taking an object and placing it in a different location.

"Errands train the infant child in the prepositions of location (on, under, between)," Zeitlin wrote. "They teach the child to follow sequential instructions, carry and care for objects, and learn the layout of the neighborhood. They also teach the social skills needed for verbal and commercial transactions. In errands and other material transactions, social accountability is stressed. Children are taught to report to their parents any kind gestures of others and to show them the gifts received; they must gradually learn to be honest without being a tattletale."

• • •

IN MOST SOCIETIES at some point in time, children have been expected to work. Among the Giriama people who live in Kaloleni, Kenya, the term for a toddler is *kahoho kuhuma madzi:* "a youngster who can be sent to fetch a cup of water." The expectations of Giriama parents grow from there, reported anthropologist Martha Wenger. "A girl, from about eight years until approximately puberty is a *muhoho wa kubunda,* a child who pounds maize; a boy of this age is a *muhoho murisa,* a child who herds." In Tanzania, Hadza children pick baobab fruits. Scholar Gerd Spittler noted that boys among desert caravaners in Mali start caring for goats when they are four—practice for later, when they will oversee their families' herds of camels on long, arduous treks.

"Nowhere are the Euroamerican views on childhood and those of the world more at odds than on the issue of work," wrote anthropologist David Lancy in his *Anthropology of Childhood.* "While we hamstring our children to keep them from the labor force, fearing their loss of innocence and studiousness, the norm elsewhere is to open the pathway to adulthood. We will find that as soon as children can 'help out' and make an economic contribution, they do so—eagerly, without coercion, and with minimal guidance."

Lancy has watched, for example, a five-year-old girl accompany her older sisters and cousins carry water on their head from a stream of water for the evening's cooking and cleaning. He has written about children on the island of Ponam in New Guinea who at ten years of age make toy canoes and learn to take charge of their own outriggers.

"This whole notion of treating children as cherubs can, in effect, spiral out of control," Lancy told me. He admitted that he, too, indulged his daughters and was more apt to play with them than make them work. He ironically noted in a footnote in his book: "I can't help chuckling when I recall what a struggle we had persuading daughter #2 to carry her dirty socks from her bedroom to the bathroom hamper!" Still, he feels alarmed with the level of overbearing parenting these days. "At some point it's no longer in the child's interest for the parent to be so overprotective and involved. We are keeping our children in an infantile state much longer than what you see in the village, and you have to ask, is that really a good thing?"

He believes kids are more resilient and self-sufficient than we think. Lancy said that in the highlands of New Guinea, children are allowed to play with machetes and are not prevented from burning themselves in the fire—they just don't do it. "Whatever harm that is done to them they seem to survive it," he said. They live in a tough environment, but they cope.

"That is something that is similar in every village I've ever been in, and every time I get into a third-world situation. At the age in which many children in the world are functioning, independent members of society, our children are still tantruming or don't know how to behave in public."

That made sense. Suzanne Gaskins has suggested that while there are benefits, there also "may be costs incurred by our own [Western] children engaging in the sort of child-oriented world of play and nonresponsibility that we construct for them and reward them for, including such things as identity crises, social isolation or selfishness, erosion of intrinsic motivation for real-world tasks, and low self-esteem."

Lancy pointed out to me, "We know our 'elite' culture isn't all good. This elite culture has high rates of child depression. This elite culture is very costly. We're seeing a lot of problems now with college students who come in [to the university setting] with very good grades, and then they flunk out. They are incapable of handling their lives. They get in a college environment, which is not exactly the jungle, and they tank."

So now I'm brainstorming jobs for Sofia.

Laundry is piling up and I'm reminded how my own mother bragged over the phone that she recruited another of her grand-daughters to help fold clothes. I decide Sofia might have fun helping me with that task, so I stack up the clothing next to me, and she sits by my side, grinning ear to ear. And indeed, she has a great time unfolding everything I fold. I give her her own socks to work with, but she reaches for the pants I just finished and shakes them open. She puts one of her daddy's socks on her arm like a puppet and has decided the shirt that I just folded would be more fun to wear than the one she's got on. She strips naked and puts it on. While she's as cute as can be, this is not something I want to go through every time we do the laundry. I mentally note that this may be a chore for a later date.

Another day, I ask Sofia to help me make the bed. She is thrilled with this invitation but is most amused when I make the sheet

hover in the air above her. I do most of the tucking and folding
and then leave a side for her to arrange. I say nothing as she goes
about her work, copying what she has seen my husband and me do
almost daily. She grabs the bedspread and imitates my actions in
clunky, awkward pulls. After some effort she has "made" her side
of the bed. When she leaves, I straighten out the wrinkles.

I ask my husband which job he thinks we should give Sofia and
he suggests "massages."

"Or dusting," he says a little more seriously, recalling that he
used to dust while his mother cleaned.

"Yeah, and she likes to wipe stuff," I say, "but is it something
she can own, that she can really help with regularly?"

He gently reminds me that she is two. I get it. While in the
Yucatán, children's work is essential and primary, whereas in our
family our child doesn't need to do chores for us to survive. (Gaskins herself pointed out to me that I was still trying to find a
job for my daughter in a 'child-friendly environment,' a behavior
particularly Western; the families in her Mayan village simply
include children in their adult routine. The motivation and outcomes are very different, she said.)

Using detailed parent and child diaries, Sandra Hofferth, director of the Maryland Population Research Center, has been
studying how children in the United States younger than thirteen years old spend their time. She reported in 2003 that among
1,343 families surveyed, the average time spent doing housework
was about twenty-four minutes a day. That's a 12 percent decline
since 1997 and a 25 percent drop from 1981.

"In the glacial realm of sociological change, that amounts to a freefall," lamented Sue Shellenbarger, a writer on work and the family at the *Wall Street Journal,* when reflecting on those numbers. "One consequence is never more obvious than at this time of year, when hundreds of thousands of college freshmen move into their dorms and promptly begin destroying their laundry. Other studies suggest the shift may have longer-term implications for marriage and community life."

In a column, she pointed to research that shows that couples who do chores together are happier. One study by New York University sociology professor Kathleen Gerson found that 90 percent of sixty women between ages eighteen and thirty-two said they hoped to share housework and child care with spouses in a "generally egalitarian relationship based on mutual support, long-term commitment, and work-family balance." The Pew Research Center says that 2,020 U.S. adults placed "sharing household chores" as the third most important factor in a successful marriage, just behind faithfulness and a happy sexual relationship.

Most people these days are spending less time doing manual chores. Women who might have been domestic goddesses in another life are now bringing home the bacon. Mom and dad both would rather hire someone else to do those yucky chores, if they can afford to. They don't want to spend a lot of time harassing kids to do them, either. In other words, manual labor is no longer a priority for the middle class—that's not the American dream. Our hard-laboring forefathers and mothers broke their backs in the factories so that we could get educated and live easier.

Yet I see the benefit of my daughter being included in the daily grind. Growing up, I was always expected to fold laundry and vacuum, and my brothers weeded and worked in the yard. I babysat and worked as a hostess. I was eager to enter the workplace and make my own money as soon as I was old enough because it made me feel productive and self-sufficient.

Marty Rossmann, emeritus associate professor of family education at the University of Minnesota, conducted a long-term study of eighty-four young adults and determined that "the best predictor of young adults' success in their mid-20s was that they participated in household tasks when they were three or four." She found that by involving children in tasks, parents taught them a sense of responsibility, competence, self-reliance, and self-worth that stayed with them throughout their lives. Other studies have shown that real work and chores encourage a sense of the common good, as opposed to the every-man-for-himself ethos that captivates our society. Alice Rossi, a professor of sociology at the University of Massachusetts at Amherst, argued that participation in domestic chores "encourages a general tendency toward greater expressivity and nurturance in adulthood" and makes people more likely to get involved with volunteer work later.

I asked Gaskins how the time she has spent living with other Mayan parents affected her raising her own three children, who are now grown.

"I think one way my work has had an impact on my parenting is to make me aware of how much I try to organize and manipulate my children's time and interests rather than supporting what

they themselves choose to do," she responded. "The Maya, starting with infants, watch their children carefully and offer support,
but they give their children tremendous agency to make choices
and to make mistakes. In that sense, their relationships with their
children are more collaborative than you often see in the West,
where parents interact with specific goals in mind and children
come to be dependent on their parents' attention and approval."

MY HUSBAND AND I value work, and I want my
daughter to understand this. I want her to feel invested in our
household, as well as to grow up being self-sufficient, to know
how to keep up her own home. The best I can do is to keep looking for little ways to start and to remember not to eliminate
chores when faced with choices on how to spend our time. I word
my requests more carefully. Instead of making chores something
that results in punishment or reward, I simply say, "I'd like you
to do this" or "Please help Mama make the bed."

I ask her to help out, just a little, with everything. As for her
uniquely designated chore, now I'm thinking nature; I like the
idea of her establishing some kind of relationship with the environment as much as possible in the concrete jungle that we
live in. She and her daddy regularly feed her Chinese fighting
fish, Bubbles, but I want something more. We decide that Sofia
will try watering the flowers, something she already enjoys doing
(though not on a regular basis).

Even in the winter months, the sun beats down on our brick
terrace, scorching countless so-called sun-loving plants, including

petunias, begonias, and mums. (Her father and I have been woefully neglectful in their daily care, so we accept the blame, too.) Perhaps if we make it our job to remember to make Sofia do her job, she'll eventually remember for us. I like to hope that it will develop into a habit, like brushing her teeth before bed or washing her hands after using the bathroom.

After her nap on a chilly autumn-cum-winter afternoon, we bundle up and head for the terrace.

Monte asks her, "What are we going to do upstairs?"

"I'm going to play. With toys," she answers.

"No," he encourages. "What did we just talk about?"

"Plants," she says. We walk upstairs, and she joyfully exclaims, "Fla-ders!" when she spots our parched flora.

Monte hands Sofia the water hose and directs her to each plant, trying to help her avoid splashes. I follow behind them, guiding the hose over chairs and tables and other barriers. We are squinting in the wind, shivering, and I think to myself that I once again have unwisely decided to teach my daughter something that would have been better saved for warmer months. She waters each plant, slowly and too much, and takes pride in every drop. We are three, doing the job of one in ten times the amount of time, but it is for a good cause. Finally, as we are frozen to the bone, Monte finishes the job, watering the plants on the mantel before the wind chases us indoors.

The Talents of Tots

Here is a sampling of the impressive precocity and work skills of children, as cited in *The Anthropology of Children:*

- Ache children by the age of eight can find their way in the seemingly impenetrable (to outsiders) trails (consisting of "bent leaves, twigs and shrubs") in the rain forests of Paraguay. They also get their first bow and arrow at the age of two, though they won't master the hunt until around ten years old.

- Zapotec kids in Oaxaca, Mexico, can name many of the hundreds of local flora as well as some seasoned ethnobotanists.

- In Liberia and Ghana, Kpelle children at the age of five carry messages to other people's homes.

- On the Tobian islands of Micronesia, boys begin fishing at the age of seven.

- From the age of seven, Hazda girls in Tanzania are gathering more food than they eat.

- In the grasslands of Tibet, kids as young as six tend to herds of *dzo* (a type of cattle), yaks, sheep, and other animals.

- Down under, in the Torres Straits islands, youngsters start using toddler-sized spears to harpoon sardines for bait and collect shellfish on the reef between six and seven; those who take up the interest with heart can be as efficient as an adult by the time they are ten to fourteen.

~11~

How Asians Learn to
Excel in School

One of my good friends likes to tease me for asking a lot of Sofia.

"You are so demanding!" she has told me more than once. "She's only two."

What do you mean? I asked her. And she rattled off a list: teaching the ABCs from her earliest months, disciplining from the time she was about one, training her to use the toilet early. We used to use flashcards to help Sofia learn words. I frowned, feeling a bit defensive. I'm not one of those parents who fuss over my daughter's developmental milestones! I hadn't even thought too much about what I was teaching her and how—it mostly evolved from what Sofia seemed to like. Yet I found myself stumbling around trying to explain why I wanted her to be able to read (at least a little) by the age of four.

My friend laughed at me. "You ask a lot of your daughter, just like you ask a lot of yourself. Maybe I'll be that way when I have kids," she said, smiling sympathetically. In her eyes, I could see it wasn't a giant leap that I would become a kind of scholastic slave driver, a piano mom, or maybe even a spelling bee fanatic.

When I was working as a Washington correspondent, the National Spelling Bee was an annual event on my beat. Each year I'd have to follow the local speller as he or she nervously prepared for the big competition and spelled words I'd never heard of and couldn't pronounce, such as *pfeffernuss* (which, according to spelling bee officials, is one of the kids' favorite words). I'd sit, hypnotized and tortured by each round of the competition, sympathizing with the agony of the spellers. I was astounded at the intelligence and poise of these kids and their ability to stare down the stern pronouncers and the glaring eye of live television. And year after year, I was amazed at the racial breakdown of the spellers who made it to the top twenty.

Asians simply dominated. In 2008, seven out of the top twelve finalists at the National Spelling Bee were of some sort of Asian descent. The finale was a showdown between Sidharth Chand and Sameer Mishra, American children of first-generation immigrants from central India who said they wanted to be neurosurgeons when they grew up. In 2009, Anamika Veeramani, an eighth-grader from North Royalton, Ohio, outside of Cleveland, won by spelling *stromuhr,* becoming the eighth child of South Asian descent to win the bee in twelve years. That's extraordinary, given that less than 1 percent of the nation's population is Asian Indian.

Statistics show that Asians do better in school. The average SAT score for Asians in America in 2009 was about 1,623 out of

2,400. (Caucasians, Latinos, and blacks average 1,581, 1,364, and 1,276, respectively). While they make up only about 5 percent of the population in the United States, they constitute 15–20 percent of graduates from Ivy League schools such as Yale, Harvard, and Princeton. In *Beyond the Classroom: Why School Reform Has Failed and What Parents Need to Do* psychologist Laurence Steinberg wrote, "Of all the demographic factors we studied in relation to school performance, ethnicity is the most important . . . In terms of school achievement, then, it is more advantageous to be Asian than to be wealthy, to have non-divorced parents, or to have a mother who is able to stay at home full time."

More advantageous to be Asian? I'm Chinese American and always got good grades, but this statement intrigued me. Truth be told, the proficiency of my race in academics was a mystery to me, too, because I'd grown up with Caucasian parents. Part of me figured perhaps it was the "model minority" myth, a stereotype that reduced Asians to nerds. But after examining the results on the spelling bee stage year after year and the hard statistics on Asian performance in school, I couldn't help but think that there were some real lessons here. What were the secrets behind such consistent success? Did Asian parents do or say anything different from my parents? What motivates these students to want to do so well? It was easy to think back to the literature and films I'd seen depicting a tyrant Chinese mother forcing a kid to play piano, a South Asian father goading his kid to become a doctor, and a tortured Japanese student studying for exams. Yet I sensed that coercion and punishment weren't the only forces that compelled many of these kids to excellence. Those spelling bee contestants surely felt pressure as they struggled to spell *appoggiatura* before the rolling ESPN cameras, yet they didn't seem to fear or resent their parents, who were sitting on the edge of their seats, sounding out the words and sweating along with their young spellers. After all was done, and the kids finished tenth, eighth, third, and first, they hugged and kissed and thanked their parents over and over.

Sameer Mishra, the sassy bespectacled eighth-grader who at age thirteen emerged victorious, dedicated his win to his mother. The kid from West Lafayette, Indiana, told reporters that his parents always encouraged him to stay "calm, cool, and collected," and added, "I don't know how I pulled it off. Definitely with my parents' support, my sister's pushing me to study hard, my hard work and effort." He went on to tell reporters that the spelling bee had been a great educational experience and a fun, albeit intense way to learn English. His parents took off time from their jobs to help him prepare word lists, look up the definitions and pronunciations, and quiz him. Sameer's sister, Shruti, competed in the national bee three times, and her acing of a different contest in math won her scholarships at top universities.

Sameer's very simple answers to press questions offered insight into his success. When asked what advice he had for other spellers, he told the BBC, "Keep working hard. Even if you don't win you will always learn something new."

Scholars have observed that many emigrants from Asian countries—especially those who were educated professionals—bring with them the standards of academic excellence that prevailed in their homelands. Traditionally, in countries such as India, China, and Japan, good grades and high scores on tough standardized tests were not only essential to a young person's future but often the meal ticket for their entire family to the middle class and a comfortable lifestyle. Doing well in school from a young age was a matter of individual pride or career aspiration, and also of survival for one's clan. That kind of pressure has a deep impact on the value of academics.

The result is a consistent message inside and outside of the home: You must try hard and do well in school. And *well* doesn't mean average. It means close to, if not perfect, 10s, all A's, and gold-star stickers.

Maya Garg remembers the pressure faced by some of the people she knew in the south Delhi neighborhood of Nizamuddin East, where she grew up in the 1980s.

"We had friends whose parents used to lock them in their rooms until they finished their homework and things like that," Garg told me. "I mean, they'd get serious beatings if they didn't do well. In India, tutors are a big deal. Some kids used to have them six or seven days a week." Other friends would do poorly on exams and she wouldn't see them for a long time because they couldn't come out and play.

Yet that sort of legendary academics-by-force wasn't what Garg—and several other people I spoke with—actually experienced. She might get grounded for a bad grade, but most of the time she received a friendly but firm message from her parents, grandparents, and other relatives. Life was very structured, Garg said, "whether it was eating meals on time, or taking the shower on time or finishing your homework. In school, it was structure: you went to school, you learned, you came home, did your homework and did it well. You knew that you put in 100 percent of your effort and you got good grades . . . It wasn't yelled and screamed at us and it wasn't threatened, but it was just very clearly expected." Her mother was always around to help them and encourage them with their schoolwork, and her parents contracted tutors when she had trouble in classes. Even outside her family, among her peer group, kids presumed that everyone did well. No one called you a nerd if you got all A's. In fact, they felt a little sorry for the child who was struggling and wondered what was wrong.

On the other side of the world, at about the same time, another friend of mine, Aisha Sultan, was growing up with the same acute consciousness about grades. Even from a young age, Sultan, like Garg, was well aware of how hard her parents worked and how much they'd sacrificed hoping for a brighter future. They moved from Lahore, Pakistan, leaving their families, community, language, and way of life; her mom spoke hardly any English when she arrived in America in 1973. Communication with relatives was limited to blue aerogram letters, and the high cost of travel made returning home difficult. While Sultan's childhood was full of simple joys, such as playing with cousins and neighbors, her parents consciously integrated academic lessons into everyday life outside of school, hoping to ensure that their girls realized the success they'd envisioned for their family. When she was in about third grade, for example, her father suggested she read the dictionary and write down the words she didn't know and their definitions.

"I made it midway through the A's," she recalled to me. "It did give me a life-long love of words. [Dad] would also give me topics and ask me to write essays on [them]—not for school, just an extra thing to do. When my cousin's grandfather would come from Pakistan to visit in Houston, he would bring grammar books and teach us during the summer, usually five, six hours at a time. He was *tough*. We were scared of him, but I think we learned a lot. My mom was teaching me to memorize multiplication tables in kindergarten until the teacher told her to stop."

Her parents' focus never made her feel resentful. If anything, Sultan loved the feeling she got when she made her parents proud; while she was not at the top of her class in high school, she was an honor student. What did bother her was the strictness in her house: she wasn't allowed to date or hang out at the mall with friends, and she could never go to sleepovers, dances, or parties. She hated it then but understands it now. "I think they were so afraid of us becoming 'too Americanized' and losing their values that they made us focus on education as much as possible."

Now that Sultan, a journalist living in St. Louis, is raising a daughter and son, she imagines she will be more lenient regarding their social lives, but she also knows she has inherited the "academics DNA."

"I started teaching [my daughter] Ameena to read shortly after her fourth birthday, and within months she was reading. Now she's in second grade and loves to read. I asked her teacher to send home extra homework for her every week (which she does). With my 5-year-old son, I waited an extra year before starting the same program. The key: I want my children to internalize high expectations."

THE SO-CALLED ASIAN advantage has been studied again and again by psychologists, anthropologists, and scholars. Despite vast differences in their home countries and cultures, Asians have consistently been found to outperform other students. Punjabi students in California, despite having problems fitting in with their classmates—their different language, customs, beliefs, religion, and lifestyle make them targets for all kinds of racist comments—were still expected to do well in school. David Lancy wrote in *Anthropology of Childhood,* "They couldn't blame the teachers or the 'system.' If students fell out of line, parents forced them into early marriage and/or put them to work in fruit orchards." Families also tend to call on controversial emotions to compel their kids to study hard. In some cases, that might be a sense of duty: if the kid does poorly, it reflects not only on the child but on the family, the school, and the community. Other research has shown that Korean students outperform U.S. students by a wide margin on objective tests of achievement, despite the government spending less than half of the funds on education and despite much larger class sizes. One of the clues to understanding these differences is that "guilt in Korea has a positive aspect . . . that promotes filial piety [and] achievement motivation," Lancy wrote.

In 1985, Laurence Steinberg, an expert in adolescent psychological development at Temple University, put together a multidisciplinary research team made up of psychologists and education and child development specialists. They set out to understand why American students were performing poorly in school and cared so little about it. For more than ten years, they studied twenty thousand teenagers of varying ethnic and class backgrounds in nine American cities and analyzed mountains of data on performance and test scores. They focused intensely on the students' experiences in the home, in their peer groups, and in their communities. The intention of the study was not to focus on ethnic differences, but the trends they uncovered couldn't be ignored.

"We were struck repeatedly by how significant a role ethnicity played in structuring young people's lives, both inside and outside of school. Youngsters' patterns of activities, interests, friendships were all influenced by their ethnic background," Steinberg wrote. The statistics repeatedly showed that Asian children performed better than white students, and significantly better than black and Latino kids, no matter the income category or parental education, in the worst and the best schools.

Steinberg doesn't buy the theory that academic achievement, or even an aptitude for subjects such as math or science, are genetic. Study after study has failed to prove this, he told me. But what is measurable is the *culture:* the high regard that parents, family, and community have for academics and how they choose to teach and enforce that value in their children. Asian students, from a very young age, tended to have higher standards for themselves than other ethnic groups, researchers found. And while students of all ethnic backgrounds understood the payoff of doing well in school, Asians worried more about the consequences of doing badly.

"When we asked students what the highest grade was that they could bring home without their parents getting angry, the average among Asian students was an A–," Steinberg told me. "No other group came remotely close to that." White students tended to say that somewhere around a B was okay, and Latino and black students said B– or C+.

"I suspect that this explains a great deal about why Asian adolescents have such a high standard," he said. "And when asked whether there would be bad consequences in life if one did poorly in school, Asian students were most likely to agree. My guess is that there are bad consequences at home for doing poorly in school as well.

"I think that Asian parents simply put achievement above everything else and do this from an early age, so that by the time high school rolls around, it's not even an issue," he explained.

Observers say these are not just authoritarian families who demand, punish, and shame children into doing well—though many of those do exist. Some young people are devastated by extreme pressure from their parents, which some believe is a major factor behind a worrisome suicide rate among young Asian Americans. Yet experts believe the most consistent, successful model—Asian and not—seems to be resolute and strict parenting, encouraging but not buddy-buddy. Children are praised but not promised money or gifts when they do well on tests.

"I remember my mentor Urie Bronfenbrenner [a well-known Russian American psychologist] once telling me that his Asian students at Cornell could not believe that their Caucasian peers did things like go bowling with their parents," Steinberg told me. "My guess is that Asian parents are warm without being 'friendly.' It is also the case that Asian parents (like Asian adults in general) are more likely to attribute success and failure to effort rather than ability. So kids just internalize the belief that if they do poorly, it must be because they aren't working hard enough."

In his book, Steinberg wrote, "Students, teachers, and parents in other parts of the world are far less likely than Americans to use the language of ability when discussing student performance. They are more likely to attribute differences in achievement to differences in student motivation (how much they want to succeed), effort (how hard they exert themselves), or behavior (how much time they devote to their studies). Success, in their eyes, is not the outcome of inborn talent, but the product of systematic, motivated, hard work."

On the other hand, American kids and parents were much more likely to attribute good academic performance to better opportunities, natural intelligence, or a teacher's favoritism and blame low achievement on a lack of opportunity or innate talent for a subject, unwieldy class size, or a bad teacher or school.

The focus on study ethic in some families is not always directly

stated; it's often projected subtly. Po Bronson and Ashley Merryman, authors of the book *NurtureShock: New Thinking about
Children,* highlighted the research of University of Illinois scholar
Florrie Ng, who conducted an experiment with fifth graders and
their mothers in Illinois and Hong Kong. Ng put mothers in the
waiting room while half of the children were given a hard test,
rigged so that they could answer only about half of the questions
right. After they finished, mothers were told the results and let
into the room to speak to their kids. The Americans were careful
to avoid negative comments and spent much of the time talking
about things other than the test. The Chinese moms were more
likely to talk directly about the test and its importance, and said
things like, "You didn't concentrate when doing it" and "Let's
look over your test." After this interaction, the kids were given a
test again, and the Chinese kids' scores improved 33 percent, more
than twice the gain accomplished by the American children.

Bronson and Merryman used Ng's research to show how encouraging a child to work harder can have a greater impact on
success than inflating his ego by telling him he's smart.

"The trade-off here would seem to be that the Chinese mothers acted harsh or cruel—but that stereotype may not reflect
modern parenting in Hong Kong," they wrote. "Nor was it quite
what Ng saw on the videotapes. While their words were firm, the
Chinese mothers actually smiled and hugged their children every
bit as much as the American mothers (and were no more likely to
frown or raise their voices)."

Psychologist Richard Nisbett, in his book *Intelligence and How to Get It,* which documents how culture impacts achievement, argued that the intense influence of the family is a key motivating factor in Asian students.

It is hard for someone steeped only in European culture to comprehend the extent to which achievement in the East is a family affair and not primarily a matter of individual pride and status. Like the ancient candidate for mandarin status, one achieves because it is to the benefit of the family— both economically and socially. Although there may be pride in personal accomplishment, achievement is not primarily a matter of enriching oneself or bringing honor to oneself.

And—here's the big advantage of Asian culture— achievement for the family seems to be a greater goad to success than achievement for the self. If I, as an individual Western free agent, choose to achieve in order to bring myself honor and money, that is my decision. And if I decide that my talents are too meager or I don't want to work hard, I can choose to opt out of the rat race. But if I am linked by strong bonds to my family, and fed its achievement demands along with my meals, I simply have no choice but to do my best in school and in professional life thereafter. And the demand is reasonable because it has been made clear to me that my achievement is a matter of will and not just innate talent.

Parul Pratap Shirazi, a thirty-four-year-old senior web content writer in the New Delhi region and mother of four-year-old Alison, grew up knowing that her only option was to "to go to school and do well." Her parents would praise and occasionally reward a big achievement, such as being the top in her English class, and when she didn't do well, she might be grounded. But what inspired her to achieve academically was less the need to please her parents than concerns about disappointing them. Respect for elders is an important traditional value in India, as well as in East Asian societies where Confucian ideas of filial piety and respect have shaped generations.

Shirazi recounted, as she played with her daughter at home in the gated community of Gurgaon, "I just couldn't bear the thought of seeing [my parents'] faces if I failed a subject or class. I remember when I intentionally dropped a year in college, I waited for them to go back from visiting me so I would have to tell them this news over the phone and not in person. That was totally a respect thing. I had too much regard for my parents and even grandparents to mess up." It was partly, too, about sustaining the middle-class lifestyle that her parents had worked so hard to give her and her siblings. Her mother, on top of being a housewife, designed and made kids clothing and ran a small home catering business. Her father traveled often but always made time for them.

"I grew up thinking all hardworking people do well," Shirazi said, and it's a value she's trying to instill in her own daughter. They, like many middle- and upper-class families, have a maid, but Alison must help clean and clear the table after meals, neaten her own desk in class, and assist in the school cafeteria. When she has trouble with a lesson, her mom and dad insist gently that she keep trying until she gets it right.

IN HIS DOCUMENTARY *Two Million Minutes: A Global Examination* (named for the amount of time a student has to spend—or waste—during his high school years), Robert Compton, a businessman and entrepreneur who spent time in India, followed two American university students, two Chinese students, and two Indian students, of similar education and economic backgrounds. The movie highlighted a startling difference in study habits and values. The two American students were writing papers and cramming for tests at the last minute between social events. ("Occasionally I do homework, like over the weekend mostly," said Neil, an American student, as he cruised Facebook.) Meanwhile, one of the Chinese students was studying all the time; every day he read *Strength in Numbers,* an advanced calculus text, in order to get ahead. An Indian student, Rohit, said, "In India, once you get into this academic course and you're serious about it, you don't have much of the option of to choose between academics and something else. It's either academics [or] . . . nothing else." While the American students—who seemed bright and ambitious—viewed their academic experience as individual and as only part of the path to becoming well rounded and successful, the Indian and Chinese students were motivated by the competitive nature of their schooling and of the global economy. The contrast in hunger to do well was astonishing.

While there are always shining examples of academic success at almost any American school in any given every year, our
society has struggled with the overall mediocre, and sometimes
abysmal, academic performance of its students over the last century. Despite some improvements, the United States continues
to fall behind many other developed countries in reading, math,
and science. A survey by the Organisation for Economic Co-
operation and Development, based on testing of a half-million
fifteen-year-old students in seventy countries and other partner
economies in 2009, found that the United States ranked seventeenth overall for reading, twenty-third for science, and a below-
average thirty-first for mathematics. Korea and Finland ranked
at the top for literacy. The U.S. high school graduation rate was
third from the bottom of the list, better than only Mexico and
Turkey. India, a country that has long struggled with disparity
in academic achievement, was not included in the survey. But as
Compton pointed out in *Two Million Minutes,* even if India and
China fail to educate a large portion of their populations, those
they do educate vastly outnumber and outperform American
students. U.S. president Barack Obama, speaking in the Rose
Garden of the White House in October of 2010, described the
urgency of the situation this way: "There's an educational arms
race taking place around the world right now—from China to
Germany, to India to South Korea. Cutting back on education
would amount to unilateral disarmament. We can't afford to
do that."

Parents, educators, scholars, and politicians point every which way when trying to explain the performance gap: underspending, poorly allocated money, flaws in schools, faults in the system, the failings of teachers, and the apathy of children and their families. In reality, plenty of American parents are very concerned with how our children are doing in school. We buy the right learning toys, move to neighborhoods where the schools test higher, and enroll our kids in the right preschool before they are even born. The biggest worry of parents in a 2008 BabyCenter.com poll of twenty-four-hundred parents was that their child "won't get the education and opportunities she needs to reach her potential."

After researching Asian achievement standards, I found the tone and wording of this very statement fascinating. In that BabyCenter article, Pamela Paul, who examined the mammoth baby products marketing machine for her book *Parenting, Inc.*, blamed that fear in part on the lucrative baby products industry that insists parents buy their products to get the one-up. She added, "Underlying a lot of parents' fears is a broad sense of economic insecurity. Parents are afraid that their children won't have an easy go of it because *they* aren't having an easy go of it. Many parents today are struggling to make ends meet, and they want a different kind of future for their kids."

Opportunity is important—I'll always push to enroll my kids in good schools with good teachers. But I began to ask myself, how much of this worry time are we devoting to instilling in our children the value of studying and working hard to achieve what they want and to overcome any so-called barriers or lack of opportunity? Many of us would like excellence to come easy—I admit being seduced by web articles that tease "Is your child gifted?"—but I wonder if we should be asking instead, "How can we encourage our children to aspire to do their best and to try and try again if they don't?" Perhaps a little tough love is in order. It also seems worthwhile to ask ourselves if we believe that academics should be less or more important than all the extra activities that fill our kids' lives. Personally, I don't want grades to get lost in my own enthusiastic efforts to help Sofia be a creative, happy, well-rounded person. (We've already enrolled her in an art workshop, dance class, and summer camp.) Some experts believe that sometimes parents feel more comfortable relating to their children through sports (tossing around a baseball) rather than academics (teaching a child to read), so they undervalue the grades.

Because my own parents were teachers, school was very important in my family. My mom insists that she and dad never had to push us, but they, too, were encouraging but unwavering about achievement. I grew to expect a lot from myself (some of my friends might say *too much*). I was the geek who read Hamlet on my summer vacation during junior high, I loved to study and relished burrowing into an alcove at my university library to memorize Spanish vocabulary for four and five hours at a time. I hardly ever missed a class, not even when I was sick, because I enjoyed going.

I find that our society doesn't seem to value classes, school, or academic success as much as it does other things, such as being attractive, rich, or good at sports. I used to feel such pride for the spelling bee winners as they beamed before the lights of dozens of television cameras, momentary national superstars. At the same time, I imagine that when they got back home, many of their classmates and playmates would ignore or downplay their accomplishment or even beat them up for it. A nephew of ours got punched for being the only kid in his class to complete an assignment correctly. Despite being cheered on by my parents and teachers growing up, I didn't want to be known for getting good grades. I recall vividly the time a popular (and pretty stupid) boy criticized me for using "big words." Even if I knew better, I was embarrassed to be chosen smartest and most likely to succeed during class elections. There are exceptions, but most peer groups from childhood to high school aren't likely to worship a math whiz.

Pop culture doesn't help. Aside from the occasional movie or book celebrating the geeky heroes of the digital revolution, the media doesn't glamorize the American of any race or ethnicity who makes his mark through hard-earned, bookish achievement (unless he makes billions). We idolize the populist, the movie star, or beauty queen turned politician, the Everyman who labored his butt off in factories or conquered the Wild West or sold drugs and made a fortune on the mean streets. We prefer our heroes to be brawny, beautiful, and talented rather than brainy and toiling.

"It is really a shame that our culture is so fascinated with stories of individuals who 'made it' as adults despite having had poor records of academic achievement as children," Steinberg wrote in *Beyond the Classroom*. "Yes, there have been adult millionaires who dropped out of high school, geniuses whose talents were overlooked by their teachers, and successful athletes and actors who, even as adults, can barely read and write. But these stories are exceptions to the rule, and we do our children a disservice by overstating their frequency and maintaining the myths surrounding them. Doing well in school is still one of the best—if not *the* best—predictors of later success, whether measured by the quality or quantity of one's higher education, the prestige of one's occupation or the income and wealth that one accumulates as an adult."

This tendency for lower aspirations in academics is something that apparently rubs off on immigrant families eventually. Several studies have shown that educational attainment tends to increase from first to second generation—these are the groups who are motivated by their immigrant parents' expectations and also their own perceptions of sacrifice—but then declines in the third generation. The census has reported that while the number of high school graduates among immigrants (of any race) increases from the first to second generation, the number declines in the third generation.

SOME PARENTS LIVING in Delhi today told me the approach of middle-class Indians and their children is changing. The exam system has been overhauled. In 2011, the Central Board of Secondary Education is expected to do away with the formal boards that caused so many so much pain and move forward with a revamped official evaluation system. More children are getting involved with activities outside academics, including theater, music, and sports. Parents are recognizing a wider range of careers aside from the traditional favorites of doctor and engineer. Rohit and Vanessa Ohri consider themselves part of a new generation of parents who are more sensitive to the desires of their children. For example, they encourage their eighteen-year-old son Revant's interest in photography and their thirteen-year-old daughter Ravia's talent for painting.

"As parents we always warn our kids about how competitive the world is today and hence are keen to help them hone every talent," said Vanessa, who quit her job as a copywriter to parent full-time. "The result is a flurry of afterschool activities that include tuitions [like tutoring sessions] as well as dance, art, music and sports classes."

Rohit, who is a vice president at an advertising agency, added, "I feel that as parents we sometimes find it difficult to accept that our kids could be average or below average in studies, even though they show exceptional aptitude for other activities."

He acknowledged, "The pressure has and always will be there because we as Indians have a deeply ingrained habit of looking over our shoulders to see how fast our neighbors are catching up. As a people, we are highly competitive. Despite whatever individual steps we might take in our homes to ease academic tension, societal influences ensure that the pressure keeps mounting."

Ravia said of school, "There is a lot of homework to do every day and it gets harder every year, but I know that if so many people from my school did it, then so can I."

I'VE BECOME MORE conscious about the language and tone I use when I teach Sofia. It's always been easy to call her "such a smart girl"—and I still do that—but I try to encourage and push her a bit more when it comes to solving problems. When she is having trouble writing a letter or finishing a maze and tries to hand me the pencil, I tell her, "Try again, and then Mommy will help." She often responds with the right answer; she likes to be challenged, too.

It's not that I think my daughter needs to go to an Ivy League school, but like Aisha Sultan, I'd like her to assimilate reasonably high expectations. The lesson that I took away from my conversations with parents is that when sensibly balanced, expectations and a measured dose of tough love can be good. It isn't always a bad thing to make a child try something she doesn't think she wants to do and to work a little harder than she thought she could.

So I go ahead and continue to fill my house with books and buy puzzles and toys that focus on the alphabet. Between playing with dolls and Play-Doh, we take the time to practice reading and writing. My husband and I dedicate a little time most days to drilling letters, making a game of it by singing and drawing, but when she's wrong, we correct her and explain why. At two years and nine months, she spells *Sofia* aloud with pride and recognizes it when it is written out. (She's particularly possessive of the letter *S*.) She can write most of the letters in her name, though not together or right side up. I applaud her effort, though, and ask her to try again. She usually obliges. If sometimes we reach an impasse, we rest and give it a go once again the next day.

Grading the Countries

The Organisation for Economic Co-operation and Development in Paris published a study comparing the 2009 test performance of fifteen-year-olds in reading, math, and science among its thirty-four mostly wealthy member nations plus thirty-one other countries and regions. China was represented by the city of Shanghai and the administrative regions of Hong Kong and Macao. They are ranked from highest to lowest.

Reading Performance

Shanghai	Canada
Korea	New Zealand
Finland	Japan
Hong Kong	Australia
Singapore	Netherlands

The United States ranked seventeenth, ahead of Britain and France and above average for all regions tested.

Math Performance

Shanghai	Finland
Singapore	Liechtenstein
Hong Kong	Switzerland
Korea	Japan
Taiwan	Canada

The United States ranked thirty-first, below average for all regions.

Science Performance

Shanghai	Korea
Finland	New Zealand
Hong Kong	Canada
Singapore	Estonia
Japan	Australia

The United States placed twenty-third, about average for all regions.

Conclusion

⟨─᛭─⟩

Travel changes you. As you move through this life and
this world you change things slightly, you leave marks
behind, however small. And in return, life—and
travel—leaves marks on you. Most of the time, those
marks—on your body or on your heart—are beautiful.
Often, though, they hurt.

—Anthony Bourdain, *The Nasty Bits:*
Collected Varietal Cuts, Usable Trim, Scraps, and Bones

In May 1997, on a balmy spring day in New York City, Annette
Sorensen, a thirty-year-old actress from Denmark, left her
fourteen-month-old child in a stroller just outside the plate-glass
window of a barbecue joint in the East Village while she and her
American husband drank and dined a few feet away. Onlookers
were shocked and horrified, complained to the parents, the restaurant employees, and eventually called police. Both parents were
thrown in jail and Sorenson said she was baffled by the reaction
to a practice commonly seen in her hometown of Copenhagen.
Eventually, charges of endangerment were dropped, but the arrest
set off an international debate about whether the actions of the
New York police were extreme and, really, what was best for the

child. In Denmark, crime is low and children are frequently left outside to get *frisk luft,* or fresh air—something parents think is essential for health and hearty development—while caregivers dine and shop. Danes were outraged at the Americans' exaggerated reaction. In New York, "where people chain even their trashcans to their sidewalks," as one journalist put it, people criticized the ignorance of American dangers and standards.

For me, the case was fascinating, not just because of the cultural differences that it highlighted, but also because it exposed the willingness of parents to jump to judge one another. That was one thing that I did not want to do in this book. While at times I might critique my own culture and my own perspective, I know my limitations. I'm neither a doctor nor a child development specialist, neither an anthropologist nor a scientist. I'm a mother who wants to do what is right for her family. I'm not trying to make any sweeping judgments or generalizations about what every parent in one culture does or believes but rather use snapshots of unique families at a given time to construct a new prism through which I could assess how I was doing.

There is, however, one sweeping observation that I feel compelled to make: I was struck by the impact that globalization has had on parenting in places as diffuse as a Mayan village in the Yucatán and the suburbs of Delhi. There is much discussion about the impact of the global economy on the environment, our politics, and our material needs, but I'd never thought about globalization in terms of parenthood. The commercialization of parenthood and childhood has changed the way people in many cultures feed, sleep, teach, and play with their children. Diapers are slowly convincing Chinese families to potty train their children later; fast food is threatening the sacred French mealtime; economic realities are causing grand extended families to break up and move away from each other. Baby bottles and formula are shortening breast-feeding times, and manufactured toys are replacing sticks and stones even in remote African villages. Modern medicine is transforming the birth experience in the farthest corners of Tibet. It remains to be seen which changes are for better or worse, but it is undeniable that parenting values and practices are morphing and that the discourse on the "right way to parent" is becoming more monotone. While the Western approach is important, I can't help but think that we need more diverse voices in the debate. For clarity in this book, I chose to focus more on the customary and indigenous practices rather than the "modern" way, even if the latter is clearly present in many if not all contexts.

Yet I realize parenting is not a static process. It evolves, because most mothers and fathers want to use the best information and tools available to help their families succeed. This book has become one of my tools. The experience of looking at parenthood through the eyes of parents in different cultures has opened my mind and challenged some of the beliefs and practices that I'd held pretty tightly. Hearing and seeing what others do differently made me rethink what I thought was right. Sometimes it reinforced what I thought, and sometimes it changed me completely. Regardless, I've collected some invaluable pieces of knowledge to compose the ideals and practices that work for us. I hope that readers have, too.

And I've reached a pretty optimistic conclusion after observing the adaptability and resilience of families in many circumstances and environments. Despite vast differences in beliefs, religion, and culture, moms, dads, and caregivers in most societies share a common desire: to raise children who can thrive in the reality in which they live. While no culture can claim to be the best at any one given aspect of parenting, each has its own gems of wisdom to add to the discussion. It's unhealthy to enclose ourselves in parental parochialism, ruled by the plaintive, guilty insistence that there is a single, best way to raise children. We may or may not adopt what another family in another culture or place does, but we can take comfort in knowing that there really is more than one good way to get a baby to sleep, transport her from place to place, and feed her. We see that, indeed, kids are amazingly adaptive and resilient creatures who will eat "strange foods," who can be potty-trained at a young age, and who can embrace greater responsibilities in our homes. While there are some universal standards of how a child should be treated, there are many ways to be a good parent in the world. This idea should empower and encourage us as our families grow.

ACKNOWLEDGMENTS

I'm indebted to the parents around the world who so willingly shared their experiences and lessons learned. Their creativity, humor, and concern for their families inspired this project and me personally. There are countless scientists who have dedicated their careers to observing and documenting the lives of families in most every country and culture. Their incredible research, little known to the public, offers perspective and important context to the global discussion about child rearing. Curious readers would benefit from checking out the works of Margaret Mead, David Lancy, Robert LeVine, Meredith Small, Suzanne Gaskins, and Sarah Hrdy, among others. Lancy's *Anthropology of Childhood* and Meredith Small's book, *Our Babies, Ourselves,* are excellent and accessible books for moms and dads new to cultural anthropology.

Appreciation goes to my editor, Andra Miller; my agents, Larry Weissman and Sascha Alper, for supporting this book; and friends Vikki Ortiz, Alex Salas, Dana Peterson, Susan Ager, and Kristina Sauerwein for offering their insight and feedback. Thanks also to Vikki in Chicago, Maryanne Waweru in Kenya, Riana Lagarde in France, Suzanne Kamata in Japan, Colleen Casey Leonard in Mexico, Colin Fernandes in India, and Uma Chu in Shanghai for their reporting and perspective in far off places when I couldn't be there. I'm also grateful for the help of

Ellen Shea at Harvard's Schlesinger Library and for the sharp eye of copy editor Jude Grant.

This book is dedicated to my husband, Monte Reel, a great partner in the marvelous and tumultuous adventure that is parenthood, to my daughter Sofia, who has filled our lives with more surprises, challenges, and joy than we could have ever imagined, and to the newest addition to our family, Violet.

NOTES

Introduction

4   "*The parental practices*"   Small, *Our Babies, Ourselves*, xvi–xvii.

5   "*By exploring*"   LeVine, Miller, and Maxwell, *Parental Behavior in Diverse Societies*, 1.

1. How Buenos Aires Children Go to Bed Late

10   "*in Buenos Aires*"   "Invertir en Buenos Aires," online.

17   "*As long as they're*"   Quoted in Hall, "Battle of Bedtime," online.

22   "*In our culture*"   Quoted in Mooallem, "Sleep-Industrial Complex," online.

22   "*stay up as long*"   Worthman and Melby, "Toward a Comparative Developmental Ecology of Human Sleep," 79.

23   "*American parents*"   Ibid., 110.

23   "*Sleep can be considered*"   Jenni and O'Connor, "Children's Sleep," 205.

23   "*It is important*"   Ibid.

24   "*customary and preferable*"   Ibid.

24   "*Clearly, there is*"   Ibid.

24   "*Are the cultural*"   Ibid., 212.

33   *In the leaf huts*   Worthman and Melby, 76–78.

33   "*Being alone*"   Ibid., 78.

2. How the French Teach Their Children to Love Healthy Food

35   *article in* Today's Dietitian   Peaslee, "Food Affair," online.

47   "*Advertising campaigns promote*"   Stallone and Jacobson, "Cheating Babies," online.

57   "*Inuit uniformly reported*"   Graburn, "Culture as Narrative," 142.

3. How Kenyans Live without Strollers

63   *Meredith Small*   Small, *Our Babies, Ourselves,* 154.

65   *"technological revolution"*   Hrdy, *Mother Nature,* 197.

65   *Maoris in New Zealand*   Phillipps, "Maori Baby's Toilet," 38.

68   *In 2002, the National*   Neergaard, "Get Babies out of Strollers and onto the Floor," online.

68   *In 2008, Pathways Awareness*   "National Survey of Pediatric Experts Indicates Increase in Infant Delays," online.

69   *A BabyCenter.com survey*   Matthiessen, "Top 5 Parenting Fears and What You Can Do about Them," online.

69   *A study released in 2009*   Finkelhor et al., "Trends in Childhood Violence and Abuse," 238–42.

72   *American babies, Super noted*   Super, "Environmental Effects on Motor Development," 562–66.

76   *"There are customs"*   Quoted in Wax, "An Idea Still Looking for Traction in Kenya," online.

4. How the Chinese Potty Train Early

88   *"as inarguable as"*   Wang, "Secret of the Chinese Potty-Training Method," online.

88   *"Could take own"*   Ibid.

90   *"Your whole life"*   Caliri, "Relieving Myself," online.

95   *In 1947, most*   Schmitt, "Toilet Training," 107; and Martin et al., "Secular Trends and Individual Differences in Toilet-Training Progress," online.

96   *Working parents embraced*   "Global Market for Disposable Baby Diapers to Reach $26.6 Billion by 2012," online.

97   *"Manufacturers of disposable diapers"*   Schmitt, 105.

97   *"parental preference"*   Ibid., 106.

98   *A study of American*   "Researchers," online.

99   *"Annual sales"*   " 'Open-crotch Pants' Make Way for Disposable Diapers," online.

100   *One of the only*   Blum, Taubman and Nemeth, "Relationship between Age at Initiation of Toilet Training and Duration of Training," online.

5. How Aka Pygmies Are the Best Fathers in the World

108   *"It's a question"*   Moorhead, "Are the Men of the African Aka Tribe the Best Fathers in the World?," online.

110   *"There's a big sense"*   Quoted in ibid.

111   *Hewlett observed*   Hewlett, *Intimate Fathers*, 104, 105, 140.

111   *A group of men*   Hewlett, "Cultural Nexus of Aka Father-Infant Bonding," 106.

113   *"Internationally, over the past"*   Quoted in Sullivan, "Worldwide Study Heralds Global Increase in Father Involvement and Reveals Why Men Have Nipples," press release.

113   *Baby titi monkeys*   Batten, "Psychology of Fatherhood," online.

113   *Golden lion tamarin*   "Tamarin (Golden Lion)," online.

113   *Red howler monkey*   Normile, *Alouatta seniculus*," online.

114   *"As a rule"*   Lamb and Lewis, *Role of the Father in Child Development*, 109.

115   *Hrdy dug even deeper*   Hrdy, *Mothers and Others*, 149–51.

117   Lamb and Lewis wrote   Lamb and Lewis, 120.

125   *"From trendy central Stockholm"*   Bennhold, "In Sweden, Men Can Have It All," online.

6. How Lebanese Americans Keep Their Families Close

128   *"not a by-product"*   Shryock, *Arab Detroit*, 574.

135   *In her book*   Hrdy, *Mothers and Others*, 277–80, 286.

136   *In Mexico, large*   Vogt, "Structural and Conceptual Replication in Zincacantan Culture," 344.

136   *One in five Czech*   Mozny and Katrnak, "Czech Family," 240–41.

136   *And among three hundred*   Bigome and Khadiagala, "Major Trends Affecting Families in Sub-Saharan Africa," 9.

138   *Even the neighborhoods*   Taylor et al., "Return of the Multi-generational Family Household," online.

141   *A study of ten thousand*   Macklin, "Grandparents Helping Make Children Smarter," online.

141   *Interactive Autism Network*   "Grandparents of Children with ASD, Part 2," online.

141   *A 1985 University of Alabama*   Dressler, "Extended Family Relationships, Social Support, and Mental Health in a Southern Black Community," 39.

141   *"Aunts and uncles"*   Milardo, "Uncles and Aunts," online.

145   *"extended financial families"*   Hall, "Living Together," online.

145   *In 2008, an estimated*   Taylor et al., online.

145   *An analysis of census*   Jayson, "Multigenerational Households Changing Family Picture," online.

148   *In Botswana*   Howell, *Kinning of Foreigners,* 50.

148   *Erdmute Alber observed*   Alber, "The Real Parents Are the Foster Parents," 33–36.

148   *Among the Zumbagua*   Weismantel, "Making Kin," 697.

149   *"In societies"*   Howell, 55.

7. How Tibetans Cherish Pregnancy

152   *Physicians during the Buddha's*   Jayasinghe, Eames, and Jaya-singhe, "A Buddhist Perspective on Women's Health Issues," 12.

156   *"the mixed sperm"*   Arya, "Tibetan Embryology, Part 3," online.

156   *Scientists have demonstrated*   University of California–Berkeley, online.

156   *A Slovenian study*   Zorn et al., "Psychological Factors in Male Partners of Infertile Couples," online.

157   *A study of eighty*   Gürhan et al., "Association of Depression and Anxiety with Oocyte and Sperm Numbers and Pregnancy Outcomes during In Vitro Fertilization Treatment," online.

157 *"Some eat the small"* Craig, "Pregnancy and Childbirth in Tibet," 154–55.

158 *"parents might give"* Ibid., 155.

159 *"after the birth"* Arya, "Tibetan Embryology, Part 4," online.

166 *Like Tibetans, Guatemalans* Neria, "Understanding the Health Culture of Recent Immigrants to the United States," online.

166 *A 2009 African Press* Mosota and Asego, "World Traditions," online.

166 *"snores like a hippo"* Ibid.

168 *A study published* Narendran et al., "Efficacy of Yoga on Pregnancy Outcome," online.

169 *In 2010, the National* "NIH Study Indicates Stress May Delay Women Getting Pregnant," online.

169 *"Stress-reduction techniques"* Quoted in Pal, "Stress Impairs Woman's Chances of Getting Pregnant—Study," online.

171 *"During the last half"* Central Intelligence Agency, online.

172 *Sweden was the only* "Sweden Tops Child Welfare Ranking," online.

8. How the Japanese Let Their Children Fight

176 *The irreverent authors* Tobin, Wu, and Davidson, *Preschool in Three Cultures,* 18.

177 *"trial and error"* Ibid., 22.

177 *"scrupulously avoided"* Ibid., 23.

178 *"the staff of Komatsudani"* Ibid., 28.

179 *"an example of"* Tobin, Hsueh, and Karasawa, *Preschool in Three Cultures Revisited,* 109.

179 *"a failure or"* Ibid., 110

179 *"We suggest"* Ibid.

180 *"If I think"* Ibid., 111.

181   *"moldable"*   Small, *Kids,* 154.

181   *"a child's mind"*   Briggs, "Autonomy and Aggression in the Three-Year-Old," 189.

181   *The University of North Carolina's*   "Corporal Punishment of Children Remains Common Worldwide, Studies Find," online.

182   *"corporal punishment is"*   Schmidt, "Liberian Refugees," 8.

182   *"ensure that a child"*   Ibid.

182   *"Many American Indian"*   Benedict, "Continuities and Discontinuities in Cultural Conditioning," 45.

183   *"along with a high"*   Sprott, *Raising Young Children in an Alaskan Iñupiaq Village,* 275.

184   *"hard on [the teacher]"*   Tobin, Wu, and Davidson, 30.

188   *a study in 2006*   Bear, Manning, and Shiomi, "Children's Reasoning about Aggression," 66–71.

189   *"intrinsic, rather than extrinsic"*   Ibid., 71.

193   *"Children in Punam Bah"*   Lancy, *Anthropology of Childhood,* 178.

9. How Polynesians Play without Parents

196   *University of Hawaii professor*   Martini, "Peer Interactions in Polynesia," 75–84.

197   Te Henua Enana   Les îles Marquises, online.

197   *In 2007, almost*   "ISPF—Recensement 2007," online.

198   *"A plane flies"*   Ibid., 79.

199   *"Indeed in Western societies"*   Ritchie and Ritchie, *Growing Up in Polynesia,* 63.

200   *"knowing"*   Zukow-Goldring, "Children as Family Caregivers in Mexico," 903.

203   *"golden age of play"*   Chudacoff, *Children at Play,* 126.

203   *"This was the first"*   Chudacoff, "Children at Play," speech online.

204   *"Baby boomers constitute"*   Browning, "Made for You and Me,"
      online.

205   *"Mothers rarely looked"*   LeVine, "Challenging Expert Knowl-
      edge," 156.

206   *when LeVine showed*   LeVine et al., *Child Care and Culture,*
      149–50.

206   *"While enjoying"*   New, "Child's Play in Italian Perspective,"
      217.

206   *"When asked to"*   Ibid., 218.

207   *"While mothers did not"*   Ibid., 217.

207   *"The two- to"*   Ibid., 218.

207   *"What seemed most"*   Ibid., 219.

208   *In a scathing critique*   Ibid.

208   *"adults think it's silly"*   Quoted in Shea, "Leave Those Kids
      Alone," online.

10. How Mayan Villagers Put Their Kids to Work

223   *"Two Yucatec Maya sisters"*   Gaskins, "Work before Play for
      Yucatec Maya Children," 1040.

225   *"Errands train the infant"*   Zeitlin, "My Child Is My Crown,"
      415.

226   *"a youngster who can"*   Wenger, "Children's Work, Play, and
      Relationships among the Giriama of Kenya," 294.

226   *"A girl, from about"*   Ibid.

226   *Scholar Gerd Spittler*   Lancy, *Anthropology of Childhood,* 239.

226   *"Nowhere are the Euroamerican"*   Ibid., 234.

227   *"I can't help"*   Ibid.

227   *"may be costs"*   Gaskins, "Children's Daily Lives in a Mayan Vil-
      lage," 58.

229   *She reported in 2003*   Hofferth, "Changes in American Chil-
      dren's Time—1997 to 2003," online.

230   *"In the glacial realm"*   Shellenbarger, "On the Virtues of Making Your Children Do the Dishes," online.

230   *"generally egalitarian,"*   Gerson, "Understanding Work and Family through a Gender Lens," online.

230   *The Pew Research Center*   Taylor et al., "Generation Gap in Values, Behaviors," 2, 17.

231   *"the best predictor"*   "Household Chores Teach Lifelong Values," online.

231   *"encourages a general"*   Rossi, *Caring and Doing for Others,* 265.

234   *Here is a sampling*   Lancy, 238–48.

234   *"bent leaves"*   Ibid., 247.

11. How Asians Learn to Excel in School

236   *The average SAT*   Miller, "Do Colleges Redline Asians?" online.

237   *"Of all the demographic"*   Steinberg, *Beyond the Classroom,* 86.

242   *"They couldn't blame"*   Lancy, *Anthropology of Childhood,* 338.

242   *"guilt in Korea"*   Ibid.

243   *"We were struck"*   Steinberg, 78.

245   *"Students, teachers, and parents"*   Ibid., 93.

246   *"You didn't concentrate"*   Bronson and Merryman, *Nurture-Shock,* 23.

246   *"The trade-off here"*   Ibid.

247   *"It is hard"*   Nisbett, *Intelligence and How to Get It,* 161.

250   *A survey by*   "OECD Programme for International Student Assessment 2009," online.

250   *"There's an educational"*   Obama, "Remarks by the President on the American opportunity Tax Credit," online.

251   *The biggest worry*   Matthiessen, "Top 5 Parenting Fears and What You Can Do about Them," online.

251   *"Underlying a lot"*   Quoted in ibid.

253   *"It is really a shame"*   Steinberg, 16.

257   *The Organisation for Economic*   "OECD Programme for International Student Assessment 2009," online.

Conclusion

260   *"where people chain"*   "Charges Dropped against Danish Mother Who Left Child in Stroller outside New York Restaurant," online.

BIBLIOGRAPHY

Alber, Erdmute. "The Real Parents Are the Foster Parents: Social Parenthood among the Baatombu in Northern Benin," in *Cross-Cultural Approaches to Adoption,* ed. Fiona Bowie, 33–47. New York: Routledge, 2004.

Arya, Pasang. "Tibetan Embryology, Part 3." 2010, http://www .tibetanmedicine-edu.org/index.php/n-articles/tibetan-embryology-3 (accessed 2010).

Arya, Pasang. "Tibetan Embryology, Part 4." 2010, http://www.tibetan medicine-edu.org/index.php/n-articles/tibetan-embryology-4 (accessed 2010).

"Baby Strollers May Promote Obesity." United Press International, December 2, 2003, http://www.upi.com/Odd_News/2003/12/02/Baby -strollers-may-promote-obesity/UPI-84761070395189/ (accessed 2010).

Batten, Mary. "The Psychology of Fatherhood." *Time,* June 7, 2007, http://www.time.com/time/magazine/article/0,9171,1630551,00.html (accessed 2010).

Bear, George, and Maureen Manning. "Shame, Guilt, Blaming, and Anger: Differences between Children in Japan and the US." *Motivation and Emotion* 33, no. 3 (2009): 62–67.

Bear, George, Maureen Manning, and Kunio Shiomi. "Children's Reasoning about Aggression: Differences between Japan and the United States and Implications for School Discipline." *School Psychology Review* 35, no. 1 (2006): 62–77.

Beard, Lillian. *Salt in Your Sock and Other Tried-and-True Home Remedies.* New York: Three Rivers Press, 2003.

Benedict, Ruth. "Continuities and Discontinuities in Cultural Conditioning." In *Anthropology and Child Development: A Cross-Cultural*

Reader, edited by Robert A. LeVine and Rebecca S. New, 42–48. Malden, MA: Blackwell, 2008.

Bennhold, Katrin. "In Sweden, Men Can Have It All." *New York Times,* June 9, 2010, http://nytimes.com/2010/06/10/world/europe/10iht -sweden.html (accessed July 2010).

Bigombe, Betty and Gilbert M. Khadiagala. "Major Trends Affecting Families in Sub-Saharan Africa." Major Trends Affecting Families: A Background Document, United Nations, Department of Economic and Social Affairs, Division for Social Policy and Development Program on the Family, 2003–4, http://www.un.org/esa/socdev/ family/Publications/mtbigome.pdf (accessed December 3, 2010).

Blennow, Margareta, and Lotta Lindfors Lindfors. "Child Health Care in Sweden—99% of Children Attend—Why?" Paper, Fourth Annual National Forum for Improving Children's Health Care, San Diego, February 18–March 2, 2005.

Bleyer, Jennifer. "Baby's Snuggled in a Sling, but Safe?" *New York Times,* March 10, 2010, http://www.nytimes.com/2010/03/11/ fashion/11BABY.html?_r=1&src=me (accessed 2010).

Blum, Nathan J., Bruce Taubman, and Nicole Nemeth. "Relationship between Age at Initiation of Toilet Training and Duration of Training: A Prospective Study" [abstract]. *Pediatrics* 111, no. 4 (April 2003): 810–14. http://pediatrics.aappublications.org/cgi/content/ abstract/111/4/810 (accessed 2009).

Boucke, Laurie. *Infant Potty Training: A Gentle and Primeval Method Adapted to Modern Living.* Lafayette, CO: White-Boucke, 2008.

Brazelton, T. Berry. "A Child-Oriented Approach to Toilet Training." *Pediatrics* 29, no. 1 (January 1962): 121–28. http://pediatrics.aappub lications.org/cgi/content/abstract/29/1/121 (accessed 2009).

Briggs, Jean L. "Autonomy and Aggression in the Three-Year-Old: The Utku Eskimo Case." In *Anthropology and Child Development: A*

Cross-Cultural Reader, edited by Robert A. LeVine and Rebecca S. New, 187–89. Malden, MA: Blackwell, 2008.

Bronson, Po, and Ashley Merryman. *NurtureShock*: *New Thinking about Children.* New York: Twelve, 2009.

Brown, Anne Maiden, Edie Farwell and Dickey Nyerongsha. *The Tibetan Art of Parenting: From before Conception through Early Childhood.* Boston: Wisdom, 2008.

Browning, Dominique. "Made for You and Me." New York Times, September 23, 2007. http://www.nytimes.com/2007/09/23/books/review/Browning-t.html (accessed July 2010).

Burgess, Adrienne. *Fatherhood Reclaimed: The Making of the Modern Father.* London: Vermilion, 1997.

Bowie, Fiona, Ed. *Cross Cultural Approaches to Adoption.* Oxfordshire, Oxford, England: Routledge, 2004.

Caliri, Heather. "Relieving Myself." *Brain, Child* (Winter 2008), http://www.brainchild.com/winter2008-caliri.asp (accessed 2009).

Cekada, Sharon. "Hmong Shaman: Hmong Pregnancy Ceremony Good for the Soul." *Post-Crescent,* November 14, 2008, http://www.postcrescent.com/article/20081114/APC06/81114054referrer=frontpage carousel (accessed 2010).

Central Intelligence Agency. "Infant Mortality Rate." *Central Intelligence Agency World Factbook,* https://www.cia.gov/library/publications/the-world-factbook/rankorder/2091rank.html#top (accessed April 1, 2011).

"Charges Dropped Against Danish Mother Who Left Child in Stroller outside New York Restaurant." *Jet,* June 2, 1997, http://findarticles.com/p/articles/mi_m1355/is_n2_v92/ai_19487246/ (accessed 2010).

Child, Julia. *Mastering the Art of French Cooking,* vol. 1. New York: Knopf, 2001.

"Child Obesity Rates Level off in France." *New York Times,* May 15,

2008. http://www.nytimes.com/2008/05/15/world/europe/15iht
-health.4.12927785.html (accessed May 2010).

Chudacoff, Howard A. *Children at Play: An American History.* New
York: New York University Press, 2007.

———. "Children at Play: An American History." Speech, Brown
Club of Oregon. Back to Class with Brown Faculty. Brown
Alumni Association, March 27, 2008, http://www.youtube.com/
watch?v=20ihGBiFdjY (accessed 2010).

"Corporal Punishment of Children Remains Common Worldwide,
Studies Find." *ScienceDaily,* August 9, 2010, http://www.sciencedaily
.com/releases/2010/08/100809111232.htm (accessed December 14,
2010).

Craig, Sienna. "Pregnancy and Childbirth in Tibet: Knowledge,
Perspectives and Practices." In *Childbirth across Cultures,* edited by
Helaine Selin and Pamela K. Stone, 146–61. Amherst, MA: Springer,
2009.

"Disposable Diaper History." Richer Investment Consulting Service.
http://www.disposablediaper.net/content.asp?2 (accessed 2010).

Dressler, William W. "Extended Family Relationships, Social Support,
and Mental Health in a Southern Black Community." *Journal of
Health and Social Behavior.* Vol. 26, no. 1 (March 1985): 39–40.

Encyclopaedia Britannica. S. v. "doll," http://www.britannica.com/
EBchecked/topic/168246/doll (accessed 2011).

Engle, Patrice L., and Cynthia Breaux. "Fathers' Involvement with Children Perspectives from Developing Countries." *Social Policy Report of
the Society for Research in Child Development* 12, no. 1 (1998): 1–21.

Finkelhor, David, Heather Turner, Richard Ormrod, and Sherry L.
Hamby. "Trends in Childhood Violence and Abuse." *Archives of
Pediatrics and Adolescent Medicine* 164 no. 3 (March 2010): 238–42.

Flegal, K. M., M. D. Carroll, C. L. Ogden, and L. R. Curtin. "Prevalence
and Trends in Obesity among US Adults, 1999–2008." *Journal of the*

American Medical Association 303, no. 3 (2010): 235–41. http://win
.niddk.nih.gov/statistics/ (accessed April 1, 2011).

Garrett, Frances. *Religion, Medicine and the Human Embryo in Tibet.*
New York: Routledge, 2008.

Gaskins, Suzanne. "Children's Daily Lives among the Yucatec Maya."
In *Anthropology and Child Development: A Cross-Cultural Reader,*
edited by Robert A. LeVine and Rebecca S. New, 375–89. Malden,
MA: Blackwell Publishing, 2008.

———. "Children's Daily Lives in a Mayan Village: A Case Study of Culturally Constructed Roles and Activities." In *Children's Engagement
in the World: Sociocultural Perspectives,* edited by Artin Göncü, 25–81.
Cambridge, England: Cambridge University Press, 1999.

———. "From Corn to Cash: Change and Continuity within Mayan
Families." *Ethos* 31, no. 2 (2003): 248–71.

———. "Work before Play for Yucatec Maya Children." *The Child: An
Encyclopedic Companion,* edited by Richard Shweder, 1040. Chicago:
University of Chicago Press, 2009.

Gaskins, Suzanne, and Peggy J. Miller. "The Cultural Roles of Emotions
in Pretend Play." In *Transactions at Play,* edited by Cindy Dell Clark,
5–21. Lanham, MD: University Press of America, 2009.

Gaskins, Suzanne, and Ruth Paradise. "Learning through Observation
in Daily Life." In *The Anthropology of Learning in Childhood,* edited
by David F. Lancy, John Bock, and Suzanne Gaskins, 85–117. Lanham, MD: AltaMira Press, 2010.

Gerson, Kathleen. "Understanding Work and Family through a Gender
Lens." *Community, Work and Family* 7, no. 2 (2004): 163–78. http://
as.nyu.edu/docs/IO/220/genderlensforfamilyandwork.pdf (accessed
2011).

"Global Market for Disposable Baby Diapers to Reach $26.6 Billion by
2012, according to a New Report by Global Industry Analysts, Inc."
Press release by Global Industry Analysts, Inc., October 22, 2008,

http://www.prweb.com/releases/diapers_disposable/baby_infant/ prweb1503344.htm (accessed 2010).

Gordon, Stephen. "Keeping Baby Outside." Letter to the Editor. *New York Times,* May 20, 1997, http://www.nytimes.com/1997/05/20/ opinion/keeping-baby-outside.html (accessed November 2010).

Graburn, Nelson. "Culture as Narrative: Who Is Telling the Inuit Story." In *Critical Inuit Studies: an Anthology of Contemporary Arctic Ethnography,* edited by Pam Stern and Lisa Stevenson, 139–54. Lincoln: University of Nebraska Press, 2006.

"Grandparents of Children with ASD, Part 2." Interactive Autism Network Research Report No. 15, April 2010, http://www.iancommunity .org/cs/ian_research_reports/ian_research_report_apr_2010_2 (accessed 2010).

"Growing up in Australia: The Longitudinal Study of Australian Children, 2009, http://www.fahcsia.gov.au/sa/families/pubs/lsac_report _2009/Pages/default.aspx (accessed November 2010).

Gürhan, N., A. Akyüz, D. Atici, and S. Kisa. "Association of Depression and Anxiety with Oocyte and Sperm Numbers and Pregnancy Outcomes during In Vitro Fertilization Treatment." *Psychological Reports* 104, no. 3 (June 2009): 796–806. http://www.ncbi.nlm.nih .gov/pubmed/19708407 (accessed summary 2010).

Hall, Trish. "Battle of Bedtime: Children Won." *New York Times,* March 1, 1990, http://www.nytimes.com/1990/03/01/garden/the -battle-of-bedtime-children-won.html (accessed 2009).

Hall, Zoe Dare. "Living Together: Return of the Extended Family." *Telegraph,* February 2, 2008, http://www.telegraph.co.uk/property/ 3360341/Living-together-Return-of-the-extended-family.html (Accessed November 1, 2010).

Harkness, Sara, and Charles Super. *Parents' Cultural Belief Systems.* New York: Guilford Press, 1996.

Hewlett, Barry S. "The Cultural Nexus of Aka Father-Infant Bonding."

In *Gender in Cross-Cultural Perspective,* edited by C. B. Brettel and C. Sargent, 106–12. Upper Saddle River, NJ: Pearson/Prentice Hall, 2008, http://anthro.vancouver.wsu.edu/media/PDF/cultural_nexus _fathers.pdf (accessed 2009).

———. *Intimate Fathers: The Nature and Context of Aka Pygmy Parental Infant Care.* Ann Arbor: University of Michigan Press, 1991.

"History of Marbles," December 2010. http://www.imarbles.com (accessed 2010).

Hofferth, Sandra L. "Changes in American Children's Time—1997 to 2003." *Electronic International Journal of Time Use Research* 6, no. 1 (January 1, 2009): 26–47, http://www.ncbi.nlm.nih.gov/pmc/ articles/PMC2939468/ (accessed 2010).

Hofferth, Sandra L., and John E. Sandberg. "How American Children Spend Their Time." *Journal of Marriage and Family* 63, no. 2 (May 2001): 295–308.

Hollyer, Beatrice, and Oxfam. *Let's Eat! Children and Their Food Around the World.* London: Frances Lincoln Limited, 2003.

"Household Chores Teach Lifelong Values." *University of Minnesota e-News,* October 17, 2002. http://www1.umn.edu/systemwide/ enews/101702.html (accessed 2010).

Howell, Signe. *The Kinning of Foreigners: Transnational Adoption in a Global Perspective.* Oxford, England: Berghahn Books, 2007.

Hrdy, Sarah Blaffer. *Mothers and Others: The Evolutionary Origins of Mutual Understanding.* Cambridge, MA: Belkap Press of Harvard University Press, 2009.

———. *Mother Nature: Maternal Instincts and How They Shape the Human Species.* New York: Ballantine Books, 1999.

Hunziker, Urs A., and Ronald G. Barr. "Increased Carrying Reduces Infant Crying: A Randomized Controlled Trial." *Pediatrics* 77, no. 5 (May 1986): 641–48.

"Invertir en Buenos Aires." Buenos Aires Ciudad, http://www.buenos

aires.gov.ar/areas/promocion_inversiones/invertir_bsas/vivir_bsas
.php (accessed 2009).

"ISPF—Recensement 2007." Institut de la statistique de la Polynésie
française, http://www.ispf.pf/ISPF/EnqRep/Recensement/Recens
2007/TableauxEtCartes/StatsLocales.aspx (accessed 2009).

Jayasinghe, Yasmin, Mai Eames, and Daya Jayasinghe. "A Buddhist Perspective on Women's Health Issues." *O&G*, 10, no. 2 (Winter 2008):
11–13.

Jayson, Sharon. "Multigenerational Households Changing Family Picture." *USA Today,* June 26, 2007, http://www.usatoday.com/money/
perfi/eldercare/2007-06-26-elder-care-generations_N.htm (accessed
2010).

Jenni, Oskar G., and Bonnie B. O'Connor. "Children's Sleep: An
Interplay between Culture and Biology." *Pediatrics* 115, no. 1 (January
2005): 204–17.

Lamb, Michael, and Charlie Lewis. "The Development and Significance
of Father-Child Relationships in Two-Parent Families." In *The Role
of the Father in Child Development,* edited by Michael Lamb, 109.
Hoboken, NJ: John Wiley and Sons, 2010.

Lancy, D. F. "Accounting for Variability in Mother-Child Play." *American Anthropologist* 109, no. 2 (2007): 273–84.

Lancy, David F. *The Anthropology of Childhood*: *Cherubs, Chattel,
Changelings.* New York: Cambridge University Press, 2008.

———. *Playing on the Mother Ground: Cultural Routines for Children's
Development.* New York: Guilford Press, 1996.

Lee, K. "Crying Patterns of Korean Infants in Institutions." *Child: Care,
Health and Development* 26, no. 3 (2000): 217–28.

Les îles Marquises—Terre des Hommes—Te Henua Enata—Archipel
Polynésie—Infos Touristiques, http://www.ilesmarquises-archipel
.com/index.html (accessed 2010).

LeVine, Robert A. "Challenging Expert Knowledge: Findings from an African Study of Infant Care and Development." In *Childhood and Adolescence: Cross-Cultural Perspectives and Applications,* edited by Uwe P. Gielen and Jaipaul Roopnarine, 149–65. Westport, CT: Praeger, 2004.

LeVine, Robert A., Suzanne Dixon, Sarah E. LeVine, Amy Richman, Constance Keefer, Herbert Liederman, and T. Berry Brazelton. "The Comparative Study of Parenting." In *Anthropology and Child Development: A Cross-Cultural Reader,* 55–65. Malden, MA: Blackwell, 2008.

LeVine, Robert A., Suzanne Dixon, Sarah LeVine, Amy Richman, P. Herbert Leiderman, Constance H. Keefer, and T. Berry Brazelton. *Child Care and Culture: Lessons from Africa.* Cambridge, England: Cambridge University Press, 1994.

LeVine, Robert A., Patrice M. Miller, and Mary Maxwell, eds. *Parental Behavior in Diverse Societies* (New Directions for Child and Adolescent Development no. 40). San Francisco: Jossey-Bass, 1998.

LeVine, Robert. A., and Rebecca S. New, eds. *Anthropology and Child Development: A Cross-Cultural Reader.* Malden, MA: Blackwell, 2008.

Liedloff, Jean. *The Continuum Concept: In Search of Happiness Lost.* Cambridge, MA: Perseus Books, 1977.

Macklin, Jenny. "Grandparents Helping Make Children Smarter." Minister for Families, Housing, and Indigenous Affairs Press Release, September 30, 2008, http://www.jennymacklin.fahcsia.gov.au/mediareleases/2008/Pages/grandparents_30sep08.aspx (accessed December 8, 2010).

Marcano, Tony. "Toddler, Left outside Restaurant, Is Returned to Her Mother." *New York Times,* May 14, 1997, http://www.nytimes.com/1997/05/14/nyregion/toddler-left-outside-restaurant-is-returned-to-her-mother.html (accessed 2010).

Marshall, John. *Mohenjo-Daro and the Indus Civilization: Being an*

Official Account of Archaeological Excavations at Mohenjo-Daro Carried out by the Government of India between the Years 1922 and 1927. London: Asian Educational Services Publications, 2004 (originally published 1931).

Martin, John A., David R. King, Eleanor E. Maccoby, and Carol Nagy Jacklin. "Secular Trends and Individual Differences in Toilet-Training Progress" [abstract]. *Journal of Pediatric Psychology* 9 no. 4 (1984): 457–68. http://jpepsy.oxfordjournals.org/content/9/4/457.short (accessed 2009).

Martini, Mary. "Peer Interactions in Polynesia: A View from the Marquesas." In *Play and Development: Evolutionary, Sociocultural, and Functional Perspectives,* edited by Artin Goncu and Suzanne Gaskins, 75–84. Mahwah, NJ: Lawrence Erlbaum, 2006.

Matthiessen, Connie. "Top 5 Parenting Fears and What You Can Do about Them." Babycenter.com, updated June 2008, http://www.babycenter.com/0_top-5-parenting-fears-and-what-you-can-do-about-them_3656609.bc (accessed May 2010).

Mead, Margaret. *Coming of Age in Samoa: A Psychological Study of Primitive Youth for Western Civilization.* New York: William Morrow, 1928.

———. "The Ethnology of Childhood." In *Anthropology and Child Development: A Cross-Cultural Reader,* edited by Robert LeVine and Rebecca S. New, 22–28. Malden, MA: Blackwell, 2008.

Mennella, Julie A., Coren P. Jagnow, and Gary K. Beauchamp. "Prenatal and Postnatal Flavor Learning by Human Infants." *Pediatrics* 207, no. 6 (June 2001): e88.

Milardo, Robert. *The Forgotten Kin: Aunts and Uncles.* Cambridge, England: Cambridge University Press, 2010.

———. "Uncles and Aunts: The Other Family," YourKidsEd.com.au, http://yourkidsed.com.au/info/uncles-and-aunts-the-other-family (accessed December 2010).

Miller, Kara. "Do Colleges Redline Asian Americans?" *Boston Globe,* February 8, 2010, http://www.boston.com/bostonglobe/editorial _opinion/oped/articles/2010/02/08/do_colleges_redline_asian _americans/ (accessed January 2011).

Montgomery, Heather. *An Introduction to Childhood: Anthropological Perspectives on Children's Lives.* West Sussex, England: Wiley-Blackwell, 2009.

Mooallem, Jon. "The Sleep-Industrial Complex." *New York Times Magazine,* November 18, 2007, http://www.nytimes.com/2007/11/18/ magazine/18sleep-t.html (accessed 2009).

Moorhead, Joanna. "Are the Men of the African Aka Tribe the Best Fathers in the World?" *Guardian,* June 15, 2005, http://www.guardian .co.uk/society/2005/jun/15/childrensservices.familyandrelationships (accessed 2010).

"Mortality Rate, Infant (per 1,000 Live Births)." *Level and Trends in Child Mortality.* Report 2010. http://data.worldbank.org/indicator/ SP.DYN.IMRT.IN?cid=GPD_55 (accessed November 2010).

Mosota, Mangoa, and Nicholas Asego. "World Traditions: Myths and Taboos—Should We Believe Them?" *African Press International,* October 1, 2007, http://africanpress.wordpress.com/2007/10/01/myths -and-taboos-should-we-believe-them (accessed November 26, 2010).

"The Mother Blessingway Ceremony—Native American Indian Tribes," http://www.aaanativearts.com/article1503.html (accessed 2010).

Mozny, Ivo, and Tomas Katrnak. "The Czech Family." In *Handbook of World Families,* edited by Bert N. Adams and Jan Trost, 235–61. Thousand Oaks, CA: Sage, 2005.

Narendran, S., R. Nagarathna, V. Narendran, S. Gunasheela, and H. R. Nagendra. "Efficacy of Yoga on Pregnancy Outcome." *Journal of Alternative and Complementary Medicine* 11, no. 2 (April 2005): 237–44. http://www.ncbi.nlm.nih.gov/pubmed/15865489 (accessed May 2010).

"National Survey of Pediatric Experts Indicates Increase in Infant Delays: Two-Thirds of Pediatric Therapists Report Seeing Increase
in Early Motor Delays in the Past Six Years; More Tummy Time Is
Key," Pathways Awareness press release, July 30, 2008, http://www
.pathwaysawareness.org/media-room/media-room (accessed 2010).

Neergaard, Lauran. "Get Babies out of Strollers and onto the Floor." Associated Press, as printed in the *Idaho Statesman,* February 12, 2002,
http://www.healthandwelfare.idaho.gov/Default.aspx?tabid=164
&mid=1389&ctl=ArticleView&articleId=676 (accessed 2009).

Neria, Jennifer T. "Understanding the Health Culture of Recent Immigrants to the United States: A Cross-Cultural Maternal Health
Information Catalog." American Public Health Association, 2002,
http://www.apha.org/ppp/red/ (accessed 2010).

New, Rebecca S. "Child's Play in Italian Perspective." In *Anthropology
and Child Development: A Cross-Cultural Reader,* edited by Robert A.
LeVine and Rebecca S. New, 213–26. Malden, MA: Blackwell, 2008.

"NIH Study Indicates Stress May Delay Women Getting Pregnant."
National Institutes of Health Press Release, August 11, 2010, http://
www.nih.gov/news/health/aug2010/nichd-11.htm (accessed November 24, 2010).

Nisbett, Richard E. *Intelligence and How to Get It.* New York:
W. W. Norton, 2009.

Normile, R. *"Alouatta seniculus."* Animal Diversity Web, 2001, http://
animaldiversity.ummz.umich.edu/site/accounts/information/
Alouatta_seniculus.html (accessed April 5, 2011).

"Nuclear Families." Jrank, http://family.jrank.org/pages/1222/Nuclear
-Families.html (accessed 2010).

Obama, Barack. "Remarks by the President on the American Opportunity
Tax Credit," October 13, 2010. Office of the Press Secretary. http://
www.whitehouse.gov/the-press-office/2010/10/13/remarks-president
-american-opportunity-tax-credit (accessed November 2010).

"OECD Programme for International Student Assessment 2009."
    Organisation for Economic Co-Operation and Development,
    http://www.pisa.oecd.org/document/61/0,3746,en_32252351_46567613
    _1_1_1_1,00.html.

Ogden, Cynthia, and Margaret Carroll. "Prevalence of Obesity among
    Children and Adolescents: United States, Trends 1963–1965 through
    2007–2008," last updated June 4, 2010. http://www.cdc.gov/nchs/
    data/hestat/obesity_child_07_08/obesity_child_07_08.htm
    (accessed on March 1, 2011).

"'Open-Crotch Pants' Make Way for Disposable Diapers." China Daily,
    July 7, 2004, http://www.chinadaily.com.cn/english/doc/2004-07/16/
    content_349150.htm (Accessed April 2010).

Pal, Jyoti. "Stress Impairs Woman's Chances of Getting Pregnant—
    Study." Med Guru, August 12, 2010, http://www.themedguru.com/
    20100812/newsfeature/stress-impairs-womans-chances-getting
    -pregnant-study-86139309.html (accessed October 2010).

Pearson, Kimberly. "Depression and Anxiety: Do They Impact Infertil-
    ity Treatment?" Massachusetts General Hospital Center for Women's
    Mental Health, June 30, 2010, http://www.womensmentalhealth.org/
    posts/depression-and-anxiety-do-they-impact-infertility-treatment/
    (accessed July 2010).

Peaslee, Kindy R. "Food Affair—The French Approach to Healthy Eat-
    ing and Enjoyment." Today's Dietician 9, no. 8 (August 2007),
    http://www.todaysdietician.com/newarchives/tdaug2007pg44.shtml
    (accessed 2010).

Phillipps, W. J. "Maori Baby's Toilet." Te Ao Hou: The New World 10
    (April 1955), http://teaohou.natlib.govt.nz/journals/teaohou/issue/
    Mao10TeA/c27.html (accessed December 2010).

"Previniendo irritaciones y dermatitis: óleo calcáreo." Embarazo y Bebes,
    http://www.embarazoybebes.com.ar/bebe/previniendo-irritaciones
    -y-dermatitis-oleo-calcareo/ (accessed 2009).

Ray, Rebecca, Janet C. Gornick, and John Schmitt. "Leave Policies in 21 Countries: Accessing Generosity and Gender Equity." Center for Economic Policy Research, September 2008, http://www.cepr.net/ documents/publications/parental_2008_09.pdf (accessed November 2010).

"Researchers at UMDNJ-Robert Wood Johnson Medical School and the Bristol-Myers Squibb Children's Hospital at Robert Wood Johnson University Hospital Pinpoint Best Time to Begin Toilet Training for Children." Robert Wood Johnson Medical School News Release, January 8, 2010, http://rwjms.umdnj.edu/news_publications/news _release/Barone_Toilet_Training_Children.html (accessed 2010).

Ritchie, Jane, and James Ritchie. *Growing Up in Polynesia.* Sydney, Australia: George Allen & Unwin, 1979.

Rossi, Alice S., "Developmental Roots of Adult Social Responsibility." In *Caring and Doing for Others: Social Responsibility in the Domains of Family, Work, and Community,* edited by Alice S. Rossi, 227–320. Chicago: University of Chicago Press, 2001.

Schmidt, Susan. "Liberian Refugees: Cultural Considerations for Social Service Providers." *BRYCS Bulletin,* January 2009, 2–13.

Schmitt, Barton D. "Toilet Training: Getting It Right the First Time." *Contemporary Pediatrics* 21 (March 2004): 105–19.

Sen, Ashish Kumar. "South Asians Top US Spelling Contests." BBC Mobile. June 17, 2008.

Shea, Christopher. "Leave Those Kids Alone." *Boston Globe,* July 15, 2007, http://www.boston.com/news/globe/ideas/articles/2007/ 07/15/leave_those_kids_alone/ (accessed March 1, 2010).

Shellenbarger, Sue. "On the Virtues of Making Your Children Do the Dishes." *Wall Street Journal,* August 27, 2008, http://online.wsj.com/ article/SB121978677837474177.html (accessed 2010).

Shryock, Andrew, ed. *Arab Detroit: From Margin to Mainstream.* Detroit: Wayne State University Press, 2000.

Shryock, Andrew. "Family Resemblances: Kinship and Community in Arab Detroit." In *Arab Detroit: From Margin to Mainstream,* edited by Andrew Shryock, 573–609. Detroit: Wayne State University Press, 2000.

Shweder, Richard, ed. *The Child: An Encyclopedic Companion.* Chicago: University of Chicago Press, 2009.

Small, Meredith F. *Kids: How Biology and Culture Shape the Way We Raise Young Children.* New York: Anchor Books, 2001.

———. *Our Babies, Ourselves: How Biology and Culture Shape the Way We Parent.* New York: Anchor Books, 1998.

Sprott, Julie. *Raising Young Children in an Alaskan Iñupiaq Village: The Family, Cultural, and Village Environment of Rearing.* Westport, CT: Bergin and Garvey, 2002.

Stallone, Daryth D., and Michael F. Jacobson. "Cheating Babies: Nutritional Quality and Cost of Commerical Baby Food." Center for Science in the Public Interest, April 1995, http://www.cspinet.org/reports/cheat1.html (accessed November 5, 2010).

Steinberg, Laurence, with B. Bradford Brown and Sanford M. Dornbusch. *Beyond the Classroom: Why School Reform Has Failed and What Parents Need to Do.* New York: Touchstone, 1996.

Sullivan, Jack. "Worldwide Study Heralds Global Increase in Father Involvement and Reveals Why Men Have Nipples." Press release, Fatherhood Institute, June 12, 2005, Abergavenny, Wales.

Super, Charles M. "Environmental Effects on Motor Development: The Case of 'African Infant Precocity.'" *Developmental Medicine and Child Neurology* 18, no. 5 (October 1976): 561–67.

"Sweden Tops Child Welfare Ranking." *The Local: Sweden's News in English,* December 12, 2008, http://www.thelocal.se/16300/200812/12 (accessed 2010).

Szabo, Liz. "Car Seats Can be Dangerous outside the Car." *USA Today,* October 19, 2009, http://www.usatoday.com/news/health/2009-10-19-car-seats_N.htm (accessed 2011).

"Tamarin (Golden Lion)." Young People's Trust for the Environment, http://www.ypte.org.uk/animal/tamarin-golden-lion-/181 (accessed 2010).

Taylor, Paul, Cary Funk, and April Funk. "Generation Gap in Values, Behaviors: As Marriage and Parenthood Drift Apart, Public is Concerned about Social Impact." Pew Research Center, July 1, 2007, http://pewresearch.org/pubs/526/marriage-parenthood (accessed 2010).

Taylor, Paul, Jeffrey Passel, Richard Fry, Richard Morin, Wendy Wang, Gabriel Velasco, and Daniel Dockterman. "The Return of the Multi-generational Family Household." Pew Research Center, March 18, 2010, http://pewsocialtrends.org/2010/03/18/the-return-of-the-multi-generational-family-household (accessed December 3, 2010).

Tobin, Joseph, Yeh Hsueh, and Mayumi Karasawa. *Preschool in Three Cultures Revisited: China, Japan, and the United States.* Chicago: University of Chicago Press, 2009.

Tobin, Joseph, David Y. H. Wu, and David H. Davidson. *Preschool in Three Cultures: Japan, China, and the United States.* New Haven, CT: Yale University Press, 1989.

Tseng, V., R. K. Chao, and I. Padmawidjaja. *Asian Americans Educational Experiences.* In *Handbook of Asian American Psychology,* 2nd ed., edited by F. Leong, A. Inman, A. Ebreo, L. Yang, L. Kinoshita, and M. Fu, 102–23. Racial and Ethnic Minority Psychology (REMP) Series. Thousand Oaks, CA: Sage, 2007.

Two Million Minutes: A Global Examination. Documentary. Directed by Chad Heeter. Robert A. Compton, executive producer. February 10, 2008.

University of California–Berkeley. "Stress Puts Double Whammy on Reproductive System, Fertility." *ScienceDaily,* June 29, 2009, http://www.sciencedaily.com/releases/2009/06/090615171618.htm (accessed April 6, 2011).

Vogt, Evon Z. "Structural and Conceptual Replication in Zinacantan Culture." *American Anthropologist* 67, no. 2 (April 1965): 342–53.

Vogt, E. Z. *Zinacantan: A Maya Community in the Highlands of Chiapas.* Cambridge, MA: Harvard University Press, 1969.

Wahlgren, Eric. "France's Obesity Crisis: All those Croissants Really Do Add up, after All." *Daily Finance,* November 14, 2009, http://www.dailyfinance.com/story/frances-obesity-crisis-all-those-croissants-really-do-add-up/19235345/ (accessed June 18, 2010).

Wang, Ivy. "The Secret of the Chinese Potty-Training Method." Silicon Valley Mom's Blog: A Byte of Silicon Valley Life, August 1, 2007, http://www.svmoms.com/2007/08/the-secret-of-t.html (accessed 2009).

Warren, Jeff. *Head Trip: Adventures on the Wheel of Consciousness.* New York: Random House, 2007.

Wax, Emily. "An Idea Still Looking for Traction in Kenya: East African Women Vote with Their Feet against Baby Strollers." *Washington Post,* May 18, 2004, http://pewsocialtrends.org/2010/03/18/the-return-of-the-multi-generational-family-household/ (accessed 2009).

Webster's Online Dictionary. S. v. "bogeyman," http://www.websters-online-dicionary.org/definitions/BOGEYMAN?cx=partner-pub-0939450753529744%3Avoqdo1-tdlq&cof=FORID%3A9&ie=UTF-8&q=BOGEYMAN&sa=Search (accessed 2011).

Wehby, Emily. "Childbirth and Culture: Providing Services to Latin American Families in the United States," http://www.wehbycreative.com/emily/Childbirth.pdf (accessed July 2010).

Weismantel, Mary. "Making Kin: Kinship Theory and Zumbagua Adoptions." *American Ethnologist* 22, no. 4 (November 1995): 685–709.

Wenger, Martha. "Children's Work, Play, and Relationships among the Giriama of Kenya." In *Anthropology and Child Development: A Cross-Cultural Reader,* edited by Robert A. LeVine and Rebecca S. New, 289–308. Malden, MA: Blackwell, 2008.

Wolfson, Amy. *The Woman's Book of Sleep*. Oakland, CA: New Harbinger, 2001.

Worthman, Carol M., and Melissa K. Melby. "Toward a Comparative Developmental Ecology of Human Sleep." In *Adolescent Sleep Patterns: Biological, Social, and Psychological Influences,* edited by Mary A. Carskadan, 69–117. Cambridge, England: Cambridge University Press, 2002.

Yang, Philip. "Through a Generation Lens: School Performance of Asian American Students." Paper, annual meeting of the American Sociological Association, Montreal, Quebec, Canada, August 11, 2006.

Zeitlin, Marian. "My Child Is My Crown: Yoruba Parental Theories and Practices in Early Childhood." In *Parents' Cultural Belief Systems: Their Origins, Expressions, and Consequences,* edited by Sara Harkness and Charles M. Super, 407–27. New York: Guilford Press, 1996.

Zorn, B., J. Auger, V. Velikonja, M. Kolbezen, and H. Meden-Vrtovec. "Psychological Factors in Male Partners of Infertile Couples: Relationship with Semen Quality and Early Miscarriage." *International Journal of Andrology* 31, no. 6 (December 2008): 557–64 (Epub in advance of print July 25, 2007). http://www.ncbi.nlm.nih.gov/pubmed/17651396 (summary accessed 2010).

Zukow-Goldring, Patricia. "Children as Family Caregivers in Mexico." In *The Child: An Encyclopedic Companion,* edited by Richard A. Schweder, 903. Chicago: University of Chicago Press, 2009.

———. "Sibling Caregiving." In *Handbook of Parenting: Being and Becoming a Parent,* vol. 3, edited by Marc H. Bornstein, 253–86. Mahwah, NJ: Lawrence Erlbaum, 2002.

ERIC EASON

Mei-Ling Hopgood is an award-winning journalist and writer. She lives in the Chicago area with her husband and two daughters, and is an associate professor of journalism at Northwestern University. Find her online at www.mei-linghopgood.com.